The Gamekeeper's Other Daughter

Doreen

McEwan-Burrows

B MCE

Copyright Doreen Burrows 2016

Copy Editing by Susan Denton

Cover Design by Pip Burrows

IBSN 978-0-9934546-4-6 (FCM Publishing)

Published by

FCM PUBLISHING

www.fcmpublishing.co.uk

First printed in the UK – February 2016

I dedicate this book to my late husband,
Wilfred Robert Burrows,
and my sister, Julia Caroline, who, like me,
is a survivor.

FOREWORD

This book made me laugh out loud (how can someone manage to bite their own bottom?), draw breath and shed a few tears! My work as a psychologist means I am regularly honoured by being invited to enter into people's lives and hear their stories. Doreen is one such example. When reading her story, her personality shines through and just how committed and fiercely independent this little powerhouse of a lady is. She is both feisty and strong whilst also kind, tender and a real romantic at heart, wanting to find her 'hero'. It was wonderful for her to reveal much more about her life than I knew already and being given the opportunity to know her more. Little did I know we had both taken ownership of foxes when we were growing up and called them 'Freddie'. What a coincidence! I think there will be many things that readers can identify with. I identified with her cheekiness on the one hand and her 'I can do this on my own' attitude on the other.

I think that writing this book was, in many ways, a cathartic process for Doreen. Grieving whilst she wrote it, her story was about reflecting on the life she has had before being able to forge a life ahead. Doreen is not afraid of what people think of her and her candidness and short punchy style comes across too. She is aware that not all the book makes for pleasant reading, but she feels it is important that the full story is told anyway in order to be 'real'. For this reason, in this book, Doreen is allowing you into her life and letting you walk that very personal journey with her.

Families and relationships are what this book is all about and the relationships that Doreen found difficult, both in her family and in her intimate life. We can all identify with that. Relationships are key in all our lives whether they are healthy or not healthy, positive or negative. This comes through in this book. A relationship built on trust and commitment swings both ways and requires time, time that I was lucky to be able to make in my work with Doreen and her family. Families – they are rarely what you imagine a 'family' to be, and Doreen's is no different.

Doreen knows her own mind and always has done, it seems, even as a child. The very nature of her story is one whereby she overcame all obstacles and experiences no matter how rough or tough these were. Knowing herself I think was key in that. I hope this book will encourage others to really know themselves and what makes them strong. Her story will give hope to others of how challenges can make us stronger or weaker depending on your character and knowing yourself. I have seen evidence of how Doreen's sense of self has been the thing that has kept her strong. No matter what the obstacles, she has faced these with grit, determinism, compassion, humour and love. Doreen's story highlights many unanticipated twists in the road throughout her life. Many people will identify with her, not necessarily because they have experienced similar events, but perhaps because they, too, have shared the feelings, questions and turns in the road that she has faced.

After hearing snippets of her life over the past few years, little did I know that one day I would be able to get the full story. I hope you enjoy reading it as much as I have.

Dr Elizabeth Boyd

ACKNOWLEDGMENTS

I want to thank my family for their help and encouragement whilst I was writing this book. An extra thanks to Pip for my cover design.

Also thanks to Caroline Miller, my son's support worker (and my rock in times of trouble), and the Mencap girls who also support him.

A big thank you to Dr Liz for my foreword.
And a big heartfelt thank you to Susan Denton who agreed to type and edit my story and, of course, Taryn who believed I could write.

Without you guys none of this would have been possible.

CHAPTER ONE: THE EARLY YEARS

Life has a nasty habit, it lets old age creep up on you. Suddenly you realise your date with 'the grim reaper' has moved even closer. It was that realisation that made me decide to tell my story. I found memories of my early childhood hard to recall. I imagined myself looking down a kaleidoscope, trying to see pictures instead of the shapes and colours normally seen. It was hard at first but I found that, with practice, memories came flooding back. I tried to fit them together, making a 'jigsaw' of my early years – but some of the pieces may be missing and it is hard to be sure of exact dates and times. Anyway, this is my story. I will try to tell it as best as I can.

I made my entrance into this world on 21 November 1948 at 10.00pm in the cottage hospital at Rhynie in Aberdeenshire. My mother told me the NHS was 'born' on that day too. We moved to John O'Groats when I was a few weeks old so Dad could take up his post as salmon bailiff. I had a sister, Maureen, who was five years older than me.

My first memory is that I'd woken up to a river flowing past my bed, watching all my toys float away. Mum rescued me and gave me my first pair of 'wellies'. The cottage we lived in was very close to the river and it was flooded on a regular basis. I remember seeing grass growing between the stone slabs on our kitchen floor.

My father's job had been to catch the poachers before they stole any fish. We must have eaten a lot of salmon in those days as I can't stand to eat the 'horrible stuff' now. I wonder how many poachers Dad managed to catch whilst we were there.

As I was so young, I've not many memories of John O'Groats to share.

When I was about eighteen months old our family moved

to Stonehaven and this was where I left a smelly deposit on the local shop's floor after Dad took me out with no nappy on. I didn't actually remember this but Mum did (especially when she wanted to make fun of me in front of friends).

I saw the Northern Lights in Stonehaven, half-asleep, sitting on Dad's shoulders by the war memorial. I'm afraid the beautiful spectacle was wasted on a child of my age. Dad seemed so much nicer then.

I also badly burnt my hands in Stonehaven when my parents left me to be looked after by some friends. I'd been kneeling on a low bench which was by the fireplace. I over-balanced and fell. My hand went into the hot cinders. I don't remember the pain but remember my hand being bandaged for a while.

My next recollection is at Stonehaven village school where my hatred of all teachers was born. I was only five but quite vocal even at that young age. I remember one occasion in particular. It was lunch time and my sister, Maureen, was helping to bring in the school meals for the younger kids. There are two things I cannot stand. One is any fat on meat and the other is rice pudding. The teacher would walk around the tables making sure everyone ate everything on their plates. She stood over me whilst I struggled to swallow the fatty meat. I did manage it and then they brought in the pudding. Yes, you guessed right, lumpy rice pud. There was no way on God's earth that I was going to eat that. I picked up my plate and threw it into the fireplace. The teacher now had me by the scruff of the neck and began to shake me whilst bellowing in my face. The shaking was not a good idea. I threw up all my lunch over her shoes and the floor. As she let go of me I took off at great speed out of the door, across the yard and round the corner to our house where I sat sobbing until Mum found me a short while later, sitting on the doorstep.

I think Mum either got fed up of fighting my corner or just realised that, small as I was, I would always fight for myself.

The next thing I remember is visiting my sister in hospital when she had scarlet fever. We were not allowed to go into her room. We just waved to her through the glass.

Maureen was poorly a lot. When she came home from hospital they had cut her hair short. She used to have her hair so long that she could sit on it. Mum said the doctors thought it was draining her strength, so they cut it short. I thought that was rubbish, but have kept my own hair short ever since.

Dad had a job as an underkeeper on the estate owned by Major Cowdray. I guess he was hoping to work his way up so that he could eventually get a gamekeeper's job. The good thing about this sort of work was that the accommodation came with the job. We had a house near

Stonehaven. Dad worked on the Dunecht Estate so travelled daily to and from work on his motorbike, not the best mode of transport but better than walking. It did, however, leave him at the mercy of the harsh, inclement weather on a winter's day. The darkness of night comes early in winter. It was on such a night that Dad and his trusty bike parted company. There had been a heavy fall of fresh snow and underneath it was sheet ice. Poor old Dad was doing his best to get home out of the cold. He had his head down, no helmet (it wasn't a legal requirement back then), half blinded by the falling snow he hit a lump of ice on the road and was thrown through the air. As his bike disappeared over a high wall, he followed it, but managed to cling to the top of the wall. He was hanging there for quite a while. It wasn't a busy road so passing cars were few. When he saw a car approaching he began waving frantically. I can only imagine his anger when the driver waved back! He began to lose hope of ever being found. His leg was giving him so much pain he knew it must be badly injured. Luckily for Dad the driver of the car stopped to tell the local bobby that he had seen a man who appeared to be stuck on top of a high wall.

Without this Good Samaritan, Dad could have frozen to death or died from blood loss. His kneecap had to be sewn back on. There was no sign of his bike. The police took us to the hospital. Mum was in a right old state, pacing up and down the corridor. Maureen and I sat on chairs, swinging our legs. We were too young to realise how serious it was. Dad was in theatre so we went home to return the following day to see how he was. The good thing to come out of it all was that Dad bought an old banger, which made his journey to work warmer and drier, but perhaps no safer as this unlit road was a well-known accident black spot. The car wasn't safe for me. I fell onto the road when the floor gave way!

I think we must have lived near a stone circle. I can remember playing hide and seek amongst these stones. Maybe that was when I became a heathen. Dad was always calling me a heathen, this stemmed from the fact that I had never been baptised. It became a bone of contention between Mum and Dad. In those days if a Catholic married outside their faith any children must be baptised and brought up as Catholic. I don't want you to get the idea that either of my parents were regular churchgoers. I can't ever remember Mum attending a church service. She was Church of England, as was Maureen. Mum had given birth to Maureen before she married. I think this happened a lot during the war. Boyfriends couldn't always get home to marry their sweethearts when they got the news that they were going to be fathers. The girls whose fellas never returned were left with a hard choice – adoption or stand the shame of being an unmarried mother. I don't think my mum would have been very bothered what other people thought, although it might have been the reason why my gran hated dad with a vengeance. She had no time for him at all and, according to Dad, the feeling was mutual. But, getting back to me, 'the heathen', Dad was kicking up a fuss because the local priest was giving him a hard time. The priest descended on our house once a week. His purpose was to teach me the catechism. My purpose in life was to avoid him at all costs and as soon as I spotted him pedalling towards our house like a demented big black crow I fled. The man terrified me. I couldn't understand a word he said. Mum was sent to look for me. The times she found me were very few. In the end the priest just gave me up as a lost cause. The Catholic Church got me eventually but it was on my terms.

Dad always looked very smart during the shooting season in his plus fours. The long woollen socks he wore were knitted by Mum on four short needles. I would sit and watch her, fascinated by the sock as it grew ever bigger. It had a patterned top which was folded over to conceal the garters worn to keep the socks up. The outfit was completed by a tweed jacket and flat cap. Two new suits were part of the yearly salary, as were the heavy brogues he wore. He was Major Cowdray's personal loader during a shoot. The Major had lost an arm which prevented him from loading his own gun.

If you had known my dad in later years you would never have guessed that he'd been a very funny man and enjoyed the time he spent being a member of the local amateur dramatics group. Oh yes, he'd trod the boards in his younger days. I was taken to see him perform in a very funny play. He also claimed to play the mouth organ (I never heard him play a tune). I often asked Mum what part Dad played. She always said, laughingly, "The Village Idiot." There was a genuine fondness between them in those days. It was so very sad to watch that change dramatically over the years.

Dad nearly managed to get himself killed again when he was trying to control the ever-expanding rabbit population by putting strychnine pellets down the burrows. This stuff was deadly to man and beast. He had been given a face mask to wear but, throwing caution to the wind, he stuffed his mask in his jacket pocket. The wind responded by blowing some of this deadly concoction back in his face. He was found later, by an estate worker, staggering about like a drunken fool, although on this occasion he was stone cold sober — another lucky escape. He seemed to be living a charmed life.

I was never told that Mum had been unmarried when she had Maureen. However, there came a time when I needed my birth certificate. Mum was very unwilling to give me this, pretending she had misplaced it. When she discovered me writing to Somerset House to obtain a copy it suddenly turned up. It was obvious that someone had tried to alter some dates. When I 'took her to task' over this forgery she was very angry, saying she had no idea what I was on about. This was how I learned that Maureen was two when they married, so maybe Mum was concerned about what people would think.

Dad was in a bad state mentally when he returned home from the Army. He had been on the beaches at Dunkirk and spent a short time in a Japanese POW camp, which left him with some nasty flashbacks. Soon after they married, Mum woke up choking one night. Dad was trying to strangle her — he thought she was a prison guard. Maybe that was why he found talking about his Army life distressing. I never saw his medals. They had hung on the wall in a special box that he had made but he claimed one of his brothers had stolen them. To the best of my knowledge the medals never turned up again.

When we first moved to Stonehaven I was quite small. I was fascinated by Dad's ferrets. When one of them had babies I would sit looking in the cage for ages, hoping to get a glimpse of the little ones. Dad warned me, on a daily basis, not to touch as ferrets have needle sharp teeth and they bite. One day I forgot that warning. I spotted one of the babies and opened the cage. When he found me later I had all the ferrets sitting with me. He was really cross. I didn't get bitten. The male ferret was in a different cage. I didn't like his colour and so hadn't opened his cage. Dad told me that the male ferret was very savage and showed me a scar on his finger where he claimed the ferret had bitten right through to the bone. I don't think I believed him. If it had bitten him, I'm sure he would have killed it.

Dad also had a very strange encounter with some doubtful mushrooms he had picked. Mum questioned the fact that they were mushrooms. She wasn't very happy cooking them for his breakfast but he insisted. Later on in the morning he began to feel and act in a very strange way. They were, in fact, magic mushrooms. He was as 'high as a kite' all day. Mum was right. She reminded him about it many times over the years, saying,

"Good keeper you were. You didn't even know your mushrooms."

We moved on then to a town in West Yorkshire. I must have been about seven years old, but as I said before, dates and ages are hard to remember. Dad had got a job as a gamekeeper for Lee Feather, one of the big mill owners. Mr Feather lived in a very large house with massive grounds and an orchard down at the bottom with apple and pear trees, which were heavy with fruit. We lived in the gatehouse. Dad was working as Mr Feather's driver just until our house on Keighley Moor was ready. I did like Mrs Feather. She used to call me into the house and give me sweets and cakes. I thought that she must be very rich to have such lovely things. I was allowed to roam about in the garden as long as I didn't speak to anyone unless they spoke to me first. I also had to remember to be very polite. Dad used to call Mr Feather 'Sir' so I thought he must be a very important man. One day, down by the orchard, some boys were stealing apples. I took to my heels and went charging straight into the big kitchen to tell Mrs Feather that some boys were stealing her apples but I ran straight into Mr Feather who was having his coffee. I stood there petrified. I didn't know what to say or do so I said nothing. He turned out to be very nice. He gave me a biscuit. It tasted strange but I ate it anyway and whispered, "thank you sir." He laughed and patted me on the head and then pointed to his wife who was in the kitchen garden picking peas. I did tell her about the boys but she just smiled and said there was such a lot of fruit that a few apples didn't matter. I don't think Mr Feather told Dad because I would have been in trouble if he had. Across the road from the gatehouse was Victoria Park. Mum and Dad took us to the fair there. Dad won a goldfish, but it died. Many, many years later when my husband and I were recalling childhood memories he told me that they often went scrumping apples in the self-same orchard and I often wondered if he had been one of the boys.

I had a cairn terrier, called Trixie, before we moved but couldn't take her with me because Dad said she was having puppies. He said that the family he had sold her to would send me a puppy. I didn't believe him. He always told lies. I remember standing sobbing as they took her away. (I had many more Trixie's through my lifetime.) I forgot all about my promised puppy until one day Dad took me to the railway station to pick up a parcel. I thought it was kippers as Dad's sister used to send him boxes of kippers from Aberdeen. He would have them for breakfast. I wasn't prepared for the parcel we picked up. It was a box with holes and it was making whimpering noises. When we got back home Dad opened it. Inside was my cairn puppy. Guess what I called her – yes, 'Trixie'. She was to have many litters of puppies and would return to the village we came from when we crossed back over the border.

We were to move to Higher Intake Farm. The summer holidays were nearly over so Mum was taking us shopping that Saturday for school clothes. Maureen needed school uniform. There was that dreaded word again, 'school.' When we returned later there was an ambulance by our gate, people rushing to and fro. Mum spotted the figure on the grass. She went drip white, uttered a screech and rushed over. Dad had been asleep in the chair when we left. Someone had left the gas on. He had been overcome by the fumes. I somehow got the blame for playing with the cooker switches. I wondered years later if I had been trying to polish him off to save the rest of us from the grief and mental torture he was to put us through before we reached adulthood and learned how to fight back. Perhaps you think I am being a bit hard on him. Believe me, I'm not. Dad was at Dunkirk on the beach waiting for rescue. He came home. So many young men were lost never to return to their family. He never talked about any of it. The only thing he told me was that they caught rats and cooked and ate them as they were so hungry. He said the rats tasted like chicken. He must have seen some horrible sights. Perhaps it turned his brain. I can never remember him showing affection to any of us. He suffered mood swings and could be nasty one minute and nice the next.

The house move had been postponed until Dad was discharged from hospital. He had to go to Chapel Allerton Hospital in Leeds for some tests on his stomach. Mum said they thought that he had an ulcer. Dad had been gone a few days so we went to visit him.

Mr Feather arranged for someone to drive us there in one of his cars. The car that arrived was posh. Mr Feather's new driver was taking us to see Dad. He wore a uniform and a cap. He put his cap on my head but it fell down past my ears – that proved I wasn't a 'big head' despite what Dad had said.

The hospital was very big. When we got inside it smelt horrible. Mum said it was special stuff they used to kill any germs. I asked if I could stay in the car and wait for her there. I didn't like the place. Mum insisted I go and see Dad. There was a lot of noise in there. I could hear men swearing and shouting and someone screaming. I was glad when we got to Dad's ward as it was quiet in there. I don't know why I bothered to go. Dad didn't say a word to me. One of the nurses told me off for hopping on one leg up the ward. I was told to sit quietly. That was a tall order for a child. Well, I sat quietly but I did sing a little song. I thought it might cheer Dad up. On our way out to the car the noise was even worse than before. Mum said the men in the ward upstairs were poor souls who had fought in the war and had bad nerves. I wondered if Dad's nerves were bad as he shouted and swore a lot. Maureen said that he was just bad tempered. I hoped I didn't have to visit him again. Mum said that Dad would be home in a few days with medicine to help his tummy. I fell asleep in the car on the way home so the journey seemed so much shorter.

We moved a few days later to the new house. I wondered if I'd have any friends there. I did have Trixie dog to keep me company. I wanted her to sleep on my bed but Dad said that dogs slept in the kennel. Mum told me off for pulling faces behind his back because it's very rude. "Your middle name is trouble," she'd said. Looking back, I'd have to have agreed with that. Had ASBOs been around then I'd have picked one up for sure.

CHAPTER TWO: INTAKE FARM

Our new home was Higher Intake Farm on Keighley Moor. The nearest village was Oakworth, which was a few miles from us. Our nearest neighbour was an elderly farming couple. They were very nice. I used to walk there and get fresh eggs, butter and sometimes cheese. If I was lucky the farmer's wife would be baking and I would get a scone straight out of the oven. They melted in your mouth – delicious. One day as I was leaving the kitchen she gave me a hug. Her collie, that had been lying in the sun, jumped up and sank its teeth into my arm. I didn't cry, I was in shock. I'd played ball with this dog, sat with my head against her tummy in the sunshine. I thought she was my friend but I'd made the big mistake, overstepped the mark. This couple had never had children and this dog was their baby. I stole her limelight and she didn't like that. The poor woman was very upset. Her husband drove me home in their car. Mum was not too pleased. Dad just said, "Dogs bite." I didn't get an anti-tetanus – I guess they didn't have them then. Mum bathed the wound in Dettol and then put some stuff on that really stung. I kept it covered up for a few days and it healed. Tough cookie I'd been in those days.

The road up to the farm was really not a proper road, half-way up was the ruins of a house that had been destroyed by fire. Dad said it was called Lower Intake. There was a tree and just the shell of a building. Dad said that someone had hung themselves on that tree and that on a moonlit night you could see them swinging in the breeze. Every time we drove up that road in the dark I closed my eyes. I really didn't want to see anyone swinging in the breeze. Mum said Dad was talking a load of rubbish but I made my mind up never to walk up that road in the dark.

Intake Farm was a beautiful place to live. In the summer you could smell the heather. The scent drifted in your windows at night and for miles the foliage formed a purple carpet. You could see the peat bogs. They showed up very black. Dad said these were very dangerous. Sheep and other animals used to get trapped in them and sink down and drown. It made me extra careful where I put my feet. Dad expected everyone to do their share of work and although I was a small child no exception was made. Dad used to cut squares of peat to burn on the fire along with logs in the winter. We had to stack the peat in a certain way, allowing the air to circulate and dry the squares out so that they became quite dry and hard like bricks. Dad would drive the Landrover to the bog and we would fill sacks with the peat to last us through the winter. It was a hard and very dirty job. He used a special spade to cut the squares of peat, which was curved at the bottom, not straight like a garden spade. He also had to keep bracken under control. He did this with a scythe and we had to use a sickle (a very sharp curved blade on a short handle). When I think about it, I was given very dangerous implements to use and could have cut myself badly but, luckily, I never did. We piled the bracken in heaps and Dad would burn it when it was dry enough. You had to be very careful as the last thing you wanted was a moor fire as it would spread so fast, destroying everything in its path and devastating the wildlife.

I don't want you to think we worked all the time. There were a lot of fun days too. Like the time we helped a neighbour with the haymaking. It was a long, hot day. I got to sit on the top of the hay wagon all the way back to the barn. Then there was the evening meal which was all cold things like pies, sausage rolls, ham and homemade bread rolls filled with cheese and homemade chutney. As I sit here writing I can taste the bread. Nothing tastes as good as bread you have made yourself.

The summer soon passed and the nights were drawing in. The peat bricks made a good, hot fire to warm your toes on a cold evening. Soon the snow would come. I thought it would look very different, all dressed in white. Yes, I must say, it was a good life. You could roam for miles, get very dirty and nobody said a word. Nobody told me off! I began to wonder if I had become invisible. Then Mum went and spoilt it all by mentioning the dreaded 'S' word.

School was to start the following week and then I wished I was invisible. Mum had been told that Oakworth Primary School was a lovely school. Yeah, right. I was not convinced. My sister was going to the senior school in Haworth (that's where the Brontes had lived). Dad promised to take us to see Wuthering Heights. I don't know what I expected to see there but it wasn't a tumbled down ruin that had seen better days. On the moors in the winter months the mist could suddenly come down. It was cold, damp and soaked you through in seconds. You could easily get lost by losing your sense of direction. OK, I must admit that Wuthering Heights with the mist coming down did look very spooky. You wouldn't have been surprised to see Heathcliff striding towards you out of the mist. Wind was whistling through the sides that still remained. It had been someone's home a long, long time ago. I'd been very pleased to get back in the Landrover and make for home. As we drove up the road past Lower Intake, I would quickly cover my eyes. I could hear the branches of the tree creaking in the wind and I wasn't risking seeing someone swinging in the breeze.

Our house was always quite warm. We had an open fire in the sitting room and a range in the kitchen which was kept alight winter and summer. We had a porch and when you opened the front door the stairs to the bedrooms were straight in front of you. I didn't like the stairs. At the top there was a small window which was kept slightly ajar. The curtains would always be open, billowing out with the strong winds that blew from the moorland. This frightened me a lot. When I went to bed I rushed up the stairs along the passageway which was always in darkness because I was too little to reach the light switches. We had three bedrooms. One was really big but the one I shared with Maureen was quite modest – just enough room for a dresser and the double bed. There were built-in cupboards where you could hang your clothes. The windows had very big sills, wide enough to sit on but quite high up. I couldn't reach them to see out. The little boxroom just held a single bed. I asked if I could have that room but Maureen didn't want to sleep on her own. The electricity came from a generator in the large barn where the Landrover was parked at night. There were some steps up to what would have been a hay loft and was now used as storage space.

First day at new school: Dad gave us a lift to the bottom of the road to catch the school bus. My stomach was full of butterflies. I thought I'd be sick on the bus. I had hoped Mum and Dad would take me into school. After all, I didn't know anyone. But, no, chucked in at the deep end as usual. I had been warned by my parents that they didn't want any complaints about me. I thought I was getting a complex and that it was their fault. I asked Maureen if she would take me in but she couldn't because she had to carry on to Haworth and the bus wouldn't hang about waiting for her. I decided that if I didn't like it, I'd just take myself off somewhere. All the smaller kids got off the bus at Oakworth. Nobody paid any attention to me. I saw there was a park across the road. I thought that maybe I would go and explore the park, it would be much more interesting. Just as I prepared to escape a tall, thin lady standing at the school gate called my name. I didn't answer. I hoped she wouldn't notice me, but she did. I followed her into school. She showed me where to hang my coat. I went and sat at a table. None of the kids spoke to me so I just sat quietly. This was all new to me. I'd been a free spirit all summer and now they sent me here. It wasn't fair. The lady did seem quite nice but I wasn't fooled. I decided to give it a few days and see if what Mum had said was true. I did OK until lunchtime then I panicked. What if I didn't like the food? I would be in trouble on my first day. Well my fears were unfounded. The dinner was OK. You didn't get to pick what you wanted to eat. In my day they cooked one meal and one pudding. It cost five shillings a week for school lunch. If you didn't like what was on offer, you did without. After lunch was playtime. I just sat on a bench hoping everyone would leave me alone. It may seem hard to believe, but I made no friends at that school. Don't get me wrong, there was nothing wrong with the school. All the other kids seemed to enjoy their day but I was a loner. I'm afraid to say that I didn't put myself out to try and fit in even at that young age. I had put up the barriers to protect me. I had to, nobody else would. The day passed and home time came. It hadn't been too bad really. I managed to get home in one piece. Also, I hadn't upset anyone. I gave myself a pat on the back. Doreen had survived.

The newness wore off quite quickly. Soon I wasn't the new kid any more. That honour moved on to someone else. I showed no interest in the school day. When no-one was watching I would slip away out of the back gate, across the road and into the park. I would hide in the caves and keep out of sight in case anyone saw me and wondered why I wasn't in school. Nobody seemed to miss me. I always waited until I'd had my dinner, no point in being hungry. I thought it was too good to last. One afternoon I lost track of time and didn't get back into school in time to catch the bus home. Maureen had to get off the bus to look for me. The driver left without us. It was going to be a long walk home. Maureen was so angry that she didn't speak to me for ages after that. We set off walking as nobody would miss us until we didn't arrive home at the normal time. It had already started to get dark. We passed the graveyard on the corner. I was petrified, my active imagination was running riot. I tripped up and nearly fell. That was the final straw for Maureen. She shouted really loudly, "Open your eyes and watch where you're going." Little did she realise how true that was. I had been stumbling along with my eyes firmly closed. I didn't want to see any ghosts or goblins. We had got a bit further along the road when Dad drew up in the Landrover. "Why the hell weren't you two on the bus," he yelled. Maureen said, "Ask her," giving me a shove into the middle seat. She slammed the door so hard it made my teeth rattle all the way home. Dad moaned about the darts match. He was too late to go. I just thanked my lucky stars that I wouldn't have to walk past Lower Intake.

I couldn't face someone swinging in the breeze, not after the ghosts and goblins. What I didn't see was the clout round the ear from Dad for causing him grief. Mum didn't say a word. I made myself be very quiet that night. Mum thought I was sickening for something.

Things at school started to improve. Now I was paying attention, I was finding the lessons more interesting. We also had a new addition. Dad came home with this strange creature. It was in a very fancy cage. He had bought it from a pub that was closing down. In the cage was a pom-pom hat. This little mouselike animal with a long tail and hands rather than paws slept under the hat during the day and then woke up at night. She had very big, round eyes. We fed her meal worms. She was so tame that she would take the food from your hand. She also ate special white chocolate drops and we mixed up a milk powder for her to drink. Her name was Mitzi. She was a bush baby. At night Mitzi would sit on my shoulder while I did my school work. On her fingers she had 'sucker like' things and she would pat my face but would 'pee' all over you if she got frightened. We had her for a while. Then one night, when I got home, she'd gone. My dad would sell on anything if it made him a profit. She went to a new hotel that had opened as an attraction for the guests. I'm surprised he hadn't thought of selling me, but then I thought I probably wasn't worth anything, so no profit there for him

To make extra money Dad trained sheepdogs. He was

very good at this and his dogs made him a lot of extra cash. His best dog was a bitch called Tip. A farmer bought her as his own dog was getting too old to herd sheep. However, he bought her back a few days later, saying she was no good. Dad couldn't understand what was wrong so gave the farmer a demonstration. Tip did everything he asked of her with no problems. It turned out that the farmer had no teeth. Dad trained his dogs by whistle. He put two fingers in his mouth and could produce all different types of whistles. To solve the problem he retrained her to voice commands and then had the cheek to charge the man for her extra tuition.

Sadly, one of Dad's sheepdogs turned rogue and killed all the turkeys Mum was fattening up for Christmas. Dad told Maureen to hold the dog's lead as he was going to shoot it. Mum saw what was happening and went mad. She tied the lead to a fence post and took Maureen, who was very upset and crying, indoors. The dog had to be destroyed. Once they had killed livestock there was no going back. Dad couldn't see that it was cruel to make Maureen hold the lead. But he had a soft side which was seldom seen. One day he shot a rabbit and then found a nest with her babies in it. He brought them home and gave them to me. I put them in with my tame rabbits. They were about six weeks old so survived OK. When they had grown a lot bigger, I released them back into the wild. Off they hopped without a backward glance. That's gratitude for you!

One of the strange things that baffled us was the case of the missing puppies. It was a sad tale. The local farmer had two dogs give birth in the same week. One dog was a show bitch and she had four puppies. The other was a working dog, she also had four puppies. The poor working dog was deprived of her puppies. They were destroyed so she could carry on working. The show dog kept her puppies. They were worth big bucks. When the farmer checked his dog next morning the puppies had gone and so had the working dog. He informed the police, assuming they had been stolen. He just couldn't understand why they had taken the wrong bitch. The weeks passed without a trace of evidence. One morning Dad went intothe barn and found a dog feeding her puppies. He knew where they belonged so returned them. The farmer was very pleased. The puppies meant a lot of money to him.

The poor working dog was to be destroyed. Dad said he would take her. She was an excellent sheepdog. Dad had no problem finding her a new home and made money as well. Perhaps next time she had babies she would be allowed to keep them. She was so unhappy that she stole another dog's babies.

So really, all things considered, the school wasn't too bad.

Sometimes I was glad to go. Mum and Dad always seemed to be rowing in those days. Well, Dad did the shouting and Mum just ignored him. He had started putting whiskey in his cup of tea. Mum wasn't amused. Come to think of it, he went out to the pub most nights as well. I heard Mum telling Maureen that it was a good job the Landrover knew its way home as most nights he was too drunk to be driving. He also bought an old American army jeep from somewhere. He was teaching Maureen to drive. She was also learning to shoot. She nearly blew Dad's head off when climbing over a style without unloading the twelve bore she was carrying which went off. A good job it was pointing at the ground or Dad would be singing with the heavenly choir or maybe not! I think he would have been sent to the fiery furnace or wherever they send people who are not nice.

Poor old Mum was not too happy. She had been to see the dentist as she had a problem with her gums. He said she had to have all her teeth out. She got an appointment the following week. Gran came to stay to 'hold the fort'. Dad had gone to collect her and I thought that they would probably kill each other before they get back. Gran did not like Dad, she never had and Dad couldn't stand Gran. She was about the only person that could put him in his place and get away with it. It was a case of light the blue touch paper, stand back and watch the fireworks. I'd planned to just get on with my chores. That way everyone would forget I was there. That's what usually happened. Things were very quiet while Gran was there. Dad hadn't gone to the pub or got drunk for nearly a week. If only it could have been like that all the time. Mum had her teeth out and was very poorly. She couldn't eat anything. Her mouth was in a terrible state. I felt so sorry for her. Gran did a fine job of keeping Dad in order but my sister and I had to do all Mum's jobs. By the time we got to bed we were so tired. It seemed we had just closed our eyes and it was time to get up again. It was so funny watching Dad trying to be nice to Gran. He had to take her into Keighley to do some food shopping. He'd asked Maureen if she wanted to go with them. She'd had a suitable excuse ready. I was nowhere to be found. So off they went. Gran was a really good cook. Even Dad said so. She was always trying to persuade Maureen to eat more as she was very thin.

Mum soon improved and would be getting some false teeth. I supposed Gran would be going home then. She didn't like me a lot. I told Mum that she didn't like me. Gran said I was a lot like Dad. I had a look in my mirror. I just looked like me. Perhaps it was because she was quite old and had bad eyesight. It had been enough to give me nightmares, saying I was like him.

Mum was very pleased with me because I hadn't been in any trouble for ages. Maureen said I should polish my halo. I wasn't sure where my halo was so I just ignored her. The weather had turned very cold. When I got into bed I pulled the covers over my head until I got warm. We had some really long icicles hanging from the house. They seemed to get bigger every day. Gran had gone so things were back to normal. That is if you can call the way we lived normal. Dad had been making fun of Mum's new teeth. She was having a few problems learning to eat with them. He had been having a laugh about it, so Mum decided to tell us about the problems Dad had experienced with false teeth. He was on his third set. His first set he lost when he was sick after too much to drink. He forgot to take his teeth out and lost them down the toilet. So he'd got into the habit of taking out his teeth and putting them in his hip pocket, this was usually when he had a lot to drink. He wanted to make sure he didn't lose any more down the loo. He was at a dance and slipped on the dance floor and landed on his bottom. He had broken his teeth but had also bitten his own bum. He had to go to the hospital to have stitches put in the cut. So, technically speaking, my Dad was the only man to have bitten his own arse! By the time Mum had finished her story we were helpless with laughter. Dad never spoke about Mum's teeth again. It was right what Mum said: Dad would laugh at others' misfortune but hated to be laughed at.

I'd woken the following day to a very different scene.

Someone had painted my windowsill with lovely shapes. When I got downstairs all I could see was a complete white wilderness. Mum had told me that Jack Frost painted windows. I wondered who made the snowflakes. I didn't even bother getting dressed. I rushed outside in my 'wellies' and coat. I couldn't believe it was so deep. Dad was out already hunting rabbits and foxes. He remembered where all the tracks were and then he would set traps and snares to catch what he considered vermin. The traps were very sharp and anything caught would chew off their legs to escape. He used to find them later and put them out of their misery.

There would be no school until they cleared the roads. That was typical, I was just starting to get the hang of the school thing. I decided to make a snowman. Mum thought it would be a good idea to get dressed and have breakfast first. So I'd trudged indoors again. I never got to make my snowman. Maureen was poorly again so I'd got all her jobs as well as my own. If there had been Childline then I could have reported them for slavery. I didn't know what was wrong with Maureen. She was so quiet those days. She was no fun any more. Mum was always telling her off for not eating her meals. Mind you, seeing Dad prancing about in his underwear was enough to put anyone off their food. He was always coming in our room in the morning acting the fool and diving under the blankets. I made a quick exit when I heard him coming.

The snow lasted and lasted but the snow plough had been along the main road now so it would be back to school.

Somehow the snow was not the same when people had walked on it. The magic disappeared. I had all the dogs to feed. It took ages. Maureen and I used to prepare the dogs' food together. We had to strip all the meat off the sheep's heads, these had boiled overnight in a big copper.

Being an evil child, I would pop out the eyes and ping them at her. She'd run screaming out of the shed and tell

Mum. That would get me into trouble again. At least that day I wouldn't. Well, I'd done everything myself so I wasn't in trouble that night. If there had been a 'naughty step' then I'd have got haemorrhoids from prolonged sitting on it. It's funny how I decided the snow wasn't such a miracle after all. When I had to plod through it to catch the school bus my feet were wet and my toes frozen. I had to walk home as well so, by the time I got there, I wasn't in a very good mood. Anyway, Maureen appeared to have recovered so that was good news.

It would soon be Christmas. It's funny, out of all my childhood memories, I can only remember one Christmas. I got a Cinderella watch. It came in a little plastic slipper. I kept that plastic slipper for years. I don't remember any of the others. Maybe there was a reason for that.

Things were changing. Home wasn't a place I wanted to be. A lot of the time there was trouble. Dad drank too much and started throwing things about. Sometimes the noise was so bad that I couldn't sleep. My sister didn't appear to hear any of it. She must have been deaf. Mum pretended that none of it happened and Dad was so drunk he probably didn't remember. I began to think that I was the only sane person there. I would be ten the following year. I wondered if I'd feel any different when I was older. I didn't think I would. Perhaps I could have prayed for a miracle that would have made everything change to good. I guess that would have been a pretty tall order for God. Anyway, as Mum used to say, "If nothing alters it will stay as it is." She was always thinking up these pearls of wisdom.

I'd had a nice little sideline going then. I was the local mole trapper. I sold the bodies of these poor creatures to the school bus driver for one shilling each. He, in turn, passed them on to someone who made moleskin gloves.

A shilling for each mole had seemed like a fortune to me. Dad had showed me how to set the traps. The trick had been to find the biggest molehill and then dig carefully, clearing away the earth until you found the junction of the tunnel, that was where you set the trap. The handles of the trap were above ground so you would know the next day if the trap had been sprung. I hardly ever found the traps empty.

I had a big problem with Mum's new cockerel. It was an evil bird. When I went to feed the dogs it tried to attack me, flying at my legs and pecking me with its sharp beak. As I had a dish of dog food in both hands, I couldn't defend myself. I told Dad. He just laughed. One night I threw the dogs' dishes at it but it still managed to get me. It was very clever. It hid behind the shed and waited to attack. I asked Mum. She came up with a cunning plan. The next night I put some corn in my pocket but had to put down the dog food to throw the corn so the hens ate the dog food and the corn so I had to go back and get more dog food. I got so fed-up with this bird. Dad decided to clip its wing so it would not be able to fly at me. If you clip just one wing it makes the creature off balance. It worked. Why didn't he do this before? My poor legs were really sore.

I hated the winter. It made everything so much harder to do. I still liked to see the snow falling, it's just when you had to go out in it. You would rather stay by the warm fire. The magic soon disappeared. I thought I was depressed. The other girls at school didn't have loads of work to do before and after school. Mum said it was the price you had to pay if you wanted to live out in the wilds. I thought the price was too high! Mum said it would soon be spring. I wondered what difference that would make?

My parents had decided to tarmac the yard. Mum was so pleased. No more muddy floors. I hoped it didn't take too long. I plodded my weary way to the school bus. When I got back in the evening half the yard was finished. So it would be finished by the weekend. It wasn't, in fact, it took another two weeks before it was completed.

I needed a pair of roller skates. I hadn't got much of my mole money left. I wondered if Mum would put the rest of the money in and then I would pay her back when I'd caught some more moles. I asked nicely. It didn't make any difference. She said I must wait and save the money up. Well I could wait. She'd be sorry when she saw me dashing past the kitchen window on my skates.

I saved every penny I got, even my sweetie money. When I'd got enough I asked Mum to get me the skates when she went shopping. She forgot and I had to wait another two weeks. I hoped she didn't forget next time. Hurrah, she got them. I thought I would be straight out the following morning. I would whizz about everywhere. I was up with the lark ready for my skating. Then I was back in bed. Thought I might as well have a lay in as it had snowed really heavily overnight. That was Mum's fault. I hoped she was really sorry. When I did get to use my skates it didn't last long. Dad put a stop to it. He said it was making horrible marks on the new tarmac. Well, I kept the skates and took them to school. They weren't bothered about marks there.

CHAPTER THREE: MAUREEN'S KNICKERS AND THE MURDER THAT WASN'T

Well, let's deal with the knickers first. Maureen always wore white cotton knickers. She used to boil them up in an old pan once a week to make sure they stayed white. She had developed a thing about being spotlessly clean. I was sitting in the kitchen reading a comic. She asked me to keep an eye on the pan to make sure it didn't boil dry. I mumbled a reply then, like children do, I forgot all about it and wandered outside. The next thing I knew, there was smoke coming out of the kitchen window and Dad was bellowing for me.

"What's up," says me. "What's that awful smell?"

By this time Dad was red in the face, coughing and swearing. Mum arrived back from feeding the chickens and stood open-mouthed. I was looking from one to the other. Then Maureen came downstairs.

Mum said, "Were they your drawers in that pan?" I tried to make a quick exit but Dad grabbed me as I passed.

"I asked her to watch the pan," sobbed Maureen. " Now I have no underwear, only the pair I'm wearing."

Dad stood shaking his head. Maureen was still screeching. I was trying very hard not to laugh.

Mum stormed into the kitchen, threw open the windows

and chucked the pan out in the yard.

"Right," she said. "Get ready, we're going shopping." She turned to Dad. "Well what are you waiting for?"

Dad went to get the Landrover. I was beginning to think I'd got away with it, but no such luck. She turned to me and pointed to the kitchen.

"I'll expect that to be cleaned up before I get back. Don't disturb Maureen. She's having a rest after the shock she's had."

So they went shopping. I went scrubbing and Maureen slumbered on.

So justice was seen to be done. I reminded Maureen about it many years later when we were both grandmothers but she still didn't see the funny side of it. I think I must have had a warped sense of humour, but me and Mum laughed about it many times over the years.

The more serious case of the murder that wasn't sort of turned the tables on me. I had just got back from school.

As I crossed the yard there was a trail of blood which increased as I followed it into the house, through the kitchen and right up to the bathroom door, which was locked. I checked upstairs. All was quiet. Nobody around and the Landrover was out front so Mum and Dad hadn't gone out. I must admit that by now I was feeling a bit scared. Very slowly the bathroom door opened and Dad emerged wearing his big rubber apron. He had a large kitchen knife in one hand and an axe in the other, both dripping blood. He stood with a weird stupid look on his face. I was getting ready to run.

"He's gone mad and killed someone," I thought. Then Mum walked in behind me.

"For God's sake," she said to him. "Get cleaned up and wash out the bath."

I was really scared and worried now. Was she in on it as well and who had he chopped up in the bath? I have heard people say they have been frozen to the spot. Well that was me. I couldn't move a muscle. We were all there in the kitchen except one.

"Oh, my God, he's killed her," I thought. There had been

a row the previous night after I went to bed. Maureen had slammed the door and run upstairs. She had been asking if she could go to the dance on Saturday with a friend. Dad said 'no'. He never let her go anywhere. I was going to stay at Janet's house. She was a new girl who had started at my school. First friend I'd had. I would go to school on Monday from her house. I think Mum and Dad were glad to have me out of the way. I sprang into action, pushed past Mum and rushed upstairs, heart pounding and scared to death. I decided that I would go to Janet's house and ask her father to tell the police what Dad had done. I heard someone coming upstairs. "That's it," I thought. "Oh, my God, he's coming to get me now." The door slowly opened and in walked Maureen.

"I thought you were dead," I gasped. "Who's he chopped up in the bath then?"

It was one of the rare occasions I heard her laugh. Panic over. Dad had knocked down and killed one of the farmer's lambs and was chopping it into joints. They were going to share the meat. I hate lamb. I didn't eat any of it and haven't enjoyed eating lamb to this day. I don't eat much meat at all now. I sometimes have chicken or turkey but that's all. Maureen did get to go to the dance. Dad took her and picked her up when it was finished, so all turned out OK in the end.

The next big thing was that we were having visitors. Peter and Pauline (my Mum's sister's children) were staying for a week. I can't really remember what we did that week. It can't have been very exciting if I don't remember it. Pauline was a bit younger than Maureen and Peter was a boy so I didn't have anything to do with him. I didn't like boys very much. Anyway the big thing was that when they had gone home Maureen kicked off big time. She claimed Pauline had stolen some of her things and taken them home. What exactly these things were I never found out. I just know it caused no end of trouble between Mum and her sister. Whatever it was that went missing was sent back so that was that.

This was also the year that Mum became a pig farmer. She had been visiting a local farm and the farmer had a runt born in a litter of piglets. He was going to knock it on the head but Mum asked if she could have it. A tea chest appeared in our kitchen with newspaper in the bottom and lots of straw. Mum had managed to fix up a heat lamp to keep the animal extra warm. It was a sow. Mum called her Gertie and she grew at an alarming rate. Mum decided she wanted to breed pigs and managed to persuade the same pig farmer to collect her sow to take to his boar. When he came to collect Gertie he was most put out when he saw what his runt had grown into. Mum promised him first refusal on the litter of piglets that she hoped Gertie was going to produce, but she did warn him she would want full market price for her piglets. Dad stood looking 'gob-smacked' at Mum's bargaining skills. When he was telling us about it later he quipped,

"Of course, she learned it from the master of bargains."

Mum said, under her breath, "Yeah, right, I got your father from the bargain basement."

He was half-way out of the door so didn't hear her. He couldn't understand why me and Maureen were falling about in helpless laughter.

He just looked at Mum and said, "They didn't get their brains from my side of the family."

This just made us howl louder. However, Gertie had a vendetta against Dad. He was standing talking to someone in the field and Gertie ran straight at him and bowled him over. Mum had seen this out of the kitchen window. She quickly got the pig bucket and shouted Gertie for her food.

When Dad came indoors later he said, "That pig is living on borrowed time."

"Why," Mum said. "What's she done?"

"She upended me in the field," Dad replied.

"Oh dear, I think that was my fault. I rattled the pig bucket to get her in for her food," Mum said.

Dad sort of grunted and said no more.

It was funny really, Dad's boss always bought Mum a massive box of chocolates. The boxes had lovely pictures on the front of cottages, puppies or kittens. She would hide them away and when Gertie started having her babies Mum took up residence in the pig pen with a blanket, a flask and the big box of chocs.

Dad would ask, "What's for tea?"

We replied, "Sandwiches." "Where's your mother?" he would bellow. Maureen and I replied in unison, "pig pen."

He just said, "Oh" and ate his sandwiches. He would always check to see where Gertie was before he walked down the field. I think Mum let her out on purpose sometimes. Gertie definitely didn't care for Dad. She was fine with everyone else but if she saw him she gave chase. Dad would run. He had no option. You didn't argue with an angry pig!

We had some more visitors that year. Dad's nephew, Clarence and his friend. They also stayed a week and used to set off every day with a rucksack. Mum provided drinks and sandwiches. We never saw the pair of them again until nightfall. Before they left for home, Clarence said, "I lost some money on the moor. Whoever finds it can keep it." We forgot all about it until the Annual Slaughter started. I picked up a pound note outside one of the shooting butts. I gave it to Mum just in case it belonged to one of the gentry. She gave it back to me later. It was a Scottish pound note. Clarence lived in Aberdeenshire so I claimed the treasure.

Dad amazed the gentry by showing them the method he used to train the gun dogs. He would place an egg on the floor. The dog had to pick it up and carry it to him without breaking the shell. The reward was the egg. Dad would crack it open for them. If the dog could perform this trick it meant it had a soft mouth and could retrieve game birds without damaging the flesh. His own favourite dog was Blondie. If he wanted to impress the gentry this was the bitch he used. She never made mistakes. She could pick baby chicks up and carry them to Dad. Then place them very gently on the floor. It had to be seen to be believed.

However, he would sell anything for a profit. Even Blondie if the price was right.

CHAPTER FOUR: THE ANNUAL SLAUGHTER (LOOSELY KNOWN AS THE GLORIOUS TWELTH)

The preparation for this day went on for months. Dad had pheasant and partridge eggs which he collected from the nests during the breeding season. He put these under broody chickens. (These are chickens that have stopped laying.) They would sit on the eggs until they hatched and made very good mums. Dad would check these eggs to see if they contained chicks. He got a bowl of warm water and put in the eggs. The ones that sank were rotten. The ones that floated contained chicks. The eggs would wobble about in the water. These chicks would become very tame and would eat from your hand. They were released onto the moor about a month before the shooting season started. I thought this very cruel. But, to be fair, they hardly ever got shot. They were low flying birds. The shooters had to be careful not to hit the beaters so most of the young birds lived to maturity.

In 1958 we had two helpers, both students. Ray was tall and blond and wore very thick-lensed glasses. He was going to university. The other was David. He was only about 5'4". He was working the summer for extra cash until he decided what to do with the rest of his life. Ray was very quiet. His mum owned a baker's shop. I met her when Dad picked Ray up to come to work. She had the tiniest dog I'd ever seen. It was a cream-coloured

Chihuahua. It was lovely and would lick your face. It loved to be cuddled. Ray's mum was tall, like him. She always wore polo-necked jumpers. She would carry this little dog up her jumper in the winter so that it was kept warm. It stuck its little head out of the top. I loved this little creature and vowed I would have one when I grew up. As I sit writing this story, by my feet in a basket sleeps a cream-colour Chihuahua. The difference is that this little dog thinks it's a big dog and has lots of attitude but no teeth as he is twelve now. He doesn't belong to me but to my youngest son. (You won't hear about him until much later in my story.) I hoped that neither of these young men would pay too much attention to Maureen or they wouldn't be keeping their summer jobs long. Dad made sure they had plenty to do.

I was on a secret mission at that time. Sandra, our brown nanny-goat, was due to have a kid. I wanted to make sure I got to it before Dad. If he got there first he would destroy it. This time I was lucky. I saw Sandra out of the kitchen window with twin babies, so they survived and were sold on at a later date. They didn't meet the nasty man wanting to drown them.

On shoot day I had to watch all the dogs. Maureen helped with guns. Mum was on catering. Ray and David were organising the beaters. These were men from the surrounding villages. They got £1 a day and their lunch (which was a bag containing a pork pie, a beef bap, a packet of crisps and a bottle of beer). This was their pay. They had to walk the moor waving a white flag to force the birds into the air for the gentry to shoot. If this was sport, the poor old grouse were on the losing team. Dad was always sober on shoot days. He never drank at home. We had a big storage cupboard under the stairs.

There were loads of crates of beer. This was for the beaters.

Also in the cupboard was Mum's ginger beer, slowly fermenting. We were going to get a rude reminder from this ginger beer but that will be revealed later. The shooting lodge was where the gents ate their lunch. This was a two-storey building that me, Mum and Maureen had cleaned out the previous week. Downstairs was the gun cupboard, which was locked up when any guns were in there. Upstairs were long tables covered with lovely white tablecloths. The gentry ate a much different lunch to the beaters. On their lovely white plates they had several cuts of cold meats and all the trimmings of a high-class buffet.

There was also a very rich fruitcake, which I loved, and some very smelly cheese and pickles, which I didn't. To drink they had brandy, whiskey and other strange drinks.

I hated the shooting lodge. It had the biggest spiders with really long legs. I didn't like spiders. Every cupboard in that place had a few in. When you opened the doors they jumped out at you. I used to run a mile when I saw one. When the shoot was over for the day I was on the packing. All the birds killed that day had to be graded and the young birds were put in hampers, then onto the train to be in London by midnight. These birds were headed for the big restaurants and hotels for the posh people to eat. I was quite good at this job. The young birds have a thin skull, so when pressed it shatters, whereas the older birds have a thick skull which stays intact.

Just as everyone was packing up to go home Dad gave Maureen Mr Feathers' matching pair of guns to put in the gun cupboard. Mr Feather was walking behind, talking to Dad when Maureen tripped and dropped both guns into a peat bog. It was only the quick action of Dad that saved them from sinking to the bottom. These guns were very expensive so Mr Feather was far from pleased. Dad 'got it in the neck' for letting her carry them. Also these guns had to be cleaned ready for the next day's shoot. That was one job he couldn't pass onto us. They had to be cleaned with special gun oil to stop pitting in the barrels. So this had to be done by someone who knew about guns. Dad was up half the night cleaning the peat off them. Serves him right! Mr Feather was a nice man. He remembered me and always asked me how I was doing at school.

I thought it strange really, but why did Maureen never ever get told off for anything? She was so meek and mild compared to me, maybe she never did anything bad. I wondered whether I was adopted. I thought about asking Mum but decided against it. With my track record they would be thinking of sending me back. I was always given the 'mind your manners' speech and told not to speak unless spoken to.

However the morning after the shoot something even worse happened. Mum told us that we were all going to the Young Farmers' dance the following Saturday so she would be buying me a new frock. I had spent the whole summer in my shorts and tee-shirt. The last thing I wanted was a frock. Oh, and petticoats! Mum said I looked like something from the Stone Age. I was getting a new hairstyle as well – Deep Joy. Well we were all off to trip the light fantastic. What a palaver it was getting ready.

Our Maureen had to have a safety pin to hold her knickers, petticoat and everything else up. She was terrified something would fall down and she would feel a fool.

The dance wasn't too bad really. There were some girls from school there so I had someone to talk to. Dad waltzed Mum round the floor, tramping on her feet. Mum was a really good dancer. Dad just thought he was. Our Maureen had a lot of dances with one of the farmer's sons.

There was an interval for the buffet and we were all sitting eating when a racket broke out in the men's toilets. The young chap who had been dancing with Maureen had been beaten up. His face was a dreadful mess. He was taken away to hospital. There was worse to come. When we got home the most awful row broke out. Dad went berserk, smashing everything in the lounge.

Poor Maureen was in a terrible state, drip white and sobbing. I grabbed her hand. We ran and hid in the barn. I must have been a tough cookie in those days. It was strange really how Dad would back down if I stood up to him. I realised that night that I was no longer scared of him. I was only ten but I grew up that night. I learned how to hate. I would never trust him again. Ray and David had seen it all. They felt sorry for us. Ray said we could go to his mum's if we wanted but it had to be faced up to. We waited until it all went quiet and then crept back into the house, up the stairs to bed. I could still hear Dad shouting at Mum. They must have been in the kitchen. Poor Mum, I felt really sorry for her. She never answered him back or argued with him. I decided I was never getting married, ever. Then, it seemed only seconds later that he was standing at the side of our bed in his vest and pants. It must have been morning because it was light outside. He bellowed at me, "Your mother needs you downstairs." I staggered downstairs, still half asleep.

I couldn't believe the mess he'd left behind. Mum was doing her best to clean it all up. I was so angry, why should we clean up the mess left by him? He had broken all Mum's nice china, her special stuff she kept in the cabinet. All that was left of the cabinet was a pile of broken glass and wood. I couldn't believe one person could have caused so much damage. It was then that Mum's ginger beer started exploding. Dad ran downstairs.

I think he thought World War Three had broken out. He opened the cupboard door. Bottle corks and ginger beer were flying all over. One cork caught him right in the eye.

"Winnie," he shouted at my mum. "I think I've been blinded." She just walked into the kitchen, ignoring him.

"Well," I thought, "At least Mum's got her own back, or the ginger beer had." The problem was that she had forgotten to loosen the corks and the bottles were so full of gas that they blew up. So we never got to taste the ginger beer but I didn't think Dad would forget it in a hurry. The thing that amazed me was that he walked through the mess of broken china and things and never said a word apart from telling Mum to clear up all the mess. I don't know how she just carried on as if nothing had happened. I got left with all the work that morning. I fed all the dogs, let them out for exercise and hosed down the kennels. We found out later that it was Dad who had given the young lad the beating. He thought he was paying too much attention to Maureen. He didn't get away with it completely as you will see later on. Ah, the plot thickens...

A star is born – Another big thing that happened (it may not be big to some people but to me it was), Maureen had left school and got a job in the pyjama factory at Oakworth.

 Mum was a bit concerned that the dust from the material would affect her chest. Anyway this was significant to me because I still detested school. It just took up all my free time. There was so much other stuff I could be doing. The other thing is that I had to walk down our long, long road on my own to catch the school bus. Dad took Maureen to and from work but I had to walk. But then I think Mum must have had a word about this because the next thing was that Dad said he was getting me a pony. I thought I would believe it when I saw it. However, he had made a sort of shelter at the bottom of the road. Anyway, this all pales into insignificance because I was offered a part in the school production of 'A Christmas Carol'. Hollywood beckoned! I was going to be the ghost of Christmas past. I only had to say one line but 'what the heck', everyone has to start somewhere. Did it all go to plan I hear you asking? Well, of course not. After all this is me we are talking about, the original Miss Disaster. You wouldn't believe how much I practised my one line over the next few weeks. I stood in front of the mirror wearing my suitably altered bedsheet to see if I looked scary enough. Dad got so sick of hearing it he said, "She won't win an Oscar for that performance but we should get a medal for putting up with it." I just ignored him.

The day of the big performance dawned. It didn't start off too well. Dad was in our room again that morning so I was up bright and early but it all went downhill from there. First he offered me a lift. I couldn't really say 'no'. I dawdled doing my morning chores. He and Maureen left without me. Thank God. He really got on my nerves. I set off down the road with my extra bag containing my scary bedsheet and then everything went wrong. I'm not sure if I went over on my ankle or stood on a stone but whichever it was my ankle was hurting a lot. By the time I got to school I was limping badly. When it got to show time my ankle had swollen up like a balloon. However, the show must go on. It gives a whole new meaning to 'break a leg'. I limped onto the stage, moaning and rattling my chains. "I am the ghost of Christmas past," I groaned. I'm not sure, even today, what happened next. Maybe my ankle gave out completely or I tripped over my sheet, but I hit the stage face down and was heard to utter "Oh shit." The front of Mum's sheet was soaked in blood from my lip and my nose, which I felt sure I had broken. I had bitten deep into my lip. I don't know who picked me up and carried me off. The performance, of course, continued without me. I was mortified. I don't know which hurt most, my ankle, my face or my pride. I'm pretty sure it was my pride but 'hey ho' if I was not to become a famous thespian I thought there must be several other fields that I could excel in. It seemed everything I tried was a complete disaster but the only way is up so I thought I would get on with whatever life threw at me next.

I had got my pony. He was an old boy called Auburn. Dad

was convinced that I would have broken my neck putting a pony at a fence riding anything more spirited. He said to Mum, "She already thinks she's the Lone Ranger." Anyway the idea of me riding him down to the bottom of the road, then tethering him and leaving him with food and water under his shelter until I came back from school wasn't going to work. Whatever we tried, he managed to get free and back to his warm stable long before I got home. He always ate his food first. Guess he needed the extra energy to get up the hill. He didn't like being ridden too much either. I was still only small in stature so Dad built me a step so I could mount. However, this didn't work too well either. I would launch myself from this step and Auburn would walk forwards causing me to land flat on my face. He used to turn his head and laugh at me, or, at least he looked like he was laughing. He could just as well have been preparing to bite a chunk out of me. So really we had a love-hate relationship. He loved me when I brought an apple or a titbit but hated me if I wanted to take a ride. Anyway, I was still walking to and from home in all weathers. One day, when I returned from school, he was gone. Mum and Dad told me that he had been taken back to his owner and that he'd only been on loan. They were liars! He had been shot and his body had been taken away. I saw that his bridle was still hung in the barn.

I missed him. Dad said that he would get me another pony much younger than Auburn. I never got another pony. Dad never did anything that he promised.

Dad killed one of Tricia's puppies as well. The poor thing was born with its front legs deformed. I found it on the windowsill outside the kennels. Poor Trixie knew it was there. She'd sit looking up and crying. I wrapped it up and buried it with a big stone on top of the grave so that Trixie couldn't dig it up. My father was 'Dr Death' as far as animals were concerned. He drowned a goat kid because it was a billy goat. He had told one of his helpers to bury it before I saw it. The poor lad was upset. He didn't do a very good job of digging the grave. Later that afternoon the billy goat came staggering up the field, unsteady on its little legs. I flew down the field and grabbed it. When I carried it into the kitchen Mum looked shamefaced. "Oh, Doreen," she said. "You won't be able to keep it. The goat's milk is for us. Baby goats drink a lot of milk." I was a stubborn child. When Dad came in he didn't know what to say. I'd already found a collar for Billy. He was tucked firmly under my arm. "You can't keep that Doreen," he growled at me. I must have looked very fierce standing there with my goat. I marched away, looking back to say, "He can have my milk. I'll teach him to eat grass." My shoes kept falling off. I never had any laces – why the hell didn't they buy me shoe laces?

I'd got a shed at the back of the barn. I remember thinking that I would go and live in my shed with Trixie and my Billy goat. When Billy goat grew bigger he became very naughty, eating Mum's washing and butting everyone, even me, what a cheek! I saved his life! When we got another goat for milking we called her Sandra. She was brown and white. The farmer took Billy back to his farm to be with his herd of goats. I trusted him. He had a kind face, not like Dad who snarled at everyone in those days.

Dad also prevented me from perfecting the perfect handstand. Every time I'd tried to practice Mum shouted at me, saying, "Don't show Dad your knickers." Everyone

at school had seen my knickers. They were navy blue with a pocket to keep your hanky in for when you needed to blow your nose. You flashed your drawers at whoever was standing nearby.

As I sit here telling my story, I think of three things that happened that year that always make me chuckle. The first concerned the local farmer who everybody said had a drink problem. He used to hide his secret supply of whiskey in very strange places. This was to ensure his wife, who was a very large formidable lady (the sort you wouldn't want to meet down a dark alley) could not find it. Anyway Dad took him out for a drink in the local pub. By the time they got back the poor man was 'legless'. Mum wanted Dad to drive him home but Dad did not want to cross swords with battling Bertha so he sent him on what was a short cut. To get home he had to cross a shallow stream. He was clutching a battered old newspaper parcel containing his dear wife's fish supper. All went well until he reached the stream. Down he went into the shallow but very cold water. This sobered him up a bit. He staggered in his front door calling out, "I've brought you a fish supper my love." Water from this, now soggy, parcel was dripping all over. What happened next is a bit unclear but he was seen in the village later in the week sporting a lovely black eye.

Some of the old farmers were real old misers who wouldn't pay for anything if they could cadge it for free. The one I'm telling you about is the man who gave Mum her pig. Every time he saw Dad he would try to cadge a brace of grouse. In the end Dad was so sick of him that he shot two crows, plucked and prepared them for the oven and then sent me to deliver them. Mum called after me that I was aiding and abetting a poisoner. She was sure that it would poison him. Next time Dad saw the old fella he was over the moon about his free dinner and said it had been the best grouse he'd ever tasted. In fact, he wouldn't mind some more. Dad was glad that grouse were out of season so he couldn't shoot any and thought he better not push his luck and give him the crows again.

Last but not least was the family outing to Bolton Abbey. First, I must explain that my dad invented road rage. How he ever taught our Maureen to drive and pass her test was a mystery to us all as he sent us into sheer panic when he started shouting. The journey there wasn't too bad, taking into consideration that it was a very hot day. However, on the way back he was constantly shouting at passing motorists who he thought were driving badly. I could see Mum was getting very fed-up listening to him. We stopped to get some ice cream cornets. Dad couldn't have one as he was driving so mum decided she would share hers. The next time Dad opened his mouth to bellow at some other poor road-user Mum stuck the rest of her cornet firmly on his nose. Well Maureen and me collapsed in the back seat. We laughed so much it hurt. Dad was forced to drive on with ice-cream dripping off his chin and down his front until he found a place to park. He must have been in a good mood that day because he laughed about it later and there was no payback from him as there very might well have been.

But a couple of things that happened brought real sadness. It was a very hot summer. Everywhere was bone dry. Then the worst happened. Some ramblers who were walking on the moor reported the start of a fire. It was terrible. Dad had to form a line with others to shoot whatever bird or animal emerged with their fur or feathers alight. We all had long poles with rubber pads on to try and beat back the flames. Whilst some of the farmers were digging a fire break and soaking it with water the Fire Services and local vets came to give a hand. Maureen was quite a good shot by that time so she was in the shooting line. It was so upsetting that a lot of us were in tears before the fire was brought under control. Dad used to have controlled burns on the moor as it helped the heather to grow better but this was fire out of control. Afterwards came the big clean up.

We were also saddened that year to hear that Ray had died. He was so young, what a waste. I think it was a brain tumour. He became unwell and died within days.

One thing I must say about the farmers was that they all pulled together in an emergency such as digging the sheep out of snowdrifts. We also had an outbreak of foot and mouth. At night you could see all the farm fires burning the bodies. We had all been warned to keep our dogs off the farmland. Farmers were shooting any dogs straying on their land. Dad got one of his fox terriers trapped in the quarry. It was on the local news. He was trapped for a week. Dad, myself and a couple of local farmers tried to dig him out but eventually had to blast the rocks. The explosion moved some of the large rocks.

However there was no sign of Paddy, Dad's Lakeland terrier. It was feared he was dead. Then all of a sudden a big vixen emerged from the rocks. Dad had left his gun out of reach so killed the fox with his spade. We sat quietly to see if we could hear Paddy. Dad heard fox cubs calling. Dad and the farmers started to dig them out. He would not leave them to starve to death. It wasn't his way. Then he heard barking. That was Paddy. Dad called him out. He thought Paddy had killed the babies. The terrier was very thin and it was obvious by the wounds on his muzzle that a battle had been going on between him and the vixen, who was fighting to protect her young. All was very quiet.

We began to pack up to come home. Paddy's nose needed stitching. (Dad did all this sort of thing very often. The gun dogs often ripped their stomachs jumping barbed wire and had to be stitched up.)

Then Dad heard whimpering. Swearing away to himself, he got down and crawled in-between the rocks. He found four cubs. Two were dead, probably killed by the blast, but two were very much alive. Dad would normally have knocked them on the head. Nothing was more certain, but he didn't. He handed them to me, two tiny little grey bundles of growling, spitting fur. Their eyes were open. Dad thought they were about four weeks old. The tea chest appeared in the kitchen again and the heat lamp as we tried to keep these little creatures alive. Dad thought they would be dead by morning but they weren't. I stayed awake most of the night and, by morning, I had them lapping warm goat's milk, which I had watered down a bit,

I didn't want to upset their tummies. I must admit it was very hard trying to get them to eat. I tried all sorts of things, chicken and also hard-boiled egg mixed with milk. In the end, it was sheep's heads that they liked. I cut the meat into tiny scraps and mixed it with a drop of milk.

Once they started eating they grew very quickly. The male, Freddie, stayed with me. The female cub went to a disabled girl in the village. They were both very tame but the female cub strayed onto the farmland and the farmer shot it. He said it was going to attack him. This was rubbish, the cub was coming to be petted. It had no fear of people. This is one of the bad things about keeping wild creatures as pets. Freddie stayed with us. We tried to get him back into the wild but he kept coming home. All the dogs treated him like a dog. The only person Freddie hated was Dad. Dad used to tease him when he was indoors. He would put his hand down and try to entice the fox to bite him. One day he bit him hard. Dad grabbed him by the scruff of the neck. I was terrified.

"This is it," I thought. "He's going to kill him." But he didn't. He put him in the barn and told me not to bring him indoors again.

I kept him away from Dad after that. I wasn't taking any chances.

The next thing to shake us all up was that Dad went missing. He went on the moor in the early morning after getting reports of poachers with dogs. Mum thought he was being a fool going on his own, poachers carried guns.

One young lad from a neighbouring farm had been injured a few months previously by poachers. They took game bird chick's eggs or anything else they could find. When Dad hadn't returned by 10.30 am Mum started to get worried. I was sent on Auburn to deliver a message to our neighbours. Very soon four farmers arrived carrying guns. They searched for ages but found nothing. The local bobby arrived and they set off again. They found Dad in a ditch by the quarry. He had been badly attacked. He had a cut on his head, which needed stitching, and also broken ribs and various bumps and bruises everywhere. He was in hospital for a couple of days and then came home to recover. The official story was that he had been attacked by poachers. I wondered if the young farmer had got his own back. But then I heard Mum telling Maureen about some woman who worked behind the bar in the pub, somebody's wife or girlfriend, I guess. Mum had heard stories before. She didn't seem too upset. I just couldn't see what they saw in him. Mum said he must have hidden charms. Well, believe me, they must have been well hidden because charming is one thing he never was.

Things plodded on for a while without any more mishaps until I rescued a magpie. Boy, was I in trouble. I had crawled along a ditch and rescued a call bird that one of the farmers had trapped in a cage. It was a cruel practice. The young bird would be kept in the cage, calling to other magpies to rescue it. As the other birds circled above, they would be shot down. This poor bird stayed in the cage without food or water until it died. I wonder how Dad found out about it. I had never seen him so angry. I thought about denying it but as Mum passed me to go outside she whispered, "You were seen."

I turned to Dad and said, "You always told me to stand up for what is right, well I don't think it's right to starve a poor bird to death."

"A poor bird," he yelled. "Have you ever seen a new-born lamb with its eyes pecked out? They steal the eggs and chicks from game birds' nests. You know I have to shoot them."

By this time I was getting very upset.

"Where is it?" he bellowed. I went outside to the barn

and he followed. I thought it was curtains for poor old magpie but when I gave him the bird his face changed.

"This bird has had its legs broken. Who did it? Never mind. I know who did this," he said. He took magpie into the kitchen so he could have a proper look at her legs. "Well," he said. "They are mending but she won't be perfect again." He gave her back to me. "You can keep her," he said. "She's suffered enough." Well she did recover but when I released her she just stayed around the house. She would sit on the kitchen windowsill and eat breadcrumbs and bits that Mum put there for her. You could always find her in the barn at night. She had made that her home. However, one day, when Mr Feather was there, he accidentally ran over her. She died and I buried her where I had buried Trixie's puppy.

Big things were going to happen for us all. Soon we would be leaving that place and all the freedom I had taken for granted would be gone. If I thought things could be hard there, I would be finding out how much worse they could get.

CHAPTER FIVE: THE ELEVEN PLUS LOOMS

I had decided I didn't want to go to Girls Grammar School. I didn't think I would be clever enough anyway, although Mr Evans told Dad he thought I would pass it easily. I thought they were all in for a big shock. I had seen the girls from the Grammar School in their uniforms, it was not for me. I needed to come up with a devious plan. Well, after spending days deep in thought, I hadn't come up with anything. I'd discounted a mysterious illness. That wouldn't work. I did consider saying I'd lost my memory but did not think I was clever enough to remember that I had forgot. What I meant was I'd forget to remember I'd forgot.

Well the day of the big exam arrived and my head was still empty of any grand plan. Then it came to me, I would just put the wrong answers down. I might not know the answers anyway. Perhaps I was not as clever as Mr Evans thought. I had no need to worry, as I took my place in the hall I felt physically sick. My head was empty. I wrote my name and turned the page. All the words merged together. I couldn't read them. What was wrong with me? My head was spinning. That's the last thing I remembered as I sank to the floor. I had got my serious illness. I was very ill with some sort of infection and was away from school for about a month. When I did return Mr Evans said I was to take the exam in his office and to do my best. I did try very hard but I failed. I did not think I was meant to be a Grammar School girl. I did not get to spend my last summer on the moor either. I was shipped off to stay with my Uncle Eddie in Lincolnshire to rest and get my strength back but I put myself in great danger by being the trusting child and not recognising evil when I nearly put myself in its grasp.

I roamed the village in the summer alone. I didn't know any of the local kids but that didn't worry me. I had always been a loner. I met this young chap whilst sitting on a bridge over a stream. I suppose he was about twenty years old. I don't remember his name but he was very nice to me and paid me compliments. I met him there a few times. The last time I was supposed to meet him he was going to take me for a ride on his motorbike, but I never turned up. I was on my way home. I had given him my address and he must have written because Dad spoke to me about it but, by then, it was a distant memory. Children soon forget. It could have been so very different. Something or somebody seemed to protect me and it was to protect me once more when I was a lot older and a married woman with two children, but you will have to wait to hear about that much later in my story.

Another very sad thing happened to me when I had returned home. My heart was broken. I had fallen madly in love with Janet's boyfriend. Then he asked me if I wanted to be bridesmaid at their wedding. My poor heart was broken for all of a day. Then I discovered someone else to make my heart beat faster. Ah, love's young dream. What a joke that was in the cold reality of the real world. It was only true in fairy tales. Prince Charming only existed in fairy tales. I'm afraid my upbringing had given me a very poor opinion of all the male sex. Some poor chaps that approached me in later years to ask for a date or wanted to take me out to dinner got short shrift. The few I accepted were dumped again quite quickly. I'd soon get fed-up with them or they would annoy me in some way. Men gave me a wide birth. It was only the brave who ventured near. I blame it all on Dad, of course. He was not a very good role model for the male species. I got many nicknames from my male workmates in later years including Icicle on legs, Ice Maiden, Frosty Knickers and some too rude to put into print.

Something about Dad became very clear to me that year. Maureen only had to say 'I want' or 'can I have?' and Dad would get it for her. I could ask until the cows came home and then had to soft talk Mum for anything I wanted and hope she would persuade him to buy it for me.

However life on the moors would soon be a fond but distant memory. My grandfather was ill and Dad was sent for to take over everything and to care for his father. What a joke that was! I knew who would be doing all the caring and it wouldn't be him.

"Why can't someone who is living close-by care for him?" I asked Mum.

"Because he is a pain in the arse." Mum said, "If you think your Dad is bad, he's 100% worse, a very bad person." Well that really cheered me up.

It was dark when we left. As we passed Lower Intake I risked a peep at the fearful tree. It must have been a trick of the light. Moonlight was shining down and, just for a moment, the whole tree seemed to be glowing. I could swear I saw someone swinging in the breeze. I shut my eyes tight until we reached the bottom of the road.

There, on the night train, I was already missing the open space, the absolute quiet and the way it all changed when the snow covered everything in a sparkling white blanket. I knew, in my mind, that I would never see such a winter wonderland again. We would be living in a small village surrounded by Dad's relatives. It would prove to be an unhappy and upsetting experience for me.

CHAPTER SIX: THE RELATIVES

What is that famous saying? 'You can choose your friends but you can't choose your relatives.' How true that is. My aunt lived in Aberdeen where she had a boarding house. When we first arrived she told Dad to leave me with her until they got sorted out. I loved every minute of it. I hung out with my cousins, most of them were older than me. Even today, I remember my aunt with great affection. She had a son living at home. He was in his early thirties, but he was great fun. He took me to the fair and the beach. We were late home one night. I didn't know, but Auntie had set a trap so that she knew what time we got back. As she was already in bed, she'd left all the pans that had been used that day on the table behind the kitchen door. Not knowing where the light switch was, I blundered straight into them. What a racket! She appeared at the kitchen door – hairnet, no teeth, peering over her glasses. She said, "Bed," and pointed to the stairs. Her son beat a hasty retreat in the opposite direction. He later married the priest's housekeeper. Poor Horace, he so liked a bit of fun and laughter and, unless his new wife was hiding her light under a bushel, he was in for a dull existence. His mother, being a good Catholic lady, was well pleased with her son's choice. I think she thought I was leading him astray. I was only nearly thirteen but a force to be reckoned with.

Dad came to pick me up after a couple of weeks. It would

soon be the start of the new school term. He had presumed that I would be attending the secondary modern in the next village. That was where all my cousins went. But I had to sit another exam as they had no records for me and they wanted to be sure that I was sent to the appropriate school. Yes, you guessed right, I was to go to the grammar school.

"Good God," Dad said. "She has got a brain then."

Mum replied, "Oh, yes she takes after me."

Now it was the swinging sixties. I didn't suppose I would be doing much swinging. It was my first day at the new school and it didn't help that I was related to most of the others on the bus plus the fact that I was the only one going to the Grammar.

There I was in full school uniform, carrying a briefcase. Would you believe Mum didn't think an ordinary satchel would do. "Not when you are a grammar school girl," she said. I would need it for all the books I would have to carry. The only consolation was that it was a mixed school. I could see the potential there to cause mayhem. I needed them to turf me out ASAP!

The relatives had made my ride into school that morning one that I didn't want to repeat. I mean, be fair, am I to blame if I was brainier than them? I would have cracked a few heads together but was well outnumbered. Well, I struggled through English, maths, science and even French. I normally did OK in French, could understand every word, but the 'twang' they spoke with – well, to say I had been born north of the border, I couldn't understand a word. I now spoke with a strong Yorkshire accent. After lunch I had thought about giving the rest of the day a miss. I wish I had. The first lesson after lunch was RE, or, to give it its full title, Religious Education. I was asked which religion I was and replied 'none'. The teacher got quite angry with this. "Well, are your parents Catholic?" I told her that Dad was but that Mum was Church of England. "Well," she said, "you best go with the heathens then." By then I was totally confused. She pointed me in the direction of a small group of kids. We had to walk all the way to the Catholic Church to listen to the priest waffling on for half an hour and then walk all the way back. The other kids said that this happened on a Monday and Friday. I just thought it was a complete waste of time.

The journey home was much worse than the morning one. By the time I got indoors I was so angry. Also the amount of homework they had given me was a joke. I thought I would be lucky to get to bed at all if I had all this lot to do. Mum spotted that something was wrong as soon as she saw me.

"Don't worry, I will sort this," she said and went out of the front door, slamming it behind her. She was gone quite a while. When she came back she just said, "Sorted."

I was still sitting at the table trying to plough through the 'sodding' homework. I left some that wasn't due back until later in the week.

I needed some fresh air and some 'me time'. I decided to exercise Grandad's pony and take the dogs with me. I didn't bother with a saddle. I had grown a bit taller now so could manage to mount this pony, no problem. I must explain the layout of McEwan's buildings so that you can understand my story. McEwan's buildings were in the centre of Lumsden, which was a small village. It had a pub, chemist, general store and a baker's shop. One of my cousins worked in the baker's but she wasn't into giving free buns out to family. The general store was quite large. It sold everything. I loved this small brown sweet. They called it a sweet potato, it had a charm in the middle. Mum thought they were dangerous. She said you could choke on the charm. Next door was the chemist. He doubled as the dentist.

Grandad owned a row of terraced houses. It consisted of three houses, some outbuildings and a small paddock. Mum said that, at one time, Grandad had owned most of the village but had sold it off bit by bit. He dealt in antiques and also bought and sold ponies but only had one at that time. Dad had warned me that this pony was a bit frisky so to watch out. Well the pony started to prance a bit and then, just as Dad was about to open the gate, he cleared the fence with room to spare. It was a good job I had ridden before or I would never have been able to control him. I could hear Dad swearing. I guess he thought I put him at the fence but, believe me, I hadn't. I was hanging on with great difficulty. I had the dogs with me as well. When we reached the woodland everybody calmed down so we had a good wander around and it was so peaceful and quiet that I wished I could remain there forever.

Dad had started playing loud music by then as well as drinking far too much. He had found a drinking partner who was a bit younger than him and they used to be out most of the time 'doing business' as Dad put it. I don't know what sort of business it was but Dad always came home 'legless'. He had never been a happy drunk, like some people. You could always tell, by the tone of his voice, if there was going to be trouble. He had started carrying a knuckle duster so Mum knew there was some serious fighting going on. A lot of buying and selling went on at the horse fairs with locals and young fellas from the gypsy community. They used to drink whiskey. It was a clear liquid and nearly 100% proof. I don't know where they bought it, maybe they had a still hidden somewhere. Mum said it turned their brains and made them fighting mad. I was developing another complex. I could not stand the smell of alcohol, it turned my stomach and made me feel sick. (It still makes me feel like this today.) So when Dad rolled in steaming drunk I made myself scarce. I don't know about turning their brains, I couldn't see why anybody would drink something that got them into a state like that.

There had been a bust-up between Mum and Grandad as soon as we got there. Mum told him he would have to sleep downstairs in the parlour now we were there. He refused, saying it was the room that Grandma died in. Mum insisted so he moved himself into the middle house on his own. I didn't know the full story but Mum told me one night that Grandad had been a very heavy drinker until he was forty, when he turned tee-total and became a religious fanatic. Mum had lived there before when Maureen was little. Dad had been away in the army. It had been wintertime and she and Grandad had an argument. He threw them both out. Mum, who was pregnant at the time, slipped on the ice and lost the baby she was carrying. It was born dead. It was a boy. Mum swore she heard it whimper like a small animal and she had never forgiven Grandad for this. Auntie Maggie used to live there and look after Grandad but she had some sort of mental breakdown and had tried to drown herself in the river. I'm not surprised, we had only been there a short time and he was already getting on my nerves. Mum never spoke to him. Mind you, no-one could blame her for that. I took him his meals every day but he wouldn't eat them. Mum sent for the doctor. Grandad told the doctor that Mum was trying to poison him. Well, no-one could blame her for that either! I thought someone needed to lock the silly old fool up somewhere before he drove us all round the bend. Of course, Dad was never there to look after him. It was all left to us.

However, I'm digressing from my tale. At this point, I was still in the woodland and as I make my way home the pony took off like a horse in the Light Brigade. Just as I turned the corner back to the paddock the priest stepped out into the path. There was no way I could stop in time and I knocked him back into the hedge, 'oh shit'. I thought that as he didn't know me perhaps I wouldn't get into trouble. I quickly stabled the pony and fed the dogs. I rushed upstairs to change and make myself presentable. When I came back downstairs the priest was sitting having tea with Mum. I didn't know, but apparently he always came for his tea on Sunday with Grandad so that he could watch 'Oliver Twist' which was on BBC 1. He was very fat and got himself wedged into one of the chairs.

As I came into the room he turned to look at me so I said, trying to sound very respectful, "Good evening father, I hope you are well." I had my fingers crossed, hoping he didn't recognise me but, of course he did.

"Oh, it's the banshee on horseback," he said in his Irish brogue.

"I do apologise Father. I didn't see you until it was too late," I said.

He turned to Mum and said, "You need to get this one married or sent to the convent school."

"She is only thirteen," said Mum.

"God help us all," he said, helping himself to another piece of cake. When it was time for him to leave he was wedged firmly in the chair. Mum and I pulled on his arms whilst Maureen held onto the chair. We finally managed to pull him out.

I was beginning to think that everyone in the village was drunk, senile or barmy. How I wished we hadn't gone there. On one occasion I remembered that there was some work I hadn't done which was due in the following day. So I knew I had that to do before I got into bed and I had got a really throbbing headache. Mum gave me two tablets and I sank into bed. I was exhausted. Suddenly I woke up with a jolt. "Oh God," I thought, "the fool is drunk again." All I could hear was a rendition of 'Pistol Packing Mama' followed by 'The pub with no beer'. I'd had enough. I climbed out of bed, grabbing a pair of scissors. The plan was that I would creep downstairs, put my hand around the curtain and cut the cord of the record player. But, just as I put my hand around the curtain, I felt a hand on my shoulder and Maureen whispered, "Don't do that. You will get electrocuted." We both crept back upstairs. I felt very poorly and started to cry. Maureen settled me into bed and eventually I fell asleep. The next morning I felt even worse. Mum told me to say in bed. At least I was pleased to be getting a few days off school.

Dad got some casual work driving a tractor on one of the local farms. He dragged us along to pick potatoes. Mum had done that sort of work before. I just wanted to be somewhere else. It was a boiling hot day. The sun beating down on me made me feel really nauseous. I just carried on trying to keep up with everyone else. It was back-breaking work. I'm not lazy and I did more than my fair share of work when we lived on the moor, but this was slavery. I started to feel very dizzy. I couldn't see properly. The sweat was running down my back. My head ached and I felt really unwell. I don't remember much after that. The next thing I knew I was in hospital with sunstroke. My body was dehydrated and I was put on a drip. I had bad sunburn on my arms and legs and the back of my neck was badly blistered. That was the end of potato picking for me. Mum and Maureen continued for a few weeks. Everyone thought that Maureen was the delicate one in the family. It was a big shock for them that this had happened to me. I find the sun hard to cope with, even today. I stay out of it whenever possible.

I must admit, the journey to school was OK by this time. My cousin, William, who was older than me, had taken me under his wing. He was quite good looking and had asked me to a dance in the village hall. I didn't know if I would go. I knew that if Dad was there he would just show me up. I was so fed-up with the whole situation. But I was in for a shock if I thought this was bad as it was soon going to get a lot worse. At least Granddad went into hospital. That was one less thing to worry about. I felt sorry for the old chap when they put him into the ambulance. He was crying. He had lost weight and looked very frail. Just a poor old man that nobody wanted. I thought that was how Dad would be, there was no way I could look after him in his old age. I was beginning to dislike him a lot.

Dad had two brothers. There was Uncle John who was deaf due to the fact that Grandad had thrown a pitchfork at him because he was acting the fool. It lodged behind his ear and he had been deaf ever since. He was a really good singer and dancer and could play lots of instruments. I asked him how he could hear the music. He said he felt it through his feet. I liked him. He was good fun. He had three daughters. Iris, the youngest, was about my age. His wife had a very bad heart condition. She got tired very quickly and her lips were always blue. Dad's other brother was William. He had loads of kids. He also had a bad chest. He got very short of breath. He had been this way since he was a child. Sometimes he looked really ill. Mum couldn't understand how he could have fathered so many children, but he managed it somehow!

Dad had left home at fourteen to go and work on a farm.

He didn't seem that close to his brothers. They didn't like him very much. I guess it was the heavy drinking and the fact that he'd been away from the village for so long.

Mum had a good laugh about our fat priest. He had made headlines in the local paper. He was drunk and a fight broke out between him and another member of the clergy. They both got carted off and spent the night in the jail in Aberdeen. We never saw him after that. I think he must have been moved to another parish. Everyone in our area had read about his fall from grace.

Then we got a new priest. He was over six foot tall. He was very nice to talk to and had recently returned from a mission abroad. He started taking all the kids for trips in the mini-bus. It could be quite entertaining, hearing stories of his adventures in foreign lands. I was telling Mum that he seemed to have some sort of problem. He would stop in mid-sentence and, after a few seconds, would carry on with what he'd been saying. We all thought it a bit strange. Dad thought that he might have got some sort of tropical disease which had left him like this. Mum though it could be a sort of neurological disorder. I was wondering if it was safe for him to drive the 'bloody' mini-bus. Mum then dropped the bombshell. She had volunteered me to go and help with the kids on the trip to the convent.

"Oh, this is just great. I'm stuck with a load of noisy kids and a priest who has got yellow swamp fever or something worse. What a wonderful weekend I'm going to have," I thought.

If you have never been in a convent it's an experience you could well do without. The silence is deafening. I found myself on tiptoe, trying not to make a noise. We got a tour round the chapel and also the cells where the nuns slept.

They had their own veggie plot and, behind the building, was a small graveyard where the deceased nuns were buried. It struck me as very sad. Imagine spending your life there, scared to make a noise with everything done on the ring of a bell. You got up when the bell rang and had food when it rang. The amount of time you spent on your knees praying! I don't know who scrubbed the corridors and polished them, but I wouldn't have liked the job. We came across a group of younger nuns in the garden, all dressed in white. I wondered what made these young girls give up on life and go there. The Mother Superior was a small woman who tucked her hands inside her wide sleeves. She had a wide belt with lots of keys. I was fascinated by the silver cross that she wore around her neck. It looked really solid. I asked her if it was heavy.

She told me that we all had heavy crosses to bear. Some people went to the convent for peace and solitude. I found it very creepy. The small rooms the nuns were expected to sleep in offered them no comfort at all. They all wore silver wedding rings. They were 'Brides of Christ'. The priest went there once a week to hear confession. For God's sake, what possible sins could you commit in there? I was very glad when it was time to leave. The Mother Superior did say that I would be welcome to come back any time. I did not think that I would bother!

Later that day I was telling Iris all about it. She had a good laugh. "Don't go back there," she said. "A girl from the bakery went there with an order and she was never seen again."

When I got back home Dad was entertaining a young RAF chap. He was very smart in his uniform. He had blonde hair and a lovely suntan. Dad was telling him that Maureen needed a partner for the dance. (I had decided that I *would* go to the village dance that Saturday as I thought it might be a good laugh.) I wandered through to the kitchen for a sandwich.

"Who's the fella Dad's talking to," I asked.

Mum shrugged her shoulders, saying, "He came back with

Dad last night. He's home on leave and has nowhere to stay. Dad said he could stay next door. I've lit the fire in there."

"Is he taking Maureen to the dance?" I asked.

"I shouldn't think so," said Mum. "She's going with a lad she used to go to school with, he's in the RAF too. Maureen is going to write to him when his leave is finished."

I never thought any more about it until later. Dad was ranting on about something. I didn't know who was taking Maureen to the dance, but Dad wasn't happy about it. For once, she stuck to her guns and went anyway. It wasn't too bad a 'do' for a small village event.

I wondered when the fireworks would start. Dad had found out about the letters. I hadn't seen Dad much since the dance. He was out during the day doing what he called 'business' and drinking the rest of the time. Mum said that his insides must be pickled.

I heard him at night when he started with the loud music. I would stick my head under the pillow and tried to ignore it. Maureen said she had a deaf ear. She didn't hear him. She was lucky, I didn't seem to get any sleep.

Mum started keeping a fire lit next door to stop it getting damp. One day I took my school work in there to get some peace. I went to have a look upstairs but I couldn't, the window at the top was open and the curtains were blowing about. I was frozen to the spot and felt very strange. I could hear Dad's voice. He was up there talking to someone. I ran back out and slammed the door. As I rushed into the kitchen I nearly knocked Mum over.

"What's up with you?" she said.

"It's haunted next door. I heard voices and I felt really strange," I gasped.

She started laughing. "It's your Dad. He's in there sorting out some stuff, Maureen's helping him." Why did I feel so strange when I saw that curtain? It was just the same when we lived on the moor.

CHAPTER SEVEN: NEW YEAR'S EVE (SCOTTISH STYLE)

There was an Elvis lookalike in the village. I saw him one day, he winked at me. (I thought I was in love.) I went to look for Iris. She knew everyone in the village. I thought I would get the 'lowdown' from her.

By that time I didn't have any problems with the relatives on the school bus. They didn't hassle me. I'd got my protector, my cousin William. He even carried my briefcase full of books. Everyone knew about Dad's antics so felt sorry for me. That's the trouble with living in a small village – everyone knew your business.

Anyway Iris knew all about 'Elvis'. He was home for the New Year festivities. His mum lived in the village. He was at least thirty and that made him an 'oldie' as far as we were concerned. But I still thought he was 'drop dead gorgeous'. Maybe I was looking for a father figure.

Iris said that 'Elvis' was the one who did all the 'First Footing'. I hadn't the faintest idea what she was on about. So she explained in great detail what happened on New Year's Eve. To give you a brief rundown: 'Elvis' went to each house just after midnight. He knocked and they let him in (with his piece of coal). He got a free drink and then took his coal to the next house, etc, etc. By morning he would be 'legless' and it hadn't cost him a penny. No wonder he came home every year! It's funny how quickly you can go off someone.

You have to see New Year's Eve in a small village to believe what goes on. It starts on New Year's Eve and carries on for a week. The majority of men in the village are 'three sheets to the wind'. The bonus was that we didn't see Dad for days and the house was blissfully quiet and peaceful. I took the opportunity to catch up on some 'shut eye'. When he finally turned up he was in a nasty frame of mind. Maureen and I headed for the hills. (We actually hid in Uncle William's toilet.) When all was quiet we sneaked home. Mum was sitting by the fire, clearly very upset. The bird-cage that usually hung in the kitchen, containing Dad's bullfinch (that bird would sing all day), was now smashed and stamped on so that it was totally flat.

I stood open-mouthed with horror. "Where's the bird?" I said. Mum shook her head. I searched the broken wreckage, checking for his little body, but could find nothing. Maureen found him hiding under the sink. We took him outside and set him free. I watched him fly away and smiled, at least he would get his freedom. I decided in that moment that as soon as I was sixteen I, too, would fly away.

"What are we going to do about Dad?" I asked.

Then Mum came out with another pearl of wisdom, "What can't be cured must be endured."

"Well, I won't be enduring it much longer," said Maureen.

"I have had enough." She ran upstairs crying. Dad was sleeping it off in the bedroom, he never heard a thing.

Dad hadn't visited our bedroom since Maureen had screamed at him to get out. This was the first week that we moved to the village. Mum had rushed in. Dad was standing, looking very stupid, in his underwear. Mum just looked at him and he left without a word. At least we didn't have to put up with him acting the fool. It had made me feel very uncomfortable.

The village was slowly returning to normal. What is 'normal'? I thought it was a strange place to live.

I asked Mum who lived in the big house across the green. Mum said that the occupants were quite old and had a son who was not right. "Why is he not right?" I asked. Mum didn't know but told me that 'rumour had it' that they tied him to a tree in the garden in the nice weather and that he was fed like a dog. People had said they had heard him howling. I was incensed by this. How could anyone treat another person in this way? Mum didn't know if he was still living there. I was short of something to do so decided to find out if the rumours were true. I made my way down there with Trixie on her lead. I didn't normally put her on a lead, but she had developed a habit of disappearing to the pub. No, she hadn't started drinking! She knew the kitchen staff would give her titbits. Honestly, you would think she never got fed at home. That dog had no loyalty! I met Iris *en route*. She knew a bit about the lad at the big house and told me that he didn't live there any longer, nobody did. Apparently the local kids used to climb on the wall to throw stones at this poor lad. His parents got too old to care for him and he was taken away. It suddenly hit me how cruel people can be to anyone who doesn't fit into the 'normality bracket'. I remember when I first went to school that I was quite chubby. Mum said it was baby-fat and would soon go. The other kids used to call me horrible names. Then the relatives gave me a hard time on the bus just because I spoke differently. It doesn't take a lot for people to single you out for special treatment.

I made my way home then wished that I hadn't bothered. Dad had gone into 'meltdown' again. He had found out that Maureen's childhood sweetheart had been writing to her. He had a go at Mum and then collared me as I came in the door.

"Do you know anything about Maureen's boyfriend?" he asked.

I just stood looking stupid. "I didn't even know she had one," I replied.

"Well, he better not come round here," yelled Dad. "I'll shoot the bastard."

I said nothing and went upstairs. Maureen seemed to get more depressed every day. She never ate a proper meal, always salad. No wonder she was so thin. Mum said she was really worried that Billy (that was Maureen's boyfriend) was due home on leave and that if he came to see her there was going to be murder committed.

"Don't be stupid," I said. He's all talk. Even he can't get away with blowing someone's head off."

It seems I was right to a point. When Billy did appear Dad tried to run him over instead! He went completely barmy that night and went for Maureen with a kitchen knife. She was petrified. She ran behind me. I shoved her out of the back door and we ran down the main street to

Uncle Johnny's house. Iris hid us in the bedroom. Dad came looking for us but Iris said she hadn't seen us. We went back home in the morning. Mum had locked Dad out. He had slept next door. We didn't see him for days. Mum was worried because there was no food in there. Maureen said, "Let him starve."

I was glad when school started again. I was just sick and fed-up with the whole situation. I didn't know that Mum had a devious plan that would set in motion a train of events that was to have a long-term effect on the whole family. I suppose one good thing about living in 'la la land' was that my workload was nothing compared to what I had to do daily when we lived on the moor. This gave me more time for myself. I would sit drifting off into fantasy land. I had this wonderful life planned for myself in years to come. One thing was for sure, it didn't include Dad or any other male. I was not going to get married, ever. There was no way I was having any children. I would take myself off somewhere and live in peaceful isolation. What a joke that turned out to be. The reality was that isolation was very hard to find. Also, men were to play a part in my life but, hopefully, on my terms. One day, believe it or not, I would run home to my parents to give me time to recover and lick my wounds. I found I wasn't such a tough nut after all. I did have a heart but there was a little piece of me that belonged only to me. That is what stopped me being totally devastated when things didn't work out as I had planned. I always promised myself that no man would ever break my heart or treat me badly. In the real world this wasn't the case. Prince Charming only existed in fairy tales. I did find my hero eventually but even he had a 'sting in his tail'.

CHAPTER EIGHT: LOVE'S YOUNG DREAM

When we left the moor we brought along Trixie (my Cairn terrier), Blondie (Dad's golden retriever) and two of Blondie's offspring. Maureen had acquired a white Peke. She bathed it and powdered it on a regular basis but it loved to get out, run with the other dogs and get really dirty with all kinds of debris entangled in its lovely white coat. Maureen would go mad if I let her dog out and allowed it to be a normal little 'woof'. Yes, I must admit, I was a very annoying 'little shit' in those days. I may have been only five foot two inches in height, but I could cause mayhem without even meaning to. I am surprised that no-one ever gave me a serious slap but I only ever did things for a laugh, there was never any malice intended.

This was the summer when I met Lee. He was staying with his gran for the summer. He was slim, tall and had dark curly hair. He was very good-looking. We spent most of the summer together. Mum said we must be joined at the hip. We walked miles, listened to music and had fun. It was Lee that got me interested in reading. I discovered a way to lose myself in a good book and be so caught up in the storyline that I didn't want to put the book down, and felt sad when it was finished. I'm surprised that Dad didn't have anything to say about the amount of time I spent in Lee's company but he was always too busy stressing out about Maureen and any spare time was spent exercising his drinking arm. Maureen was still writing to Billy. I presume that he was writing back. Dad went out of his way to waylay the postman, so how the letters got through to her is still a mystery to me. Those that he did intercept ended up in the fire. He had a dammed cheek really. She was surely entitled to receive her mail. To give Billy his due, he wasn't scared off by Dad. He came to see Maureen when he was home on leave. Mum took a lot of flack because of it. I pleaded ignorance if Dad spoke to me about it. The only downside to spending a summer day with Lee was coming back home to the same old 'crap'. Thinking back on it all, I don't know why Mum tolerated all the hassle but, in those days, women didn't leave their husbands, no matter what.

The next big event in my life was to be baptised into the Roman Catholic faith. I was put under pressure at school and by Dad's family. In the end it was really getting me down. I did it for all the wrong reasons but, apart from having to attend mass every Sunday, it meant I got some peace and quiet. As far as going to confession was concerned, there was no way I was doing that. What gave the priests the right to forgive sins, surely that was God's job? I didn't believe that anything I ever did was a sin, stupid maybe, but of no great concern to any priest or God. I have my own beliefs as far as God goes.

The summer holidays were drawing to a close and Lee would be leaving and I would be back at school and the situation at home wouldn't be any better. Everyone thought I would be devastated when Lee left but that wasn't my style. My barriers surround me and as long as I don't let anyone climb over them they will protect me. I learnt at a very young age that people could be nasty and hurtful. I also learnt that the male of the species were not to be trusted. I put myself first. I made a promise to myself to never put myself in a position where I was dependent on any man. As far as the Catholic faith was concerned, I would rue the day I became a Catholic.

When Lee went I had no plans to write to him or anything like that. I told him that I would look him up if I got to Aberdeen. I think he was a bit disappointed that I didn't intend to keep in touch. To be truthful, by the time I had been back at school a week or two he was a pleasant but distant memory. I wonder what he did with his life.

I can't remember at what point Grandad passed away, but die he did. I started having bad dreams about the funeral. I dreamt that the pall bearers had dropped the coffin when one of them stumbled carrying it down the steps from the kirk. It slid to the bottom, the lid came off and he was half in and half out of his box. I used to wake up in a cold sweat. It was because of this dream that I was not allowed to attend his farewell. I remember going to the funeral of Uncle Eddie's little girl. She died at a very young age, a beautiful little girl with blond, curly hair. When she was sleeping she looked like a little doll. I wasn't allowed to go into the room to see her in her coffin but I remember that the sweet smell of the flowers in there spread all through the house. Mum said the iris was always known as the funeral flower in days gone by, the smell of the blooms covered up the smell of the corpses.

It may have been true long ago, but not these days. I sat in the garden talking to her pet rabbit. She was buried in the local churchyard. When I stayed with Uncle Eddie the summer after I had been ill, I went with the family to lay flowers on her grave. I don't know how people cope with the death of a child. To watch that little white coffin being lowered into the ground must be heartbreaking. I was at the graveside when she was buried, but was very young so it didn't affect me as much as it did the older people there. I did wonder how they could all tuck into sandwiches and cake afterwards, chattering away, the sorrow soon forgotten. Another of Mum's pearls of wisdom was, "You can't live with the dead." Just because people are getting on with everyday life doesn't mean they care any less. Mum told me about twins in Dad's family who had passed away. They were buried in the graveyard at Rhynie. Iris and I took ourselves off there to see if we could find their grave. We found it and also my grandmother's. She had been in her forties when she died. That seemed so young to me. She'd had a hard life. Every day she walked from Lumsden to Rhynie to get her food shopping – a return journey of eight miles. Grandad only gave her enough money to buy food for one day. Perhaps he thought that if she had more money she might go and not return. I know I would have done.

When Mum had told Grandad that he would have to sleep in the parlour, he refused. This was the room his wife had died in. He was scared that she might come back to haunt him. He was not a nice person to know. When he stopped drinking he developed all these high moral standards. From what Mum had told me about his life, I think he had a 'bloody cheek'. Just because he stopped drinking, it didn't make him into a saint.

Dad never stopped the booze but developed the same high morals. When I look back now, knowing what I know and what I have seen, I believe he was an evil man. How much Mum knew about what went on I can never know. I was kept completely in the dark. She had never told me anything. I tried to give her the benefit of the doubt but found that hard to do. I thought that maybe one day I would be able to ask her.

Getting back to the graves, we found they were both sadly neglected. I resolved to come back soon to tidy them up. I never got the chance as we were soon to be on the move again. In fact, when I returned from school the following Monday, I got the biggest shock of my life. Maureen had 'flown the nest', taking her little white Peke and all her belongings. Mum was saying nothing but I think she had got a bit of help from her 'fly boy'. I wondered what Dad would say when he got home and learnt she had gone. I thought that one thing was for sure, it would be Mum and I who would get it in the neck.

"Well," I thought, I'm not taking any more crap. Why should we be punished just because Maureen decides to leave home?" I couldn't get my head round it – kids left home to get married or get a place of their own – what was Maureen's reason? However, I believed that she should be allowed to live her own life and that he should be set straight. I didn't think we should be expected to pick up the pieces. "Roll on the time I leave school," I thought. "As soon as I'm old enough to leave I shall be doing just that." I didn't think Dad would be bothered anyway.

Mum and I sat there just waiting for the fireworks to start. My stomach was turning somersaults. I totally blame Dad for the way my stomach reacts, sometimes I'm physically sick when I get any stress. I did not think it was fair for any one person to treat people this way. I fell asleep in the chair and woke up with a jolt as the back door slammed. "Oh, God," I thought. "Here we go." Dad stormed into the room. He already knew. Some well-meaning nosey neighbour had filled him in on all the details.

He started ranting on at Mum, saying, "Why didn't you stop her?"

Mum yelled back for once, "She's old enough to make her own choices."

"Where's she gone?" he shouted. Mum just shook her head.

I lost my temper with both of them. "Why the hell would she want to stay here?" I yelled. "All the trouble and no sleep from your loud music, not able to have a life of her own. Why can't you just let her get on with her life?"

Dad tried to shout me down but I stood my ground. I should have learned how to duck. He backhanded me across the mouth. "You deserve that," he yelled.

I still stood my ground. "Don't ever hit me again," I shouted, "or I swear to God I'll finish you off while you're asleep." He shoved me out of the way and went clattering up the stairs. He came down later on. He had packed a bag. My face was red and you could see the finger marks.

"Where are you going?" Mum asked.

"Start packing our stuff. When I get back, we're moving to Keighley. I'm going to bring Maureen back. She belongs with me." With that he left, slamming the door so hard the house shook.

"Oh, dear," sobbed Mum. "I hope he doesn't make

trouble at your gran's. She's an old lady."

"She must have known that was a sure possibility when she let Maureen move in," I replied.

Dad would never have even noticed if I had left home. In fact, he would have probably said 'good riddance'. I felt reassured by this. At least I wouldn't have him chasing after me. Mum, of course, knew where Maureen was. Dad soon figured it out too. He went to Horncastle and camped out on Gran's lawn, just made a nuisance of himself in general. Gran must have felt really shown-up with the stupid fool sleeping out on her lawn. I thought he had "flipped" and was sure he'd gone barmy.

Maureen managed to get herself a job. Mum's youngest brother, who still lived at home, used to escort her to work and back so that Dad couldn't molest her. I'm surprised Maureen didn't crack up with all the stress and aggravation.

Dad got arrested twice by the police. They told him to go home. Of course, he took no notice. In the end he was told to make himself scarce or he was going to be in big trouble. Maureen was not a minor so if she wanted to stay with Gran there was nothing he could do about it. That would have been a bitter pill for Dad to swallow. He thought he had her brainwashed. He imagined she would just go home with him. Both myself and Mum were surprised that she didn't. She stuck to her guns and sat it out. Meanwhile, back in 'la la land', Mum had been getting our affairs in order ready to move.

I decided to rehome Trixie. She was getting on in years. I thought it unfair to uproot her again. She could wander about in the village. Everyone knew her. She got plenty of strokes and petting. When I took her bed, dish and things over to the pub it broke my heart. She was my best friend. I told her all my troubles. She was a good listener. I knew the people at the pub would take very good care of her, but she was all I had of my own. I said my goodbyes.

As I walked across the village green she ran after me. I cuddled her and explained why I couldn't take her with me. She would have a better and more peaceful life in the village. She turned and went back to her new home. She had just wanted to make sure it was OK with me. I made my way home struggling to see through the tears. I sat a few minutes on the swings to compose myself. By the time I got back indoors I was the hard-faced bitch that everyone knew.

I did check on Trixie later on. She was fine and had attached herself to the pub landlords' grandson. She had found a new special person. I wasn't so lucky. I wondered where my special person was. I needed a hero.

I have racked my brains and I have no recollection of how we got back to Keighley. Maybe my brain gave up under the pressure of the whole situation. It was quite a few years later before I had any contact with Maureen again. Mum kept in contact somehow, but to tell the truth I wasn't interested. Maureen had chosen her life. I just hoped it was what she wanted. I was still stuck there. Dad left me to my own devices but he did stupid things to try and get me in trouble with Mum.

CHAPTER NINE: WHAT NOW, I WONDER?

At that moment in time we were staying with Edie and Jim. Jim was a friend of Dad's. Jim was blind. He was also a Buff. This was some sort of secret society, a bit like the Masons. They had weird ceremonies and stumped around with buffalo horns on their heads. They wore a special pin in their lapel, it was shaped like the horns of a buffalo. Other members recognised them by this pin and the special handshake. "Still," I thought, "while they are being water buffalos us lesser mortals can get on with our humdrum lives." To be fair, I think they did some good things for charity, but someone should have told Dad that 'charity begins at home'.

I was sleeping on the floor and it was not very comfortable – but better than a cardboard box!

Another new school for me. Mum had told the authorities that I had been attending grammar school so they, in their wisdom, sent me to St Anne's Secondary Modern Catholic School. On day one I was caned by Sister Mary Campion, the nun from hell. Everyone was scared stiff of her. My crime was that I hadn't handed any homework in. When I got a chance to explain that it was my first day she just said, "Make sure you hand your work in on time in future." I thought that she wouldn't get a chance to punish me again, she needed to look out. She was on my 'hit list'. The other kids had warned me to take care but was I frightened of her? Not me, I'd tackled someone swinging in the breeze, not forgetting Heathcliff striding out of the mist. It would take more than an evil penguin to faze me.

I needed to get Mum on my side. I wanted out of that school ASAP, the penguin was becoming a pest. I found out that I could transfer to Eastwood School if I wanted to take up nursing and I set about convincing Mum of my chosen career. She spoke to Dad, he wasn't bothered where I went to school. So after the summer holiday I was to start at Eastwood Secondary Modern.

Another amazing thing happened. Mum shocked us all by announcing that she was having a baby. The look on Dad's face was classic. He choked and starting spluttering. When he could speak, he said, "How the hell did that happen? I thought you were too old for that." Mum was forty at the time. Just goes to show how much men don't know about women's bodies. Anyway Dad had done us a favour this time. As Mum was with child the Council gave us a three-bedroomed flat in a new multi-storey block of flats in Parkwood Rise. So Leylands House on the fifth floor was to be our new abode. There are no unlucky places to live. It's not the places, it's the people that make them unlucky.

On the last day at the school from hell Sister Mary Campion called me into her office to give me my report card. It was a really bad report. She said that she knew I had no intention of taking up nursing and that if she had her way I would remain at St Anne's. I wondered how many other kids she had terrorised. I was glad to be leaving. As I walked out of her office I gave her one of my best smiles, it more or less said, "one to me, you didn't win this time sister."

Dad was to prove he was still an 'arsehole' even though he was going to be a father again. I had gone with Mum to the antenatal clinic. When we got back Dad was laid on the floor outside our flat. By the state of the door it was obvious he had been kicking hell out of it because he couldn't get in. As we got inside he started yelling at Mum. I yelled back at him, "It's not our fault you didn't take your key." He rounded on me, telling me to 'shut my fucking mouth or he would shut it for me'. I stood and glared. He must have seen the look of pure hatred in my eyes because he shut up and took a step back. When I returned to the kitchen later Mum was trying to clear broken glass out of the sink. She was crying. The 'bastard' had smashed the bottles of orange juice they had given her at the clinic. I made her some tea and cleared the rest up for her. I was livid and thought that I would 'swing for him' one day. I thought that it was to be hoped that he never needed my help ever because he 'sure as hell' wouldn't get it.

Later in the week I had gone to the cinema with Jean. She lived higher up in the flats. Dad came home and told Mum that he'd seen me outside with a fella but she was wise to him. "What coat did she have on? Are you sure it was our Doreen?" she asked.

"I'm positive," he replied. "She had her black coat on, the one with the fur round the hood." Mum walked through to the bedroom and came back with my black coat on a hanger. "Well, I'll be damned, I could have sworn it was her. She must have a double," Dad said. No, I didn't have a double, just an 'arsehole' for a father.

I didn't have many problems at Eastwood School. I still took myself off somewhere if I felt the need. One really sunny day, after lunch, I decided to go and sit in the park. I would only be missing PE and games – not my favourite lessons. I spent a lovely afternoon getting some sun. As I set off to go home I noticed some young kids throwing stones at the pigeons. I shouted at them. They replied with abusive language. As I was leaving something hit my head. The little swines had chucked a stone at me, good job it wasn't too big. I felt something running down my neck. When I looked down the front of my school shirt was covered in blood. It's always the case that you never have a hanky when you need one. A young woman pushing a pram stopped to ask if I was OK. She kindly gave me some tissues to mop up with.

I had to think of something quickly as I knew that Mum would want to know what had happened. I couldn't tell the truth as then she'd want to know why I'd been in the park. So I just said that a lad had chucked something at me as I walked past. When Mum had a look it was only a very small cut. It shows how much you can bleed if you hit your head.

I had an invitation to go to the youth club. Dad wouldn't let me go. He thought the youth club was a den of iniquity, full of teddy boys. I didn't make a fuss, just waited a few weeks until he had forgotten and then went anyway. I could do all the ballroom dances but had never learnt to jive. I just had no sense of rhythm, it really wasn't my scene.

When the time came for Mum to go into hospital I stayed at Jean's. There was no way I was staying on my own in the house with Dad. Mum called him 'Jocky Boy' for a bit of fun, not sure he liked it a lot. She gave birth to a girl. "Another bloody girl," Dad said when I told him. Mum was in hospital for ten days, this was the normal amount of time years ago. Not like today, you step on the 'conveyor belt' as you go into the labour ward and then step off at the exit with your new 'bundle of joy'. Dad visited the hospital once. Mum said that he reeked of booze. I hadn't seen him since Mum had gone into hospital. It was heaven to sleep all night without waking up to Jim Reeves or whoever Dad was listening to. I realised that this was how normal people lived – no rows, no 'aggro'. I wondered why my family couldn't be normal people. It brought to mind what the nun had said to me in Lumsden, "We all have our crosses to bear." So I guessed that Dad was our cross. Well, at least I was getting nearer to my sixteenth birthday so I did not think that I would be 'carrying my cross' for much longer, God willing.

CHAPTER TEN: NEW BABY IN THE HOUSE

Every parent knows how traumatic it is when you have a new baby in the house. You can imagine how it was when Mum brought the new addition home. When I knew she was being discharged I had enrolled Jean's help to clean up the flat. There had only been Dad there – how much mess can one man make? Well, you wouldn't believe what I found. Apart from a sink overflowing with dishes, the bathroom was filthy and there were dirty clothes all over the bedroom floor. He'd burnt the bottom out of Mum's favourite pan, the one she used to make soup. She made soup the old way with bacon ribs, veggies, pearl barley and dried peas amongst other things. It was delicious. We were going to attempt to make some so I tackled the housework and washing-up. We'd changed the bed, so I put some washing on. Jean went into Keighley to try and replace Mum's beloved pan, she was hoping to pick up some ribs for soup. When Dad brought Mum and new baby home the house was near presentable and the soup bubbling on the stove smelt rather good. I just hoped that it tasted as good as it smelt. Dad made a quick exit. He didn't want to miss valuable drinking time. Jean couldn't stay as she had got an evening job in the supermarket stacking shelves. So it was just us three. At least we saved Mum coming home to a terrible mess. She looked round. "Has he been living here while I was away?" she asked. I said that I presumed he had but I had not seen him. Mum thought he hadn't because the place was tidy. I didn't want to cause any upset for her so I told her that me and Jean had done a bit of cleaning so she didn't have to bother. "Was it very messy?" she asked. "Not too bad, plenty of washing-up," I mumbled. I couldn't look Mum in the eye and tell a fib. She had called her little girl Julia Caroline. I thought it was a lovely name, she'd got it out of a book she had been reading in hospital. Well, his lordship wasn't pleased with anything. The name was 'stupid' he had said and he couldn't cope with Julia crying as babies do. Well, I thought that was tough for him because, short of gagging her, there wasn't a lot we could do about that.

It was a good job that I had got plenty of sleep in whilst Mum was away because she went downhill fast. She would sit for hours knitting little dresses, cardigans and suchlike but the rest of the baby's care fell to me. In the end I had to speak to Dad, I had my school work to do. I couldn't be there all the time, he was going to have to take a share of the work. Mum was nervous of doing anything for Julia. She would give her the bottle but, as for changing her, bathing her and anything else, she was just too nervous to cope. Well, I might as well have spoken to the wall. Dad was useless. He did nothing for Julia at all. I hadn't been out for any enjoyment since Mum had come home and everyone needs some 'R and R' from time to time.

Mum became very depressed. She would sit and cry about nothing but could never tell you why she felt so down. Well, it was obvious, wasn't it? Living with Dad would make a saint depressed. Without giving me any warning, Dad had arranged for a psychiatrist to visit Mum. She had started pushing Julia in the pram down to Eastwood School. I would have to leave my class and take her home. It couldn't continue. Well, this chap asked

Mum all sorts of questions such as her name, age, who was the prime minister, who was on the throne, etc. When he had gone, leaving me with a script for diazepam to help her, I went off with Julia in her pram to pick this up and, hopefully do some food shopping as supplies were running low. The weather was warming up and most of the pubs had their doors open. As I walked past the 'Market Arms' I glimpsed in and there was his lordship with a woman – they were obviously together and, by the glasses on the table, had been there quite a while. I was fuming. I had to be careful how I handled this. I didn't want to cause hassle for Mum. Julia was asleep so I put the brake on.

Walking into the pub took a lot of courage from me – I hated pubs. When Dad spotted me he went drip white. Then he said, "Oh, hello darling." I nearly turned to look who he was addressing. "This is my daughter, she's a treasure, we couldn't manage without her," he announced to anybody who would listen. He then asked if I wanted a drink. If looks could have killed he would have been stone dead. "No thanks," I replied. "The doctor has just left. I'm going to pick up Mum's pills and do some shopping. Your baby daughter is asleep outside." He thought I was going to leave her with him. No way, I wouldn't have trusted him to look after a dead dog.

"This is Jim's daughter," he said. "You remember Jim." Oh, I remembered Jim all right. This young woman was nowhere near the right age and also Jim didn't have a daughter. I picked the first name I could think of. "Oh, you must be Christine," I said. "Yes," she replied.

"Pleased to meet you."

"Well, I must get on, lots to do. I'll tell Mum I've seen you, bye," I said.

I thought I would let him chew on that until he got home. I never said a word to Mum. I wouldn't have wanted to upset her. Dad was very subdued when he got in and soon took himself off to bed. He was very quiet for a while, then I remembered that he didn't have a conscience. So I wondered what he was plotting for 'pay back'. Mum was worried. She thought that the doctor had got the wrong impression of her. "That doctor that came thinks I'm barmy," she said.

"Of course he doesn't," I said. "I told him you were just a bit rundown."

We all knew what was wrong. She had put up with Dad for far too long. He needed locking up somewhere and for the key to be thrown away. What he did next beggers belief. I had been upstairs to see Jean. I was struggling with some homework. When I walked in the front door I knew something was wrong. It was freezing. The days were warming up but the nights were still very cool. When I walked into the front room I saw that he had opened one of the big windows. He was sitting on the sill with one leg inside and the other outside. Mum was sitting petrified.

Julia was screaming. I told Mum to take the baby into the bedroom. She was only a few weeks old. If she caught a chill I would let everyone know whose fault it was! "Right," I thought. I didn't shout. I walked over to Dad and spoke very softly. "If you intend to jump, do it, I need to get this room warm again for the baby." He just sat there smirking. It dawned on me that this was 'pay back' for me. My mind was working overtime. It would be so easy. All I had to do was give him a good shove. I could claim I had tried to pull him in. I had a devil on one shoulder and an angel on the other, one saying, "Go on, finish it," the other saying, "You'll never forgive yourself, he is your father." I'm sorry to say that the angel won. I raised my voice a bit, "We're five floors up. You have until I count to five to get your sorry arse in here. If you're still sat there after five I swear to God I will shove you out. You'll be dancing with the devil tonight." He still didn't move. I got hold of his arm and pretended to shove him. He looked very scared. I started counting. He got down and staggered to his chair.

"I'm sick of you ruining everyone's lives. You are pure evil," I yelled at him. Then he started to cry. I went into the kitchen. His sandwich was still there on a plate. I made my dysfunctional parents a cup of tea, then fed my sister and got myself into bed. I can hear you saying, 'she was a hard little bitch'. Don't think I didn't feel sorry for him, I did, but if I had shown him I was wavering he would have used it as a stick to beat me with. I did want to give him a cuddle and ask what I could do to help but, 'cut me some slack here' don't you think I had enough on my plate. What with Mum and a newborn to look after, I think I was doing my best to hold it all together. In hindsight, I realise now he had severe mental health issues, but I was only young. I had nobody to go to for advice. I knew that by morning he would remember nothing about all this, lucky him.

I lay in bed making my plans for the future. As soon as I left school and could support myself, I would be off. Mum knew this and I knew that she was not looking forward to being on her own with Dad. The trouble was that he knew Mum must be keeping contact with Maureen. He wouldn't have her name mentioned. I blamed myself for not giving Mum enough support when she was carrying Julia. But, to be fair, the only thing I could have done to help her was to hire a hit man to rid us of 'Jocky Boy'. He was the big problem. Mum was a nervous wreck and would sit in the kitchen smoking, waiting for him to return home every night, wondering what mood he would be in. With all the hassle she got from him you would have thought she would have hated his guts, but, no, she never said a bad word about him. I wondered if she felt ashamed. Maybe she thought it was her fault. But I thought that one day the 'worm would turn', he better watch out. She would see the light and make him pay.

What was this big fixation with Maureen all about? Kids grow up, leave home to get married or just to find their own space. Why should we have all this hassle regarding her? I cast my mind back to something that happened when we were on the moor. I had awoken to find Mum sitting by our bed, crying. I knew Dad was already in bed so he wasn't the problem. I whispered to her to ask if she was poorly. She shook her head and told me to go back to sleep. I wondered if she had been told something about Dad, maybe that was it.

In our family I always felt that I was the odd one out. I can never remember either of my parents showing any affection to me. I often thought there was something going on that I was being kept in the dark about.

Mum really baffled me. It didn't matter how serious the trouble got, she would get up next morning and carry on as normal. Why did she do that? Why did she stay with Dad? It was a mystery to me. The only time I had seen him visibly upset was when he sold Blondie before we returned to Keighley. I was amazed. The dog walked away, looking up at her new owner. She never looked back once. Perhaps she was glad to go. She deserved a peaceful retirement. The dogs had to work hard on shoot days. I had bathed her feet many times as they were sore with the constant work. Heather is not very kind to dogs' pads. I hope she lived out her life in peace.

Most people can find a skeleton in the cupboard, we found a bloody graveyard full when the truth finally emerged.

Dad continued to question me regarding Maureen's whereabouts. I told him straight, I hadn't had any contact with her since we left Lumsden. I said I wasn't really interested in finding out what she was up to now. Mum hadn't mentioned her to me. I had posted an airmail letter for her the previous week but I didn't look to see who it was addressed to. I wasn't getting involved in it all again.

In the meantime me and Jean were having a great summer. We were very wicked really. If we were out and spotted a girl with her fella one of us would go over and whisper to him, just loud enough for the girlfriend to hear, "Thanks a lot for Friday, I enjoyed every minute." Then we would stand back and wait for the fireworks. If you said Friday you could be sure he wouldn't have been with her that night. It was a tradition, Friday was lads' night out, girlfriends stayed home and washed their hair or met up with their mates. We thought it was a great laugh. My only excuse is that we were young and stupid.

I got the tables turned on me later in life, it was not funny after all.

When I started at Eastwood School, I had a new strategy. I planned to keep my head down, stay out of trouble and work hard. God, that would be a first for me. Perhaps I was getting some sense in my old age. The truth was that I had enough hassle at home. I didn't need it at school too. In eighteen months time I would be leaving school and I thought that, hopefully, I would be able to change my life for the better.

We then appeared to be in calmer waters. Mum had pushed Julia in her pram down to the building site where Dad worked. He had to finish early to bring her home. He didn't want that to happen again so this stopped him causing any upsets for a while. Peace and tranquillity reigned. Mum became her old self again and all was right with the world.

Dad came up with another new scheme to make extra money. He had started a new job at the foundry. The work was hard, he was getting older. I shared my room with Julia so he decided to rent out the spare room. Our first lodger was an Italian lad called Tony, better known as 'Tony Guitar'. He was very good-looking and he knew it.

Dad had an allotment. You could see it from the kitchen window. He had a few chickens and grew some vegetables. He also had a lurcher cross dog. He shared the allotment with a chap called Nick. Dad was always boasting how fast the dog was, it didn't go unnoticed. The local gypsy lads were always on the lookout for a dog with speed. Dad got a lab cross dog to keep the lurcher company. Mum had said that it wasn't fair to keep the dog on its own. Anyway I was taking the dogs up the woods for exercise. Tony was just returning from work. He called out to me, asking if he could come along. "Be my guest," I replied, "but your shoes will be ruined." I had boots on. He was wearing some really nice black slip-ons.

Anyway he came along. The previous night he had been giving us a few songs and serenaded me with Elvis' 'Old Shep'. He was quite a good singer. Dad said that the pubs were full on the nights he entertained. Anyway, we stopped for a sit down while the dogs had a run around. He played the gentleman, putting his jacket down for us to sit on. He started to get a bit too close. I remembered Mum's advice. This was another of her pearls of wisdom. She said that men were just out for what they could get and to "keep your hand on your ha'penny our Doreen and you'll be OK." I'll leave you to figure that one out for yourselves. I asked Tony if he knew how old I was. Being under sixteen, I was what they referred to as 'jail bait'. Anyway I gave him the benefit of the doubt. I didn't like to label anyone a dirty old man unjustly. I didn't say anything to Mum. After all a kiss wasn't a big thing, was it?

Later in the week he asked if I wanted to go to the cinema that Saturday. It was a film I really wanted to see, so I said 'yes'. We went to the Ritz. When we got there his girlfriend was waiting for him. She was really put out to see me. To add insult to injury he told her he was baby-sitting for his landlady. It was payback time. He wanted to make a fool of me because he didn't get his wicked way. Well, he was going to learn that you didn't mess with me. When we got home, I had a quiet word in Mum's ear. She gave him a week's notice to quit his room. The 'Italian Stallion' had been gelded. When Dad wanted to know why he had left, Mum said that he wasn't the sort of man you wanted around with a teenage girl in the house.

Next to take up residence was Brian. He was a postman, a really nice chap. He decided to teach me to drive his old van. Soon enough he discovered that I had no sense of direction. If he said 'left', I had to think about it. He would laugh. "You'd better wait until you get a wedding ring on, then you'll know which is left."

"There's no chance of that," I replied. "I'm never getting married."

"Why, what's wrong with marriage?" he said.

I turned the tables on him. "Why aren't you married then?" I asked.

"I'm waiting for you to grow up," he replied.

"You'll be waiting a long time. I'm like Peter Pan, I'm never growing up." I tried to look serious but ended up laughing. He was a good mate.

Brian stayed with us a long time. Then him and Dad had a fall out about something. I learnt later that they were both chasing the same woman. No fool like an old fool. Anybody who found my dad attractive must have been very hard up.

I had found out that I wouldn't be able to leave school the following year. They had changed the rules and no-one was allowed to leave at Christmas so I would have to carry on until the following July.

Mum got a shock. Dad had been asked to play Santa at the local hospital. I thought this was a joke and that someone should tell him that charity began at home. He was totally different when he was out and people thought he was a really nice chap. They should have seen him at home. That would have changed their minds.

Brian became quite attached to me. Wherever I was going he'd ask if I wanted a lift. He could be a bit of a pest at times. We went in a cafe in Keighley. The girl serving asked if my Dad took sugar in his coffee. He looked taken aback. It just reminded him how young I was. Also, I didn't look my age so that made the age difference more obvious. He still wasn't put off though. He tended to tag along. Mum mentioned the age gap and said he was far too old for me. I told her that we were just good mates. Well we were as far as I was concerned. Jean told me to get a boyfriend, saying that this would give him the message. I started seeing a boy from school. He lived up Bracken Bank with his mum. His dad had recently died. It was such a shame, you could tell they were a close-knit family. His name was John. He had a mate who was really good-looking, called Eric. It was when we were at Eric's house one weekend that his cousin called to leave a message. That is how I met my first love, Kevin Westlake. He drove a cream-coloured Ford Anglia. I thought he was good-looking, he had really black hair, but I never gave him a second thought until a week or so later. Eric had a message for me. Kevin wanted to take me out. I wasn't sure how old he was. This would be an issue with Mum. Eric said he was nineteen. I had been fifteen on my previous birthday. So when I spoke to Mum I knocked a year off Kevin's age and hoped for the best.

When Kevin came to pick me up in his car Brian went into

sulk mode. Mum said she thought Kevin was a nice lad, he appeared a bit shy. Dad thought he was OK too. Well, he would. Kevin worked for Timothy Taylor's brewery, delivering beer to the pubs. I don't think Dad would have bothered who I was with or what I was doing. He gave me a wide berth and I did the same. Most nights he was in bed before I came home, although I was never out very late anyway. He had a new routine. He would go straight to the pub from work. He said that working in a foundry gave you a very dry throat. He would then get home about eight o' clock, eat his meal and be in bed by nine thirty. It was a very early start at the foundry. He would often wake up later and ask Mum to make him a 'piece', this was Scottish for sandwich. She said he always asked if I was in. She would tell him I was in bed whether I was or not. He was very quiet those days.

Anyway then Dad asked me if I would like to go on a driving holiday to Scotland. His friend, Danny, who was a retired jockey was going with his wife, a friend who worked as a civil servant and her son. There was one spare place if I wanted to go. I knew Danny's wife. She was a nursing sister at St John's Hospital. I sometimes went at the weekend to read to the old ladies who had no visitors.

One weekend Doris, whom I visited a lot, wasn't very well. She started making funny noises in her throat. I rang the bell. Staff nurse told me to sit with one of the other old girls for a while. When it was time to leave I popped back to see Doris. They had covered her face with a sheet. She had passed away just like that. I was shocked, how could she have gone in the short time I had been away. It scared me really. The previous week she had been having a laugh and joke about the old chap who came round with the books trolley. He must have been at least seventy. She had said that she wanted him as her toyboy. Then she was there with the sheet over her face, end of life for her. It made me aware just how quickly life could be taken away. Mum always said that life was a precious gift which should be handled with care. Doris had not looked very old. I reasoned that young people didn't die, no, of course they didn't, that was OK then. I thought I should have about another hundred years at least!

Anyway Dad said I could go on the holiday and, would you believe it, he gave me some spending money as well. It turned out to be a lot of fun. We stayed one night near Loch Lomond. I don't know about it being bonnie, it looked quite spooky after dark with the mist over the water. We visited St Andrews. It was the cleanest place I had ever seen but the shops were very expensive. Then we carried on to Aberdeen. My hosts planned to spend a couple of days there so I went to stay with Auntie Penny again. I had planned to visit Uncle Joe, Auntie Penny's husband, who had been in hospital a long time. Joe came from down south so didn't have the Scottish twang. He had worked as a window cleaner but slipped off his ladder one day and broke his back. Penny visited most days. He wasn't ever able to return home as he was paralysed from the waist down and needed specialist nursing care. He was very pleased to see me. He had heard of my misfortune with the booby trap in Penny's kitchen. He said he had fallen foul of it after a night in the pub. I felt really sorry about the whole situation. Why do horrible things happen to the nicest people? I wandered around the grounds whilst Penny spent some time with Joe. Had this happened to Joe in 2014 he would have been able to live at home with all the equipment and help available. As it was 1963 he had no choice and was, in fact, lucky to be alive, if you could have called his life then lucky. I wondered if he would have preferred to have been killed outright. I suspect he would have. He had been an active and fun-loving person.

In the evening Horace took me out to dinner. It was a bit different to the previous time we had been out. He kept glancing sideways at me. "I can't believe you're the same person I took to the fair. You've changed so much," he said.

I laughed. "That was a million years ago," I replied. "I leave school in a few months, then I can start living my life."

He asked me if I had a boyfriend. "Not really," I said. Then I remembered Kevin. Well we only went out once so he wasn't really my boyfriend. It would surprise me if I ever heard from him again. Oh well, his loss.

We got home very late. There were no pans to fall over this time. I had hot chocolate with Horace. He told me of his plan to get a house of his own quite soon. He had been romantically involved with the priest's housekeeper for a while so I guessed that they would marry. The highland air certainly made you sleep well.

We left the following morning for two days in Edinburgh. The civil servant lady and her son decided to take the train home early. I hoped it wasn't anything to do with me. There you go. I had got a complex. When anything happened I automatically assumed it was my fault. I asked Danny if they were leaving early because of me. He said the boy's asthma was playing up. He winked at me and said, "That woman's always been a snob." We visited the castle and watched the marching band returning to barracks. God, those bagpipes were so loud, I was sure I'd gone deaf. I bought Kevin a pressie. I got Dad some mealy jimmys which were oatmeal sausages that you ate with soup and also some bradies. They were morning rolls. You warmed them and ate them with butter. I got Mum some Edinburgh rock. It is soft and crumbly, she loved it.

When I arrived back it was early evening so I thought I'd take Kevin his tankard. Brian, of course, was only too pleased to give me a lift. We went the back way past 'The Vine' pub. I spotted Kevin's car. "Stop," I shouted at Brian. He glared at me. "I'm deaf. You just blasted my eardrums," he said. He still had the sulks as far as Kevin was concerned, I think.

"Go in and see if Kevin is there," I said to Brian. He just sat there, looking at me.

"Well," I said. He still sat there. "Look," I said, I can't go in. I'm underage. People think I'm about twelve." He went in grudgingly.

I sat in that van for ages. When he did come back I yelled, "Where have you been, I've been here for ages."

"Well, I had to have a pint, didn't I? It would have looked odd if I didn't and yeah, he's in there."

"Who is he with?" I asked.

"How would I know?" Brian snapped back. I thought he

was very tetchy. It never crossed my mind that he was jealous. He was old enough to be my father for God's sake. Brian went on to say that it looked like a family party.

"Was he with a girl?" I asked.

"Well, said Brian, "he was sat with his arm around a rather tasty blonde."

"Can we go home now?" said Brian. I just nodded. That was that as far as Kevin was concerned. After all, he only took me out once, what did I expect. He'd only been interested in me until he found out that I was still at school. Anyway, I thought Kevin could 'get stuffed'.

A week later Eric was waiting for me at lunchtime. "I've got a message for you," he called out. Before he could say any more, I yelled, "Tell him to boil his heid."

"His what?" asked Eric.

"Just tell him." I stormed off then, turning and yelling, "It's Scottish."

The following day Kevin was waiting outside school at lunchtime. He called out to me as I walked past. I ignored him and carried on walking. As he drew alongside of me he opened the door. "Please get in," he said, looking very sorry for himself. I was still quite put out.

"Why, is your blonde busy today?" I replied.

He looked really confused now. "I have no idea what you are on about. Please get in so that I can talk to you, and why are you so angry?"

I got into the car and slammed the door so hard it made my teeth rattle.

"What the hell is up with you?" he yelled at me.

I decided that he deserved an explanation. I told him what Brian had told me. He shook his head. "It was a family party. My cousin's twenty-first birthday," he said.

"Does your cousin happen to be a blond?" I sniped back.

He was shaking his head again and started to laugh.

"Don't worry about it," I replied, "I think someone has been a bit economical with the truth."

"I'm glad we sorted that out," he replied. "What time shall I pick you up?"

I smiled and started to open the door.

"Don't you want to go out with me?" he said. "Why don't you like me? I'm a nice fella really."

"I'm sure you are, Kevin, but you're too old for me. I'm not really a pub person. It just wouldn't work, sorry. I got out and shut the door, quietly. I regretted what I had done. I liked Kevin a lot. He made me feel safe. I wished I could have taken him up on his offer but, as I said, I'm not a pub person, the smell of beer turns my stomach.

I'm afraid that's what years of living with my dad did for you. I told you that he'd given me a complex that would stay with me all my life.

"Oh well, that's that," I thought.

When I got home Brian was sitting having his tea. I sat down and gave him my angry stare. He knew what he'd done. Dad arrived home. I made myself scarce. I had some school work to do.

That Saturday I went into town to look for some new shoes. When I went into Wild's Cafe for a sandwich I saw Kevin across the road. I left my sandwich and dashed across the road just as he was getting into his car. "Oh God, I hope I'm not going to regret this," I thought. I tapped on the window. Kevin smiled and opened the door.

"Get in," he said. "Please don't slam the door."

We went for some fish and chips. He said he was glad I'd changed my mind and we arranged to go out that night, he was to pick me up at seven thirty.

Brian was still sulking. He knew I was going out. "Who are you meeting tonight?" he asked. I ignored him. He was no fun any more. "I'm sorry if I upset you," he said.

"You didn't," I replied, "and I'm meeting Kevin."

" We've spent a lot of time together," said Brian. "I hope he doesn't let you down."

I laughed. "I'm going for a night out with him, not marrying him," I said.

Well, things progressed from there. Kevin and I spent a lot of time together. I got on well with his parents. They were nice people. Kevin took me into several pubs even though

I was under age but most of the landlords knew him so it wasn't a problem and I didn't drink alcohol. I found I was OK when I was with Kevin. He never got drunk. I was out with him one night. We went into 'The Vine' pub. "Oh shit," I thought. Dad was sitting there with two other blokes. I waited for the explosion. It didn't come. He just smiled, said 'hello' and carried on with his conversation. I was 'gob smacked'. When I got home he was still up.

"Here it comes," I thought.

Mum was sat drinking her tea. I got myself a cup. "Did you enjoy your evening?" Mum asked.

"It was OK," I replied.

"You do know you are not old enough to go into pubs," Dad said. I nodded. "Well, I'll say no more but you better not let me catch you drinking before you are eighteen." He got up and went to bed.

Mum let out a deep sigh. "You were lucky to get away with that," she said.

I just said, "Yeah." He could have said a lot more but he let me off easy. I could still meet Kevin so that was fine. Kevin often picked me up from school and we went to his house for tea. I was quite happy with my life. I needed to start looking for a job. I would be leaving school at the end of the month. I had finally got there. I had been waiting to leave school since the day I threw my pudding in the fire at Stonehaven. I had made it.

When I was doing research for this book I looked through old copies of the 'Keighley News'. I live in Lincolnshire now so was online trying to check on some old friends.

What I saw saddened me very much. I came across Kevin's death notice. He had died in Airedale General Hospital in August 2010. He was only sixty-five years old, what a waste! He should have lived a lot longer. I knew he had married and then later divorced and had two children but then I lost touch. It seemed very strange that

just when I got to the point where he had played a big part in my life I should come across this notice.

Regardless of the stories I had heard about his excessive drinking and reckless behaviour I will remember him as I knew him. Kevin was a lover, not a fighter. He played a big part in my life. I loved him in my own way and would have married him if Dad hadn't kicked off big time and I left Keighley for pastures new.

Would it have worked out for us? Who knows? I will visit his last resting place if I ever return to Keighley again. I do come across Kevin several times in my story. You will just have to wait to see how it all fits into place.

CHAPTER ELEVEN: WORKING GIRL

Mum always cooked chops for Dad, me and Mum had sausage. Dad said it was only the workers that got chops. I thought, to myself, how mean he was. Poor old Mum had a job looking after him but she never got chops. I know it sounds petty, but it's the principle of the thing. It somehow made Dad more important and that got up my nose. I thought that when I started work I would give my chop to Mum. I didn't like them anyway. I'd rather have a fried egg.

Dad informed me that he had arranged an interview for me at Peter Blacks. This was the local sweat shop. I wanted to protest. I'd rather hoped I could get an office job. However, Dad went on to say that those who didn't work didn't eat and so, just to keep the peace, I went for the interview. I got a job to start after I left school. Peter Blacks made slippers, bags and other things. It would be a sewing job. Now this was bad news for me as I didn't know one end of a sewing machine from the other. Anyway, I would be paid full wages for the first two weeks and then it was piecework (so you got paid for what you did). I thought I'd better find another job before the two weeks' training ran out. The last thing I wanted was to give Dad a chance to have a go at me. I didn't 'give a shit' what he did or said, he'd lost my respect a long time ago. I knew that the next time me and him crossed swords would be the last. I was in a 'no win' situation and I would have to walk out. Before this happened I wanted to be sure Mum was well enough to cope without me. I know that makes me sound big-headed but it's true. Mum depended on me a lot. I did most of the things for Julia. Mum still wasn't confident bathing her. I think Julia got very confused, she thought I was her mum. She was a good baby and needed very little. Dad did nothing. As far as he was concerned babies were for women to look after. I think Mum had been suffering from post-natal depression but, of course, it wasn't recognised in those days.

My last week at school was sad really. I hated to admit it but I thought I was going to miss what friends I had made there. I would be starting work the following week. Boy, was I in for a shock!

Kevin understood when I explained it all to him. He said I was just a little girl trying to be very grown-up. Imagine, I'd spent all my school life just waiting to leave but then, as the time grew near to leave, I didn't want to.

So anyway, when I left, I thought, "Right, that's me now, no more school. I'm meeting Kevin tonight and going to his place." Friday was his parents night out. Kevin picked me up at seven and we got some goodies to stuff ourselves with. I was telling Kevin about my last day and how I was a bit sad. He said, "Never mind, you're a big girl now." I couldn't believe what he said next, "How would you like to do what big girls do?" he said, laughing at the look on my face.

"How would you like a smack in the mouth?" I replied. I was angry. "If you have brought me here tonight just for that reason I'm not interested. I suggest you find yourself an obliging big girl," I hissed at him.

"Hold on, hold on," he stuttered, "I was only joking."

"I wonder what you would have done if I had said 'yes'," I said. I was still very pissed off at him.

"Ah," he said, "but I knew you wouldn't."

"Oh, so you don't fancy me in that way then," I replied. He was in a hole and he should have stopped digging. Everything he said was getting him in trouble.

"It is the bloody sixties you know", he said.

"The sixties it might be but I'm not a swinger," I replied. I was finding it hard to keep a straight face. He was floundering about like a fish out of water. I know it was mean but I couldn't help but give him the full treatment.

"I've only known you two minutes and you think you are going to get in my pants. Forget it mister." I held up my left hand. "Can you see a ring on there?" I asked.

He looked very shamefaced. "I'm really sorry. I didn't mean to offend you," he said. That did it, I collapsed in helpless laughter.

I was rolling around on the floor giggling like a fool. He then made a big mistake by saying, "I forgot you were just a kid."

I stood up, grabbed my coat and bag and left. I met his mum and dad getting off the bus.

"Where is he?" his mum asked.

"Oh, he's digging himself out of a hole at the moment," I replied and jumped on the bus into town.

I was home early. "What's up?" said Mum.

"I've got a bad head. I'm going to bed," I said and filled myself a hot water bottle. I thought I had just blown any chance I had with Kevin. I pulled the covers over my head and went to sleep.

I didn't see Kevin on Saturday or Sunday. Brian asked me, "Where's lover boy tonight then?"

"I wouldn't know," I replied.

"Do you fancy going to the pictures?" he said.

"Sorry," I replied. "I've got a previous engagement."

I got myself ready and walked into town. I thought I'd go to the coffee bar and see who was around. I spent a couple of hours in there talking to Carol and Margaret from school. Margaret had a job at Woolworths. She had been working there on a Saturday for ages. Carol had a bigger problem. She was pregnant with Pete's baby. He was a lot older than her. Her parents knew and weren't too pleased about it all. "Well," I thought, "if this is what you get for being a big girl, I'll give it a miss." I thought, laughing to myself as I walked home, that Mum would have been so proud of me. Her advice was right. Men were after only one thing and I was glad I'd kept my hand on my ha'penny.

The first day at work was not too bad. I found my way round a sewing machine but what I couldn't do was sew a straight line. This was not looking good. By the end of the first week I had been to A & E twice to get a needle out of my finger – mind you, so had some of the others who started with me, so guess this was 'par for the course'. Mum knew I didn't like it there. "Have a look in the 'Keighley News'," she said. "See if there's any office jobs going."

I was looking through the paper when Dad came in. "Got the sack already?" he said.

"She's looking for something more suited to her talents," said Mum, glaring at him.

There were a couple of office jobs going, one at Emu Mills and another at Keighley Lifts. I phoned for an appointment at Emu's. I thought that it would be good if I got a job there as it was just down the road from the flats. I went for an interview in my lunch break. It went OK but they were seeing other girls so said they would let me know. The only downside was that you had to go to night school once a week to learn shorthand and typing.

I was in Driver's Milk Bar at lunchtime having a sandwich when Sandra came in. I knew her from St Anne's. She was working at the council offices. She told me that Lynda, the witch, had got a job at Emu's. "That's it," I thought. She's got my job." Lynda and I didn't get along. She was a slapper and would go with anything in trousers.

She chased everyone else's boyfriends just for the hell of it. I'd lost count of how many relationships she had broken up. She had tried it on with Pete, Carol's fella. He'd heard of her reputation and just laughed at her. Carol wasn't too pleased though.

When I got home that night from the 'torture house' I saw Kevin's car outside. I thought about hiding out until he left but didn't. He was sitting talking to Mum when I walked in.

"You've got a letter from Emu's," said Mum as she handed me a cup of tea.

"What are you here for?" I asked Kevin.

"He wanted to take me out," joked Mum, "but I'm busy tonight."

"I wondered if you wanted to go out tonight," he said.

The door opened and Brian came in for his tea. "Are we having a party?" he joked.

I turned to him and said, "I can't go to the pictures with you this evening. I forgot that Kevin was taking me out."

"I've got to work a double shift," he mumbled, so it's OK."

Kevin had a big smile on his face. "You're on a week's trial," I said.

"Don't you start," he replied. "I've been getting blasted all week by Mum."

"Aren't you going to open your letter?" Mum said.

"You open it Mum. I already know who's got the job," I said going into the kitchen so that I could hide my disappointment.

"Well done, you got it," Mum shouted. I was amazed.

I would like to say that Peter Blacks were sorry to lose me but the poor woman who was trying to teach me to sew looked like she'd won first prize when I told her. She had already checked in the offices for vacancies, terrified I was going to do myself some serious harm. It was also costing them a lot for needles and ruined work. I finished at the end of the week. They didn't want me to work any notice, they were just glad to get rid of me.

I was to start in the Order Office at Emu's the following Monday. Kevin lavished a lot of attention on me over the weekend. I must admit that I did like him a lot.

Well the first day at my new job went well. One of the girls was engaged to Kevin's mate, Stanley. She was chattering away all lunch-time about the house they were saving up to buy. I suddenly realised how much I didn't want a little house and then maybe a little, but very noisy, baby and washing, cleaning, ironing, dirty nappies and everything else. Irene wanted all of these things. She was older than me but couldn't wait for married life. "Oh well," I thought, "everyone to their own." It was the norm. You left school, got yourself a boyfriend, then engaged and married by your twenty-first birthday. I was still very clear on the marriage thing. It wasn't for me. In fact, none of it was.

Kevin and I spent most of our free time in each other's company. Friday was boys night out but he still preferred to meet me. He would pick me up from work and we would spend the evening at his place. His parents went out on a Friday. Kevin did drink but all the time I knew him I'd never seen him drunk or nasty. We were comfortable in each other's company. I felt quite happy with my life at that time.

One evening I was getting ready to meet Kevin in town. We were going to the cinema. Brian was also getting spruced up for an evening out. I wondered if he'd found himself a lady friend. He offered me a lift. We were chatting away and then he asked if I was serious about Kevin.

I quickly answered, "I'm far too young to be serious about anything."

"You want to watch he doesn't get sick of waiting for you to grow up," he said.

"That's his problem," I replied. "If he does, he does. You're looking very smart tonight. Hot date is it?"

He just smiled and opened the door for me. I walked across the square. I could see Kevin but not who he was talking to. Then I realised that he was chatting up Lynda, the witch. She was about my height with really long blond hair and I thought she was overweight. Well I would, wouldn't I? She was supposed to be going out with Gerald who was training to be a carpenter. He worked for his dad. They were doing a lot of joinery at Emu's. Guess that was where she had met him. He obviously hadn't heard about her reputation, she was a slapper.

I read Kevin the riot act once I had him on his own. It made matters a lot worse when he said that he'd known her for ages. I was livid. I said, "If you've been with her I suggest you get yourself tested. You may have caught something nasty."

When he dropped me off that night he didn't make any plans for the following day. I was glad. He was dumped. I thought that if I never saw him again it would suit me fine.

I spent all that weekend planning my revenge. Scorpios

always get revenge. On Monday I went to the cafe for my lunch. Lynda was in there sitting with Gerald. She looked at me, trying to gauge my response. I sat on my own, eating my sandwich. When I got up to leave Lynda called out to me. I walked slowly back to her table. "Oh," I said, "I didn't realise you two were still seeing each other.

When did you dump poor old Kevin then?" She sat with

her mouth open. I continued to tell Gerald all the things Lynda had been saying about him to the other girls in the office, including a very personal measurement of his manhood. He stood up, shouted, 'bitch' at her and stormed out. I turned to leave. She grabbed my arm. I turned to face her, laughing. She was just about to have a go at me so I gave her a slap. She ran out in tears. I thought that I would feel a lot better when I had got my own back, but I didn't. I was in a foul mood for the rest of the day.

Kevin didn't meet me after work. I didn't give it a second thought. I thought that I was much better on my own. I told Mum the whole story. She thought I was over-reacting. Later in the week one of the fellas from Packing asked me out. I said that I would think about it. Irene asked why I wasn't seeing Kevin any more. I just said that it wasn't working. A couple of weeks passed. I hated to admit it but I was missing his company. I had been out a few times with Ian from Packing. He really was far too old for me. There you go. Looking for a father figure. It was all Dad's fault.

I was intending to have an easy weekend. It was now well over a month since I'd last seen Kevin. I had started smoking. One of the biggest mistakes I ever made. I blamed that on Dad as well. Our house was like a stress bucket just waiting to overflow. Then I had another big shock. Dad and Brian had a mega argument. This surprised me as Brian was one of the quietest men I have ever known. He never raised his voice about anything. Anyway the outcome was that Dad told him to pack his stuff and leave. He asked if he could have until the end of the week so that he could find another room but Dad told him to vacate his room by the end of the day. Poor Brian, I wondered what he had done to upset his lordship. I was sorry to see Brian leave. He was a good mate. I saw him in town a few weeks later and we went for a drink.

"What the hell happened?" I asked him. He didn't want to tell me but I got the truth eventually. It seemed that Brian's lady friend was also seeing Dad. When Dad went round one evening and found Brian at her house they had an argument and, you know the rest! Well, well Dad never ceased to amaze me. I couldn't believe that Mum didn't know about everything but thought maybe she just didn't care.

CHAPTER 12: I GROW UP

I moved to the Wages Department. It was a bit more money and it also got me away from Lynda, the witch, who was in deep trouble herself. She had been seeing an older fella from the Mill Office. It seemed that he was married with a little boy and his wife was 'gunning' for her. It was her own fault. She always wanted what belonged to someone else. I hadn't spoken to her since the day in the cafe. Her ex-boyfriend, Gerald, was going steady with a trainee nurse from St John's.

When I went for my lunch Kevin's Mum was waiting for me. She said that Kevin was drinking like a fish since we broke up. I sent a message with her to say that I would meet him in town on Saturday lunchtime.

I stood waiting for ten minutes for Kevin to turn up. When he did he had got a big surprise for me in the shape of a ring box. Thank God he didn't do the down on one knee bit. It's then I made another big mistake. I said 'yes'. I couldn't believe that I'd said yes. What about all the plans that I'd made – my life of solitude with no man to foul up the works? Oh, well, you know what they say about the best laid plans of mice and men.

Kevin's mum and dad were very happy. My mum also thought it would be good for me. She thought Kevin might just be the one for me. Dad made no comment. It took my relationship with Kevin to a whole new level.

Mum was pleased. She thought that I would remain at home when I was engaged.

My life settled into a routine. I loved my job. I was happy with Kevin but still had no plans to marry. I was high on the cloud of romance. Young and stupid me. Guess what happened next? Yes you're right. Dad kicked off big time. I got home after an evening out to find Dad giving Mum a hard time. As I came in he started on me calling me some very choice names. Of course, I retaliated.

"Don't judge everyone by your own moral standards," I shouted. He stepped towards me. I thought, "This is where I get a serious slap."

Julia was screaming her head off. Mum was trying her hardest to quieten her. To cut a long story short, he threw us out. There was snow on the ground. It was freezing. We had managed to grab a few things but wondered what the hell to do. It was late and we had a fractious child who was getting very tired and very cold. I did the only thing I could think of. I took them to Kevin's. He gave up his double bed for us. His mum was really sweet, after all we had got her out of bed.

Next day I booked them into a bed and breakfast in Haworth for a couple of days. I didn't have unlimited funds so we had to decide quickly on a plan of action. I went home when I knew Dad would be at work and picked up the things Mum needed. He would never have noticed I had been there. The place was a tip with broken china and smashed ornaments. Well, I sure as hell wasn't clearing that up. Then I thought about Mum and Julia. They would have to come back. Where else could they go? Mum couldn't clear all that up and look after Julia as well. I thought I would get it done whilst there was nobody there so I got stuck in. It didn't take me long. I made myself a drink, got a biscuit and sat thinking 'what a shambles'. Poor Mum was stuck with that life, but I didn't have to be. I thought it was time for me to move on but to where? I could have stayed with Kevin but his family didn't have a spare bedroom and Kevin couldn't sleep on the sofa forever. I couldn't share his bed. It might have been the swinging sixties but that would have been a step too far, even for the sixties. What would dear old Dad say about that? I dreaded to think. Kevin's mum said, "Why don't you just get married?" I reminded her that I was under-age and would require his lordship's permission, which he would not give. Besides I was never going to marry, but didn't tell her this. She had high hopes for me and Kevin.

Mum and Julia returned after two days. I told Mum that Dad might realise then that she was not going to put up with 'all that crap'. She then told me that it was a letter from Maureen that had started the big row. I was furious.

"She doesn't even live here now but she's still causing trouble for us," I said. Mum never answered. "It's not fair." I said. "It's just not fair."

I knew I would have to leave. Dad would make my life a misery. Maureen was living in a place called Ramsey in a flat with her husband and daughter.

I went to see Kevin. He was far from pleased. "What about us?" he asked.

I shook my head. "I don't have all the answers but I know I have to leave for a while."

"When will you be back?" he asked. "Why can't you just move in with me?"

"Look, if I moved in with you can you imagine what Dad would be saying about me?" I said. I was getting emotional. I thought that if I moved into Kevin's I could still keep my job. I loved that job but as hard as I thought I was I didn't want Dad rubbishing my reputation.

"We could get married," Kevin said.

"I'm underage," I responded.

"I'll speak to your Dad," he said.

"Do you have a death wish," I replied. "Besides, I'm too young to get married." I was treading water there, the conversation was getting out of hand. "Look," I said. "I'll go to my sister's for a while until things blow over." Although he said, 'OK', he was not a happy bunny.

I'm afraid that at that moment in time I had to put myself first. When I got back home Mum was upset that I was still intent on leaving. I think she thought that Kevin would have been able to change my mind. I wrote a short note for my boss as way of an apology. Mum was going to take it in for me and would send on my wages and P45.

"Well, this is it," I thought. "I'm seventeen, no job, no home. Oh well, it could be a lot worse. I could be barefoot and pregnant as well." But, all joking aside, I was very uneasy about leaving.

It was an awful night, pouring with rain. Mum begged me to wait until the morning. I refused. I knew that it was now or never. I had to learn to stand on my own two feet. The trouble was that I didn't feel grown-up. I just wanted someone to give me a cuddle and tell me that everything would be OK. If I had known what the outcome of my adventure into the big wide world would be I'd have stayed where I was and eaten humble pie. But I did think that Mum would have a more peaceful time if I wasn't there. I always had an answer ready for Dad, it was fuelling his anger. He would have gone for me big time. I'm not sure what I would have done if I had got my hands on some type of weapon. After all, I so very nearly shoved him out the window. I was better off out of it. I packed and, ready to leave, told Mum that if Dad came home within the next hour or so she should just tell him that I was out with Kevin or had gone to bed. He never checked anyway.

I managed to get to the station with one very heavy suitcase. My coat was soaked. I was tired and cold, already missing my warm bed. I got my ticket and got onto the train without too many problems. As the train rumbled along in the darkness it suddenly didn't seem like such a good idea but, when I closed my eyes and saw Dad's angry drunken face before me, it made me sure I had made the right decision.

The train was empty. I must have been the only fool stupid enough to have travelled during the night. I tried to remember when I last had some food. God, I was starving. I was so hungry that it gave me a headache. My head was pounding. I thought about when Maureen had left Lumsden. She had someone with her and she had a place to go where she would be welcomed. What did I have? Nothing. There was no-one travelling with me and nobody waiting to welcome me anywhere. I was going to Maureen's. I figured that she owed me a helping hand.

All the trouble at home was caused by her letters. She had left home. It wasn't fair, she was still causing havoc. I decided I must be clear about it. I couldn't blame her. She just wanted Mum to know she was OK. It was not her fault that Dad was a 'looney tune'. I wondered why life had to be so hard. I was missing my warm bed, a good cuppa and one of Mum's cheese sarnies. What about Kevin? Yes, I was missing him as well. He had always been there to listen if I had a problem and would always come up with a solution.

Before I left I had spoken to a workmate. Her mother wanted a cleaner and babysitter and she'd offered a self-contained annexe rent-free in exchange for the duties of cleaner and dog's body. I spoke to Mum. I paid Hillary a week's rent and gave Mum the keys. I honestly thought she would leave and be glad of a safe, quiet place for her and Julia but was to learn later that she stayed with Dad. I felt sorry, upset and tearful. I had tried my best. If I'd moved in with her I still think she would have run back to the evil bastard. Maybe I should have waited and married Kevin. I've often pondered that thought over the years. Kevin often drifted into my thoughts. He was my first love and also a very sexy guy but I think he had a roving eye. My temperament would not tolerate that. I would have walked all over him. Well, so it was just me. I would have to face what life threw at me. Dad would never let me forget that I gave Mum a passport out of hell. She told me later that she went back before he could move an old slag into her home. He was a total shit. "He's your father, our Doreen," her words rang in my ears. I thought that he had best watch his back whilst I was around. Life seemed to get tougher by the minute. I thought, "Stop the world I want to get off." I needed a sugar daddy. I can't believe I just wrote that. My father was a liability I didn't need. I hope he rots in hell.

CHAPTER 13: DONCASTER BY MOONLIGHT

Well, I'd made it to Doncaster, only to discover that I was stranded there until the morning. I staggered into the waiting room as the waiting area had a useable toilet and an open fire with a good supply of fuel. So I was only thirsty, dog tired, scared to death and hungry. Then, I sat, traumatised by fear. There was a big bloke about to enter my sanctuary.

"I come bearing gifts," he said. "The old fella has sent you a mug of tea. If you smile nicely I'll share one of my Mum's cheese and onion baps."

We sat chatting by the fire. He was a sailor making his way back to his ship. He seemed nice enough. He offered me his donkey jacket to keep me warm. In spite of the open fire, I was shaking like a jelly.

"What's a kid like you doing stranded in the middle of the night on her own?" he asked.

I laughed, "I'm older than I look." I held up my left hand. He spotted my ring.

"You travelling to see your fella?" he asked.

"Not really," I replied. I'm going to see my sister."

"You need to have your wits about you, there's weird people hanging out in stations in the wee small hours."

"Well, thanks for that," I said. "You've made me twice as scared."

I'll always be grateful to the old station master, Popeye, the sailor and his mum's cheese baps. If I'm truthful, I was scared to death. I snuggled up to my sailor boy to keep warm. We talked about life in general and he showed me the ring he had in his pocket for his girlfriend. It seemed that she wasn't too keen on a sailor for a husband. The old tales of a woman in every port came to mind. I asked him, "Have you a girl in every port?" He laughed, "Not me. I save all my wages. Just want to get hitched and settled down but this is the only way I can make any money." He seemed a nice fella but in the wee small hours in a deserted station waiting room anybody, apart from Dad, would have seemed a hero. I was waiting for the train to nowhere.

"Don't worry," he joked. "I'll look after you."

The night dragged on. I fell asleep wrapped in his donkey jacket. I woke up with a jolt. A couple of lads outside the waiting room were making a lot of noise, swearing and shouting.

My 'bodyguard' whispered, "If they come in here, keep quiet and leave the talking to me."

They stayed outside and eventually went away. It suddenly made me realise that I had put myself at risk by not making proper plans. I had just wanted to put miles between me and Dad. The worst case scenario would have been that I would have ended up on some waste ground, murdered. I made a silent promise to be more careful next time I planned a journey. Me and my sailor boy watched the sun rise together. When my train arrived, he found me a seat and carried my suitcase for me. I thanked him for looking after me.

"You tell your fella to look after you proper. I may not be around next time to keep you safe," he said.

He jumped off the train and waved goodbye. I wonder what became of him. I was very grateful for his company.

I was now on the last leg of my journey and wondered what reception I'd get from Maureen. I would be letting her know how much trouble her letters to Mum had caused for all of us.

CHAPTER 14: WELCOME VISITOR (OR NOT)?

I wasn't sure what sort of reception I would get. "Oh well, here goes," I thought. I pressed the bell and waited. My sister opened the door.

"What the hell are you doing here?" she said.

"It's nice to see you too," I replied. "Your last letter to Mum caused no end of problems." I was crossing my legs.

"Can I come in? I need the loo."

When we got upstairs and I had a warm drink and some food in my stomach I told Maureen the full story. She was upset as she hadn't wanted to cause trouble for Mum.

What about your boyfriend?" she said.

"Well, he's not too happy about the situation," I replied.

"Couldn't you have moved in with him?" she asked.

"Well they only have two bedrooms. I can't expect Kevin to sleep on the sofa every night."

"You could have got married."

"As I keep telling everyone, I'm underage and besides I'm too young, I don't want to get married, ever," with this I brought the conversation to an end.

I heard the door closing downstairs. "That will be Billy. I better put the kettle on," Maureen said as she dashed off to the kitchen.

I sat on the sofa waiting to see what Billy's reaction would be when he saw me. Well, he didn't look very pleased. I didn't blame him. They were a young, married couple. I did feel I was intruding on their life.

"Don't worry. I will get a room as soon as I can," I said. Billy didn't reply, he just went to get changed out of his uniform.

Maureen had been away from home for quite a while but she didn't look a lot happier. "Doreen needs a bed for a week or two," she said.

Bill was still non-committal. I could see that it was going to cause problems having me there. The bedroom that I was going to use didn't have a separate door, so I would have to walk through their bedroom to get to my room. Not the ideal situation. I wished then that I had gone to Kevin's. His parents wouldn't have minded. Also, I had left the job I loved. What a bloody fool I'd been. You have heard the phrase, 'out of the frying pan into the fire'. "Oh dear, Doreen, you have made a ginormous mistake in coming here," I thought. I decided that I needed a good night's sleep and then I would form a plan of action.

Next morning Maureen said that she had some good news – a factory in Huntingdon had vacancies. I set off to see if I could find myself a job. Well I got set on at the factory but the bad news was that it made uniforms for the armed forces. So it was me and sewing machines again. I knew that it wouldn't be a long-term solution but it would get me a wage for a week or two. Billy gave me a lift into work and back so I saved on bus fares.

During the second week at the factory I was dashing across the road into work. It was dark and raining. A car hit me and then carried on. I was laying in the road, covered in mud, blood and my tears. I dragged myself into work, shaking like a leaf. I was drip white, cut and bleeding. My legs were a dreadful mess. My coat had a big rip in it from the mascot on the car. My stockings were in shreds. I thought I must have done some damage to my back as the pain was unbearable. When the boss saw what a state I was in he called an ambulance to take me to hospital. Someone must have rung Maureen who had then rung Billy. He arrived at the hospital whilst I was in X-ray. He was not pleased to have had to leave work to come and sort me out.

"Oh shit," I thought. "Why is it always me that gets into scrapes like this?"

I was told I had no broken bones but my ankle was very swollen and I was black and blue all over. Billy took me home and then dashed off back to work. God, I felt awful. I forced myself into the bath. I was stiffening up fast. I washed my hair, which was full of mud, blood and debris. I got myself into bed. I felt so sick. Maureen gave me some painkillers and a hot water bottle. I slept the clock round. It was two days before I tried to dress myself and get some food inside me. Maureen told me that the police were coming to see me because it was a hit and run. When they arrived I could tell them very little. I was laid in the road before I saw the car leaving.

"Did you get a good look at the car?" the policeman asked. I thought that if I had I wouldn't have been knocked down! I was getting seriously 'pissed off' with the copper. Apart from the colour of the car I could be of little help and, to add insult to injury, I got a bill for the ambulance. I never paid it. I think Maureen took care of it.

When Billy came home later he asked if I was returning to work in the morning.

"No way," said I. "That Job Is no good for me, I can't sew, the whole building is filthy. Someone saw a rat in the room where we have our sandwiches. I won't make you sick by telling you what condition the toilet is in."

"So what are you going to do?" asked Maureen.

"Get another job," I replied.

CHAPTER 16: GOODBYE KEVIN, HELLO?

I had been invited to the firm's Christmas 'bash'. I wondered what I should do. I was thinking that if I went it was unfair to Kevin but, then again, was he staying at home every night thinking of me? I thought not. Should I say 'no' to the invite or should I tell Kevin that it was over – decision, decisions. I asked Maureen what she would do. She said to tell Kevin first. Billy said I should go to the dance and then if I decided I wanted to see the lad again I should then tell Kevin. I decided to go to the dance with the fella. His name was Dudley. Again, he was older than me. He lived in Ramsey. But, I would make it clear to him that I was engaged to Kevin and that I would be returning to Keighley in the future. I could not decide whether or not to tell Kevin about it, but decided to see what happened.

Maureen offered to do my hair for the dance but as my hair had grown quite long I booked an appointment at the hairdresser. I'd also bought myself a new dress. I had my hair done in a French pleat. The evening went OK but nothing fantastic and we didn't make any plans to meet again.

Christmas arrived and was very quiet. I hated to admit it but I was missing home 'big time'. I was half-way through the washing up when Maureen shouted that there was someone at the door. I was just about to go and answer it when Billy walked into the kitchen. He didn't look very pleased. "Someone for you," he said. Kevin was standing behind him.

"How the hell did you get here on Christmas Day?" I asked.

"I managed to get a lift. I'm here until late Boxing Day," he said.

"I'm afraid we can't put you up. We haven't got room," Maureen said.

"That's OK. I'm booked in at the pub," Kevin replied.

It was a lovely day so I got my boots and coat. I felt terrible that I couldn't offer him a sandwich or anything as it wasn't my house. I need not have worried, he'd already eaten.

"I'm very pleased to see you. Why didn't you tell me you were coming?" I asked.

"I wanted to surprise you. This is my last ditch attempt. I want you to marry me. I can't carry on like this," he said.

I didn't know what to say. I wasn't ready to marry but I didn't want to lose him. I asked him to give me a couple of weeks. He agreed that he would. We went out for the evening and spent Boxing Day together. Maureen and Billy didn't invite him to share a meal with us. I thought this was really mean. I thought it was about time I returned home. I went into Huntingdon with Kevin to see him off at the station. I had been warned not to be back late and told which bus I should catch. I was getting more 'pissed off' by the minute. I waved Kevin goodbye and got myself back to the bus station, onto the correct bus, or so I thought. I was actually sitting on the wrong bus. I watched the bus I should have been on depart without me. The next one wasn't until after nine. I knew I would be in so much trouble. I sat nervously waiting for the next bus.

All I needed was Billy turning up to take me back. He would be in such a mood! Then I thought, "Hang on a minute. I'm not in his control, thank God." I found him very overbearing and I thought he could be a control freak. "Well," I thought, "not with me." I was grateful to Maureen for putting me up but I also felt very sorry for her. I hoped she was happy with the life she had chosen but she didn't look happy.

When I got back Billy was waiting. "Why weren't you on the bus?" he said, glaring at me.

"I thought I was, I honestly did, I didn't mean to miss it. I will be out of your hair soon. I'm going back home."

"Are you marrying Kevin?" Maureen asked.

"I haven't made a decision yet but I am moving back to Keighley."

I wasn't wearing my ring to work. I had more or less decided to write to Kevin, sending back his ring. I had spoken to a friend on the 'phone. Kevin had been out and about while I had been away. I didn't know who he had been seeing. I had told him that I had gone to the dance with Dudley. He didn't tell me about anybody, perhaps he thought it was OK because I was away. I thought it was obvious that I couldn't trust him. Thank God, I hadn't said I would marry him. I loved him to bits but I would always be wondering where he was and with whom.

Maureen said that Billy had been posted and that they were moving to Bedford. I couldn't have got to work from there anyway. I wrote my letter to Kevin and included his ring. By return post I had a letter from his mum begging me to reconsider.

She said that we could live at their house until we found somewhere else. It was tempting, but no, my mind was made up. A lady at work had offered me a room. She was an older lady and lived alone. Maureen and Billy put me on the train for Keighley. I got off at Peterborough. Dudley offered to meet me there. I left my stuff at his house. His mother offered to put me up for the night. I would be moving into my new room the following day.

What happened next changed my life. Accident or fate — I'm not sure. The lady who was offering me a room in her home had an accident at work. She fell headfirst down a flight of stairs and was seriously injured. She passed away a few days later. I wondered what I was going to do.

Dudley didn't want me to return to Keighley but his mum didn't want to put me up even though they had a spare room. A lady who worked with me in the lab put me up for a few days. Well, I guessed that I was homeless. I decided to go back and see Mum and Julia. Dudley was determined to go with me. I wasn't sure it was a good idea. I'd sent a letter to Mum telling her about Dudley but did not know what they would make of him. I was not sure I wanted to live in Keighley any more but I didn't belong in the south either. Dudley's parents didn't seem too keen on me. "Well," I thought, that's their problem." I was glad I hadn't got Billy telling me what not to do. I had had enough with my excuse for a father. I did not know why everyone thought I needed to be controlled. I just wanted to be my own person. I thought that if I 'cocked up' if was down to me.

CHAPTER 17: I FORGOT MUM'S ADVICE

I was making the most of my last few days in Ramsey. I didn't know why I was returning to Keighley, in fact if I never saw the place again it wouldn't bother me unduly. Kevin and I were finished, so what was the point? I didn't know it, but the man of my dreams was at that moment marrying his pregnant girlfriend in a church somewhere in Keighley, much against his will. I wrote to Mum to say that I would be home for a visit and also that I was bringing my new fella with me. Dad went ape when he saw his surname, I think he thought he was a coloured gentleman. Mum was praying he wasn't.

On our way back to Keighley we stayed overnight in Leeds. That night was to give me time to decide if I would stay in Keighley or return to Ramsey with Dudley. It changed my whole life and shaped my future.

By the time I got to Keighley the next day my mind was made up. I would return to Ramsey a married woman, much to the surprise of Dudley's family, don't think his mum was too pleased but he was well over twenty-one. I, however, needed some forms signing.

My stomach was churning as we arrived at the flats. Well, I need not have worried. Dad got on really well with Dudley. I'm afraid Mum wasn't too impressed. She thought I was making a big mistake. However, I was between a rock and a hard place so I took the only path that was acceptable in those days. I had forgotten to 'keep my hand on my ha'penny' as Mum would say. Although nobody was aware of the fact at that time, I was pregnant, even I didn't know, but when Dudley asked me to marry him I said 'yes'. Something told me, at that moment, that I didn't have a choice. Dudley returned home for a couple of weeks. I stayed in Keighley making plans. No big church do for me. I just didn't fancy walking down the aisle dressed like a meringue. I would rather have worn my jeans but mum was not going along with that, I ended up wearing a pink dress, not really my choice but mum liked it.

Before Dudley left we went for an evening out with Mum and Dad. I steered clear of Kevin's local but later on he walked into the pub we were in. He had a dark-haired, rather plump girl on his arm. As our eyes met he gave me that look that always said 'I love you baby', but we didn't speak. The big romance was well and truly over. My first love had moved on. I just wasn't sure I had, he always remained in a corner of my heart. If he'd have asked me there and then to marry him I know now I would have said 'yes' but think of the fall- out that would have caused!

The next couple of weeks passed in a blur. I hate to admit it, but I was just looking for a meal ticket and Dudley obliged. Looking back I can't even remember what he looked like. The reason Dad was all over him like a rash was that he'd realised that he was getting rid of me forever. How wrong he was. The marriage was doomed before it started. Did Dudley love me? Only he could answer that. What I did know was that I never loved him. In fact, to be truthful, I didn't even know him. I was still a little girl looking for her hero. How sad was that! Dad's fault again.

Dudley returned from Ramsey and we were getting married the following day. Mum kept telling me, "It's not too late to change your mind." She didn't know just how close I was to doing just that.

The big day arrived and went off without a hitch. I was glad when it was all over. It was then I realised that I would have to share my bed for the foreseeable future. Mum was right, I shouldn't have got married. I still thought like a little girl. I wanted my bed to myself. I liked to cuddle up to a pillow, not a fella. I thought that he may very well have to start sleeping on the sofa when we got back or I would.

Dudley had rented a caravan at Worboys, a small village between Ramsey and Huntingdon, and also had his name down for an upstairs flat in Ramsey which was going to be empty in the near future. I found myself very much at a loose end. He had a job at Hotpoint in Peterborough at that time. He left early and got back late so I had all day on my hands. The devil makes work for idle hands and it wasn't long before I was in trouble again. There was another girl on the site who was expecting her second child, she already had a boy. She was in a bit of trouble as the baby she was having wasn't her husband's. Her husband was in the forces and he knew it wasn't his. As soon as it was born she had to hand it over to the father to raise. One evening we decided to steal some apples from the orchard next to the site. Of course, we got caught. What a showing up – two pregnant ladies pinching apples. The policeman was very nice. He let us off with a caution.

"Does that mean I'll have a criminal record or not," I asked.

He laughed. "I'm not saying anything about this back at the station. I would be a laughing stock so your record will be blemish-free." Thank God for that what would mother-in-law have said?

I also got very close to one of Dudley's friends. I'm not naming names as it could cause trouble but we spent quite a bit of time together. Dudley used to go out on a Friday on the pretext of playing darts but didn't have the common sense to take his darts with him. So this was a newly married bloke out on a Friday with his mates hoping to pull a bird. This was the fella who had never had a girlfriend before he met me. Did I care? To be honest, no, I 'didn't give a shit'. It was obvious, even at this early stage, that I had made one very big blunder. I was already planning ahead. I had decided that as soon as my baby was born I would be high-tailing it back to Yorkshire. One big surprise was that Mum, Dad and Julia came to visit us.

They stayed for a couple of days. I don't know if they visited Maureen as well. I wondered if perhaps she was going to be welcomed back into the family. I thought 'well wonders would never cease'. Before they left to go home Dad took me to one side and gave me an envelope.

"That's your escape fund," he said. "It's obvious you are not happy here. There's enough money there to get you home. Put it in a safe place until you need it." That was one day when Dad went up in my estimation.

On the day I went into labour I was in Ramsey at the

doctor's. He told me I had a kidney infection and gave me some stuff to drink to clear it up. I made my way to Dudley's mother's to wait for him to return from work. As the day went on I got much worse. His mother said I wasn't in labour as my waters hadn't broken. It turned out I was having a dry labour. Well, ladies you can imagine how painful that was. I was seventeen, in pain and terrified. Dudley's mother shipped me off to the cottage hospital on my own. In fact no-one came to the hospital until the day after my son was born, weighing 5lb 4oz.

Dudley's mother had told me that eight month babies never survive (that was before I even reached the labour ward). The next day they all came to see me. I thought to myself that this was my son and nothing whatsoever to do with any of their 'clan'. I was in hospital for ten days.

When I was discharged home we stayed at Dudley's mother's for a few days. There was a big row over what to call my baby. I told them I had already chosen a name, end of discussion. I had decided that his name was to be Paul, no middle names. His parents were really peeved at this but Dudley knew better than to argue with me. I had to stop breastfeeding when I got home as he found it repulsive. That was nothing to what I felt about him.

Before Paul was born Dudley's friend got married and we had to go to the wedding. I was huge and my ankles were swollen. I felt really out of place but, of course, we had to go. The last straw was at the reception when Dudley vanished for over an hour as did one of the bridesmaids who had been hanging around him most of the day.

However, he was my husband so he should have handled

it better. Anyway, on the way out I said to the bridesmaid, "Did you enjoy your hour with my husband. You should learn to keep your knickers on in future girl?" I was livid and had a right go at Dudley. He just stood and took it.

He wasn't a big drinker and had drunk too much that day.

I never spoke on the way home. I think we both knew that our marriage was already in trouble. I'm not going to 'throw stones'. I think, to be fair, it was six of one and half a dozen of the other. He acted like a single bloke when he was out so I retaliated by sleeping with his best friend. In fact it was him who came to the hospital with fruit and flowers. It was still the sixties so I thought I was entitled to swing a bit. This guy used to stay at our flat often when he and Dudley had been out. On one occasion I was in the lounge and Dudley knew who I was talking to. He was trying to hear what I was saying, eavesdropping outside the door. As I came out carrying a tray of mugs I nearly broke my neck tripping over him. He asked his mate to go, but because Dudley was in a foul mood and had drunk a lot his mate refused to leave in case he got nasty. Dudley was in no doubt now who was keeping his wife company.

Time moved on and we went for a visit to Keighley with, believe it or not, Billy and Maureen. She had two girls by that time. It wasn't a pleasant trip. You could have cut the atmosphere with a knife. Back in Ramsey time hung heavy on my hands. I really wanted to go back to work but I wouldn't trust my boy to Dudley's mother so I offered to look after his brother's son while his wife went to work. It didn't last long as she was struggling to cope with a baby and a job. I went down to her house one day to help her out. My God, never again. She had about two weeks dirty nappies and all the rest to do. I was grateful for the practice I'd had with Julia.

I kept my promise to my 'partner in crime'. I went with her the day she handed over her baby to its father. She sat in the back of the car cuddling Paul and sobbed all the way home, her husband concentrated on his driving and never spoke a word, somehow I doubt they stayed together very long after that.

I was convinced that there was some sort of presence in our flat. I woke up in the early hours and saw a nurse in World War One uniform bending over Paul's cot. I got up to switch on the light but it wouldn't come on. I rushed into the kitchen but the same thing happened again. I was seriously freaked out by that time. I got Paul and slept in the lounge until the morning. I made a few enquiries and found out that the house had been used as a hospital for injured troops from the front. Once I knew the facts I was OK with it until something else happened. I didn't know, but the elderly man who owned our flat had passed away. I had been talking to him on the morning that he died and he was sad because he didn't have a sixpence for Paul. He always gave him sixpence for sweets. I had told him that Paul wasn't old enough for sweets but he still insisted. I only found out later that he was dead long before I spoke to him. I really wanted to move out of the flat then but Dudley said, 'no', saying that it was all in my imagination. Things came to a head one morning when he stood on Paul's favourite toy that my mum had bought him. It sounds trivial, I know, but he lost it and told me what he thought of my family. As soon as he left for work I packed and made my escape. I thanked Dad for giving me the means to do so.

It wasn't an easy journey with a young baby in a carry-cot and a suitcase. When I changed trains at Doncaster I nearly lost Paul. I gave him to a lady to hold whilst I got off the train with our luggage. I only just managed to grab him and get off before the train left. By the time I got to Keighley I was on my knees. I took a taxi to the flats, took Paul up to my mother's and returned downstairs to get my case and carry-cot. I never thought I would say it, but it was so good to be home. Julia was a very good nursemaid for Paul. She looked after him so well.

"What do you intend to do?" Dad wanted to know.

I needed a flat. The following morning I went to the Council offices with Mum. They put me on the list, saying that I shouldn't have to wait long as Mum didn't have enough room to put us up for long. Dudley arrived two days later. He wouldn't even take a day off work to come after me, he waited until the weekend. Well, he wasted his time as I was on my home turf now and that's where I was staying. Dad told him in no uncertain terms that I was very unhappy. I needed to be near Mum so I could return to work as there was no-one I would trust my son with except Mum. We talked all weekend but I stood my ground. I had tried to live in Ramsey but it wasn't working. I told Dudley that if he wasn't prepared to move to Keighley then it was over and Paul would stay with me. Dudley had never changed a nappy, done a feed or bathed Paul since he was born. In fact, Paul didn't like him. He wouldn't go to him and would scream 'blue murder' if Dudley picked him up. He really was not good with babies. I agreed to go back with him to pack up our things. Mum was not happy. She didn't trust him. She said that there was just something wrong but she couldn't put her finger on it. I was confident that I would be OK.

Dudley wasn't pleased when I said that Paul would be staying with Mum. I knew he would be safe with her. If Dudley had taken him back to Ramsey he may have tried to keep him there. Paul was my son and he would be staying with me come hell or high water.

CHAPTER 18: IT'S OVER

It was strange being back at our flat with Dudley but without Paul. The fair was in the field behind the flat so we decided to go. I love fairs – not for the rides, I don't go on the rides, but just for the whole atmosphere. Dudley wanted to have his fortune told. I declined. I didn't believe in fortune telling, they might have told him all the secrets I didn't want him to know.

While Dudley was working I packed. I had a black Silver Cross pram. Dudley's mother said she would sell it for me. If she ever did sell it I never saw a penny of the money. She was very put out that her son was leaving to live in Yorkshire. When I think about the whole situation I guess Dudley must have been interested in saving his marriage or we would have just gone our separate ways. In hindsight it would have been better for us both if we had done just that. I should have spoken out then. I should have told him it was over before it even got started.

We went out for a farewell drink with Dudley's mates. I didn't want to go but he insisted. I think he suspected that something was going on between me and his friend, but that had all finished some time ago. However, as he was as guilty as sin himself he said nothing. Was I sorry that I had done that? No, I'm afraid I wasn't. Another one of Mum's pearls of wisdom was, 'Don't get mad, get even'. That was just what I had done. I knew that Dudley had told his mates that he would wipe the floor with me. No chance – I was brought up in the school of hard knocks. I had learnt from the 'master of all evil'. I might only have been 5' 2" but I packed a punch. I might be crying inside but nobody would ever know. I had Paul and he was my main concern. I thought that the rest of them could just 'get stuffed'. In a few more days I would be back on solid ground. There had been a bit of good news at last. The Council had offered me a flat in Delph House. At least we would have a place of our own. I couldn't do with Dad for any length of time, he would always try to take over.

Well, you would have thought that Dudley was going off to war the way his mother carried on when we left. I have never been so pleased to leave anywhere in my whole life.

We had only been back in Keighley for a day or two and I already had an interview for office work at Ondura (it was a tyre remoulding company). Dudley got a job at a dye company so things were looking up. To say that me and him lived separate lives was an understatement. We weren't even on the same planet! He never wanted to go out with me and Paul. He took himself off somewhere at the weekends. I was working at Ondura then so I had my own money. I wondered if he was up to his old tricks again. I didn't know and, to be truthful, I didn't care either. I blame myself for not realising how isolated he must have been, he didn't know anyone in Keighley. I thought, "Well, he would know how I had felt now." I wondered how long it would be before he turned tail and ran back to his mum, I hoped it would not be too long.

The summer passed and the evenings grew dark. Dudley

still managed to be out all the time when he wasn't working. Mum said that I should talk to him about it. I just couldn't be bothered. Then he changed again. He started coming home directly from work and also preparing a meal for me to have when I was working late. I worked overtime a lot. We were short-staffed and it was a chance to earn extra money.

Paul had flat feet. The doctor sent him to the hospital.

Then he had to have Clarks' shoes which the hospital built up for him. Well, the shoes cost a bomb and he had to have two pairs all the time and he grew out of them so quickly. It would soon be Christmas and I thanked God that I would be at home this time. I never thought I would say that.

Little did I know when I started at Ondura that it would change my destiny. Being back at work was a real confidence booster for me. I felt like a person again, not somebody's drudge. I wasn't a bad-looking chick. I was getting a lot of attention from the men in the factory. I didn't take any notice. I'd got enough men problems without inviting any more. If I'd stuck to my original plan for my life I wouldn't have been in the mess I was then. Dudley and I hardly spoke to each other. It was like living with a stranger. I realised that I had never taken the time to know him as a person but, to be fair, he'd not played by the rules from day one. Looking back now, I blame myself for not seeing what was happening. I also felt guilty. I'd never noticed how depressed he had become. What happened next could have resulted in a terrible tragedy.

Dudley changed again. He became very secretive. Mum

asked me what the pills were for. I said, "What pills?" I didn't know he was on any sort of medication. Mum said he seemed to be popping pills all the time. I wondered if he was on drugs, that would explain his mood changes. It wasn't too long before I found out. God, I will never forget that day. He was on holiday from work and late in the afternoon he went over to Mum's. He wanted to take Paul home and get the tea ready and Paul bathed as I was working late again. Anyway, I decided not to work late that night and it was a good job I did or he would have been dead meat. I went to get Paul from Mum's as usual. She was very agitated. Dudley had come to get Paul but she wouldn't let him take him. She said that he was in a very strange mood and got a bit 'mouthy' with her but that Dad had got home from work and told him to go home. Dad said that Dudley appeared drunk, but he wasn't a drinker as such and Mum said it was probably the pills. Apparently Dudley had been on antidepressants, real heavy duty stuff. I didn't even know that he had been to the doctor's. When I went over to our flat that day I left Paul with Mum just in case there was any trouble. Dad said, "Give me a shout if you need any help." Well, I sure as hell needed help that day.

I put my key in the lock but the door was double-locked. I couldn't get in. I ran back for Dad. Something told me that this was serious stuff. Dad couldn't shoulder the door so we had to break the glass panel to get a hand in to unlock it. Dudley was laid on the sofa without a cushion and his head was at a very strange angle. I walked over to him. He was deathly white and didn't appear to be breathing. A couple of empty pill bottles in the kitchen was all the proof I needed. I felt for a pulse, it was very faint. He wasn't dead but was close enough to hear the angels singing. When the ambulance arrived they moved him very carefully, trying to keep his head at the angle it was. They told me later that it was the angle of his head that had saved his life. He'd taken enough pills to do the job.

They went to help me into the ambulance to go with him.

"I won't be coming along," I said.

"Isn't anyone coming with him?" the driver asked.

"I'll let his family know," I said as I walked away.

I can hear you all saying 'what a callous bitch'. Yes, I suppose I was. All I could think of was thank God Mum didn't let him take Paul. Would he have put some medication in his bottle? I don't know. I would never know the answer. The hospital kept ringing, wanting to speak to me. In the end I just got so pissed off with it that I made an appointment to see the doctor. He was a young chap who presumed I would be very upset about the situation. So I think he was a bit surprised at my attitude. I told him that I had informed Dudley's family and his place of employment.

"I'm sorry," he said. "I thought he was your husband."

"He was," I replied.

I left the doctor sitting open-mouthed. I thought that I had better go and see Dudley and get it over with. When I saw him laid there I must admit that I felt really sorry for him.

"Oh, you came," he said.

"I just wanted to say I'm sorry I never noticed how unhappy you must have been."

"What happens now?" he asked.

"If you want to collect your things here's the key," I said, giving him the key to the flat.

"What about us?" he mumbled.

"Dudley, there is no 'us', I don't think there ever was. It's over. I'm alone here."

I walked away, never looking back. A chapter in my life was over. I needed to get back to work. I had my son to raise. Dudley had to return home on the train. His parents never even thought to come and pick him up. Now that's what I call heartless.

CHAPTER 19: SINGLE MUM

Well, it was the works' Christmas bash. All the office staff were going to the Variety Club. I had splashed out on a new dress. Mum thought it was a bit short. The truth was Mum thought it a lot short, not suitable for the mother of a small child.

"Mum, I'm still young. I'm not going to go around dressed like a frump."

"What's a frump?" Mum asked.

"I'm not sure," I said, "but I'm not going to dress like one."

Why is it that when you're a single mum all blokes think you are 'easy pickings'? Two of the office blokes, both married, had asked me out. I said 'no'. I was having a quiet time, even I had morals. I didn't date married men. Then a lad called Alan asked if I would like to go for a meal some time. I accepted. Alan was a quiet lad. We went out for a meal and then he came back to the flat for coffee. Yes, I used to drink coffee in those days. Alan was a really nice chap, too nice for me. He knew about Paul and also knew that I was waiting for my divorce papers. I was going for complete breakdown of my marriage, it certainly fitted the bill. Dad said that I should ask for money to support Paul but I didn't want anything from Dudley, just my freedom. I didn't want him to think that he had any claims on my son. If I asked for money it gave him rights. No, I could support Paul myself. I left it at that.

I warned Alan not to get ideas about me as I wasn't in the market for a relationship. I was not getting tied to another fella, not then, not ever. I thought that I wouldn't be saying 'I do' ever again. What was Mum's pearl of wisdom for that? Oh yes, it was 'once bitten, twice shy'.

I got quite a surprise one weekend. I was over at Mum's doing my washing when there was a knock at the door.

You remember the holiday I had in Scotland with the ex-jockey. Well, the asthmatic young lad was a six foot good-looker with a beard. He'd brought some flowers for Mum. Mum wasn't keen on flowers. She always said, "I can't eat flowers," but I knew she would thank him anyway. I invited him in and made him coffee. He said he was going to work abroad for the Civil Service. I asked him jokingly if he was training to be a spy, sort of 007 thing. He was a year younger than me. He seemed so much older than that. Maybe it was because he was upper class. He asked me what I had been doing with myself.

"Well, I'm nineteen. I've a failed marriage and a toddler to show for it."

He thought Paul was Mum's.

I said, "No, he's definitely mine."

He asked me if I fancied going out that evening.

I said, "Oh, I don't think your Mum would be too happy if

you took me out."

"It's nothing to do with her," he said, smiling. "It's my last night in the UK. I don't want to be stuck in with Mum all night."

"Well, I'll have to ask my mum if she'll watch Paul for me."

Just then Mum came in the door. She knew who he was. I explained he'd brought her some flowers.

"Oh, you home to see your mum then are you, Nigel?"

"Yes, that's right Mrs McEwan. I wanted to take Doreen out for the evening. I'm leaving for foreign shores tomorrow."

"I suppose I'm wanted to babysit then?" she said.

I looked at Mum, hoping she'd realise that I didn't want to go but she never picked up on it or she just didn't want to.

"I'll just keep Paul here tonight then. No point in disturbing him later."

Nigel looked very pleased with that. "I'll pick you up at seven thirty then," he said to me.

When he had left I turned to Mum. "You did that on purpose, didn't you? What am I supposed to do with him all night?" She just raised one eyebrow and gave a stupid grin.

"He's a bit of class is that lad. Shame his mother is such a snob," Mum said.

"She'll go ape if she knows he's going out with me, he's just a kid," I said.

"He doesn't look like a kid to me," replied Mum.

"Oh shut up, you've got me into trouble. If his mother finds out she'll be on my case."

Mum just stood and laughed. "Maybe you should take a ladder, he's quite a tall chap. Put your heels on girl."

I left with my washing. "Oh well," I thought. "I could do with a night out."

I had a bath, did my hair and even put a bit of make-up on. I didn't use make-up very often, everyone thought I looked about twelve years old so why bother.

I must admit that Nigel looked very smart when he picked me up. He also had his mother's car, a lovely black convertible, really classy.

"How much younger than me are you Nigel?"

"Only a few months I think. Why, is it important?"

"No, I just wondered. I wanted a sugar daddy and I get a toy boy." He laughed. He looked really gorgeous when he laughed.

We went to a very nice pub out of town and had a lovely meal. He was a very interesting person to talk to. When we got back I invited him in for a coffee. I think he thought he was onto a good thing, but, no, he got coffee, end of. To be fair, he was a gentleman.

"I really like you," he said. "Can we meet up when I'm home again?"

"Yes, if I'm still around," I replied. "Your mother may have me killed before then."

I saw him to the door.

"Are you sure you'll be OK on your own tonight?" he said.

"I'm always on my own," I replied.

He gave me a kiss and left. I guess that was the one that got away.

It was getting difficult to keep the flat going on just my salary. I could see I would have to move back home. I just hoped that Dad didn't start taking over again.

Alan invited me for Sunday tea, saying that his mother would like to meet me. I couldn't believe it. He just would take no notice of anything I said. I thought I would sort it out so I said that I would love to come. He came to pick me up at three o'clock. He got a shock. I had Paul with me, all shiny and clean and looking very angelic. He had been ordered to be on his best behaviour. I could see Alan looked shell-shocked. He hadn't expected me to take Paul. I thought that should put an end to the whole charade. Oh, my God, his mother was a real ogress, very pleasant to your face but pulling horrible faces behind your back.

"I didn't know you had a child," she said.

"Oh, I thought Alan had told you," I replied. "I also had a husband, but that's over now."

I didn't want her thinking I had never been married. I have never been so pleased to leave someone's house as I was that day – what a battle axe. I thought that Alan would get it in the neck when he got back after taking me home.

Paul had fallen asleep in the car so I put him to bed. I would undress him later. I sat in the dark thinking that I could see Alan in a few years time with a nice little house on the same estate as his mother, working overtime to pay the mortgage. I would have bet my bottom dollar that he wouldn't be asking me out again. I thought that at least that would put an end to it. I didn't see him to talk to for a few days. I was right, he never asked me out again. Alan was such a quiet mouse, I would have walked all over him and then died of boredom. Another one bites the dust!

I was working long hours and I had moved back into Mum's. It seemed the sensible solution and so far it was working out OK. We were having a bit of trouble at work.

A big-mouthed fella had the girls in tears every time they had to take an invoice downstairs to the factory floor. Our boss had also been abused by this foul-mouthed creep so when she asked me to take an invoice down she laughingly advised me to "be careful of the caveman with no brains."

Well, he started as soon as he saw me. "Show us yer knickers," he bellowed across the factory at me. I turned and walked back towards him. When I got level with him I prodded him in the chest. He started backing away. I followed, still prodding, until his back was against the wall.

"Oh dear, I thought you wanted to play games. It's true then, the rest of you isn't as big as your mouth. Your girlfriend on switchboard must have been so disappointed to find you are not the big man she thought you were."

He stood and glared at me. I turned on my heel and walked into the office to deliver the invoice. The two blokes in there were curled up laughing as were the men on the shop floor. We never had any more trouble from him.

When I got back upstairs the girls asked what I had said.

"Nothing really. I just asked him if he had a big spanner?" I replied.

Later on in the day a guy came upstairs to fix our leaking radiator. He whispered to me as he walked by, "Be careful, you've made an enemy today."

"Thanks for the warning," I replied. "I won't be losing any sleep over it. I've eaten bigger men than him for breakfast. The bigger they are the harder they fall." He gave me a lop-sided smile and winked as he walked away.

I thought, "Now that's what I call a hunk of man." Later that day Christine called me to 'look out of your window' and there he was stripped to the waist, towel around his neck making his way to the shower block. I don't know what came over me. I flung open my window and wolf-whistled. He looked up and smiled.

"You have done it now," Christine said. "He's going to be right on your tail."

CHAPTER 20: MY HERO

Do you remember old big mouth from the Despatch Department. Well, as I said, we had no more trouble from him as regards shouting at the girls but I did have trouble when leaving work late after doing overtime. It was pitch black and very cold. I had put my coat collar up to keep my neck warm. I heard footsteps behind me. I don't scare easily, I've tackled someone swinging in the breeze and good old Heathcliff striding out of the mist, but this time I was on my own. I didn't panic. I thought it was probably someone else who had been working late. I wondered why the hell I had put three inch heels on that day. I couldn't have run even if I wanted to. Just then someone grabbed my arm. A voice said, "Not so big now, on your own in the dark." I knew it was him. I silently told myself to keep calm and that he wouldn't dare touch me. He put his arm round my neck, trying to turn me to face him.

"If you still want to have a job tomorrow I suggest you let go of me," I said.

Then another male voice said quite loudly, "Let her go."

The thug let go and I fled, my heart was pounding. I felt a lot better when I got to where there was street lighting. I thought that would teach me not to play the big 'I am'. It's amazing how fast you can run, even in high heels, if you are scared enough. I wondered who the knight in shining armour was. I never said anything at home. I didn't want Dad shouting his mouth off at my place of work. I don't think he would have bothered to anyway.

Next day I was unsure what to do. I could have reported him to the manager which might have led to him being sacked. I believed that he had been warned before about his foul mouth and vulgar remarks. Then I thought, "Why did I run. I should have turned to face him, and then brought my knee up in the appropriate place. That would have sorted him out."

There was an invoice to go to Despatch waiting on my desk. Also they had a French driver that nobody could understand. The manager wanted to know if any of us spoke French. Well, I had learnt it at school but I was not sure if I knew enough to tell this 'froggy' where to park his lorry while they were ready to load it.

Well, you would have died laughing if you had been there. It was like a comedy show. First of all the foul-mouthed fella was sporting a black eye and split lip, so I asked him if he'd walked into a wall. He said, "Your fella thumped me."

I replied, "I haven't got a fella."

He looked a bit confused. "If you haven't got a fella," he said, "the bloke who hit me thinks he's your fella."

"Oh great," I thought. "My hero has turned into a weirdo who thinks he's my fella."

I would have to find out who had hit big mouth. I went to tackle the French Casanova. I was standing outside the building using my schoolgirl French and hand signals to get this Frenchman to move his lorry into the loading bay. Between my hand being kissed several times and him attempting to whisper in my ear we finally got everything in order. The chap who had fixed the radiator in our office stood watching all this farce going on. I was sure that he found it very amusing. I went back inside to see if big mouth (whose name by the way was Peter) knew the bloke who had smacked him in the mouth. I thought he did but he wasn't prepared to tell me. Perhaps he had been warned not to tell me. I thought I would just sit back and wait to see what happened. Peter appeared to be my best friend now, thanking me profusely for not reporting him. I didn't think I would have any more problems from that area. I was working late again that night so thought I would see if 'Prince Charming' appeared again.

It had been a really long day and I was ready for home, a hot bath, something to eat and my bed. Then I saw that it was 'peeing' down with rain. At least I had my 'brolly'. There was no sign of Prince Charming arriving in his carriage. I thought that you couldn't even depend on fairy story characters to be there when you needed cheering up.

All was quiet at home for a change. Paul was bathed, fed and asleep. I reckoned I would have to stop all the overtime or he would forget that I was his mum. The trouble was that I really needed the extra money. I thought that I really needed a rich old man with one foot in the grave. I could give him a gentle shove and then inherit all his money. I did not know how much the divorce was going to cost but I was sure I'd need all the overtime to pay my solicitor. I just hoped that Dudley was not going to make a fuss about anything. I just wanted it over and then we could both move on with our lives. Dudley hadn't bothered about Paul since the day he was born so I didn't see why he would then. My life was quiet and disciplined at that time but I did not think it would last, something was bound to happen to upset the apple cart.

My boss was leaving soon to have a baby so Christine, my friend, was taking over. She was engaged to a teacher from down south but there was no sign of wedding bells. I thought that if she had got any sense she wouldn't bother with it. I sure as hell wished I hadn't although I wouldn't have wanted to be without my son. He was a ray of sunshine in my life. I loved him to bits.

One Saturday I decided to take Paul into Keighley shopping. It was a great for me to be able to spend time with him. The pigeons that gathered in the town hall square fascinated him so we sat for a while to watch them.

We were just getting up to leave when radiator man walked past, all suited and booted. He spotted me and stopped to talk. He didn't know Paul was mine. I didn't enlighten him, it was none of his business. After he had gone I reflected that he was quite good-looking in a rugged way, I imagined that he played rugby and drank like a fish. Men were off my menu at this time. I just wanted a peaceful life. Men always meant problems for me.

Christine shocked everyone when she arrived back at the office after lunch one day, dropped off by a flashy type in a red sports job, not her teacher from the south. She told me that she'd met someone new and was 'flying on the wings of romance'. Before we could draw breath she had dumped the teacher and was seeing Mr Sporty on a regular basis. I thought that it must be something they were putting in the water, making these women throw caution to the wind. Well I was not throwing caution or anything else to the wind. Remembering Mum's pearls of wisdom, 'once bitten, twice shy', I didn't want to get bitten again.

I was still no closer to finding my hero. I wondered if maybe he didn't work at Ondura and was just a brave passerby. I must have led the most boring life ever – work, bed, sleep – what happened to fun, laughter and love? Well, fun and laughter anyway. I thought, "You can stuff the love, it's only a word used in soppy romance stories about stupid people with no sense." I was becoming very bitter in my old age.

I was worried that Dudley would make a fuss about Paul.

My solicitor told me to stop worrying, he hadn't a chance in hell. If he tried getting clever we would demand all the support money he should have paid. I never wanted anything from him. I believed that I was quite capable of working to support my son and that he was nothing to do with Dudley whatsoever and if I had it my way he never would be.

CHAPTER 21: WAITING

I knew what I had to do. I had to wait. You couldn't get a divorce until you had been married for two years. I realised I was not as tough as I thought. It is hard bringing up a child on your own. Mum helped a lot and now that Maureen had been sort of welcomed back into the family Dad was behaving, well sort of behaving. I had no idea what he got up to when he was out and about. He tried the 'controlling' thing with me.

I just told him, "I'm a married woman waiting for a divorce to come through. I control my own life."

But I had to be a little bit careful. I didn't want him to kick me out. It would have been difficult to rent anywhere with a toddler in tow and also I would have had to find someone to look after Paul while I worked. It just seemed that I'd hit a brick wall at every turn. I found it very hard to take the crap Dad handed out, especially when he took the moral high ground. I thought he'd got the morals of a sewer rat. I never had been able to resist giving him glib answers. However, I was responsible for a small person and I intended to take that responsibility very seriously.

I hadn't been out in the evening for ages and thought I was becoming a 'boring old fart'. I got invited to a night out with the office girls. I was not sure I was up to that sort of thing. I thought I would rather stay at home with a good book. Told you I was boring! Anyway, I decided to get myself motivated – hairdresser and new dress in that order. I got myself a trim, wash and blow-dry and then I hit the shops. I was not sure what sort of image I wanted to portray. Was I going for the demure, very sensible look or the 'babe on the pull'. Oh, what the hell, I went for the 'babe' look. The finished product was a pale blue sparkling mini-dress and 3" heels. I knew I must remember not to bend over or everyone would get a flash of my new underwear.

Mum said, "You can't go out in that our Doreen. You'll get yourself locked up."

Dad looked and half choked on his cup of tea. I made a quick exit before he could give me his opinion.

We all met up at the Variety Club. It was absolutely packed. The evening was in full swing. I must admit that I was enjoying myself. Later on I saw radiator man standing at the bar. I found him very good-looking. When he looked at me I could have drowned in his eyes.

"Hang on a minute, listen to me," I kept reminding myself. "I'm off men. I'm not in the market for a relationship, bit of harmless fun maybe but definitely no strings attached."

I asked one of the girls in the office who knew him to find out what his situation was. I had drawn myself some boundaries, definitely no married men, I didn't want any hassle from wives or steady girlfriends. I could cause myself enough stress. I didn't need anybody else contributing.

Later on we called into a pub on our way to the taxi rank. There was someone belting out Elvis songs. It was live music night. As I told you all before, I usually stick to soft drinks so I'm more aware of what's going on. The other girls were a bit sozzled. Would you credit it? Radiator man was in there as well. On my way to the loo I passed him at the bar. "Are you following me?" I asked. He just smiled and said nothing. When I came back he'd got a blonde bimbo draped around his neck. I was not sure if she was with him or not. She was very drunk and he seemed to be trying to get rid of her. There were a couple of blokes from our office who had just come in and they headed for our table. We were all sat laughing and talking. I glanced up to see who was singing as he sounded really good. It was the radiator man. He sang 'Heartbreak Hotel'. We all clapped and shouted for more.

He got down off the stage with the microphone, perched on the middle step and gave a brilliant rendition of 'Loving You'. He started to walk with the microphone and stopped by our table. Everyone stopped talking to listen.

I thought, "Oh God, the fool is going to sing to me." I felt my face glow red.

To give him full credit though he could really sing very well. He got a lot of shouts and cheers when he finished. I made myself ready to leave. One of the office fellas offered me a lift. I said, "No thanks," as he had been drinking. I wanted to get home in one piece without being molested. I decided to get a taxi. There were quite a lot of people waiting so I sat in the town hall square and smoked a cigarette and then made my way over to wait for a taxi. I was ready for my bed. It had been quite a night.

The rest of the weekend passed quickly and then it was

Monday and back to work. I was passing the building where the maintenance men worked. Someone wolf-whistled at me. I turned and it was my 'crooner' from the other night.

"Was that whistle meant for me or have you lost your dog?" I said. He just winked and carried on with what he was doing.

When I got into the office there was a message waiting on my desk from the Wages Department. The girl who did the banking had rung in sick, they wanted me to fill in for the week. Well you know what they say, 'a change is as good as a rest'. There was a board meeting that morning and I had to get the balance sheets ready and get them in there. It was a busy morning. At lunchtime I took my sandwiches into Victoria Park. It was sunny but a bit on the cool side. My 'informant' was giving me the lowdown on the radiator man, also now known as 'the crooner'. My good mood took a nosedive. I found out that he was married and had a daughter. I decided to just mark him down as the one who got away. I was off men anyway, I thought they were all creeps.

It was a busy week. On Friday I had to do the wages run to the bank. I hoped that nobody picked that day to do a wages snatch. There I was, only 5'2", in heels, case handcuffed to my wrist. The car pulled up with the two chaps who always did the bank run.

When I got back to the office later I found that there had been a flood in the tea room. It was being attended to by my admirer. I grabbed my mug of tea and made a quick exit. As I was leaving he asked me if I would meet him for a drink.

"I don't go out with married men, not unless they're married to me," I replied.

I was sitting at my desk later when I got a note delivered. It was from him saying that he was separated from his wife. I was still not interested. I wiped him from my memory. I'd got enough on my plate without taking on someone with a failed marriage under his belt.

It was Saturday morning. I took Paul into Keighley with me. I didn't get enough time with him but if I didn't work full-time plus overtime I couldn't make ends meet. I was in the market buying some fruit. Paul wanted a little Corgi toy. He loved the cars and played for ages with them so I treated him to one. He was getting tired so I picked him up and balanced him on my hip. He was getting too heavy to be carried. I took him into a cafe. I was just finishing my tea and Paul was using the table as a racetrack when a friend of mine from Eastwood School came in. We sat chatting for a while and then I carried Paul over to the bus stop. Mr Crooner was waiting for another bus. He waved and I waved back and he walked over.

"Did you get my note?" he asked.

I replied that I had.

"You didn't answer," he said.

I decided to tell him in my own way that I wasn't interested. I put Paul down and he gave one of his lovely smiles. He looked up at Mr Crooner and held out his arms to be picked up.

"Hello little fella," he said and picked Paul up and put him on his shoulders. Paul thought that this was good fun and started giggling. Mr Crooner asked me again if I'd meet him for a drink.

"Look," I said. "You don't want to get involved with me. I'm high maintenance and come with a lot of baggage."

He was still smiling at me. Then I said, "Can I have my son back, I need to get him home, he's getting tired."

He handed Paul back and I was convinced then that he didn't realise that Paul was mine.

I headed home. I was baby-sitting that night as Mum and Dad were going out so I was watching Paul and Julia. After the children had gone to bed I get my book and fell asleep reading. I was tired out. "Roll on retirement." I thought.

CHAPTER 22: IN LIMBO

Nothing seemed to be moving forward with my divorce. I had an appointment with my solicitor after work and I thought that maybe he would give me an update but after sitting waiting for forty minutes my 'legal eagle' hadn't a lot to say. Dudley had been served with the divorce papers. My solicitor also asked me, did I think Dudley would go for custody or joint custody? This stopped me dead in my tracks.

"Not unless he's got a death wish," I replied.

He was not amused. "Do you want me to hit him with a claim for maintenance and also the back payments due to you since he left?" he asked.

Before I could answer, however, he said, "If I were you I'd keep that back, we may need a bargaining tool if he gets awkward about custody."

I left his office with my head in a spin. I hadn't given custody a thought. It had been 'crystal clear' to me that Paul was my son and that he belonged with me, end of! I went into a cafe for a drink whilst I waited for the bus. I tried to get clear in my head what the solicitor had said. I was seriously worried. I wondered what I would do if Dudley went for custody. I thought that I would kill the bastard. He had never shown any interest in my son so he had better not start playing the big man. I suddenly felt very vulnerable. I was very aware that I would have to fight this battle alone. Well, no change there then.

When I got home Mum had some good news. Dad had applied for the job of caretaker at Leyland House and he had got a letter to say that he had been successful, he was to start work the following week. This meant he would be around all the time (oh great) but he was getting older and had found his job at the foundry a bit too hard.

I had another shock when I got into work the following morning. Christine was leaving. She had given her notice and was going to marry Mr Sporty and would be moving away. I wondered who would get the job. I asked one of the managers. They told me that they had put an advert in the "Keighley News". I hoped that they appointed someone I could 'rub along' with. If not, I decided that I would look for something else.

The weeks passed and I heard nothing regarding my divorce. I was not sure if that was good or bad.

We all gathered in the local pub on the following Friday to wish Christine 'Bon Voyage'. She got lots of gifts, some too rude to mention. I had a storming headache and decided to leave early. I'm not sure if seeing Mr Crooner walk in with a beauty on his arm had anything to do with that! He said, "Hello." I ignored him and decided to stay a little longer. I wondered if he was back with his wife. They looked really pally. One of the office chaps sat down by me. He was not bad-looking really. He bought me a drink. I was feeling so pissed off that I decided to have a port and lemon. This was a bad move on my part. Not being used to alcohol, it went straight to my head. It was live music night so I got up to dance. This was unusual for me too. I tended to say sitting down and watch others make fools of themselves. I managed a slow smooch around the floor. My head started to clear and I noticed my crooner making his way over to us. He tapped my partner on the shoulder and took me in his arms. I was thinking, "What a creep who comes into a pub with a girl and then leaves her to dance with somebody else."

"Have you been avoiding me?" he asked.

"No, why?" I replied.

I saw the look on his face change when the office guy came back to claim me again.

"We're all moving on somewhere else," he said. "Do you want to join us?"

"I'm going to call it a night, thanks," I replied and stayed in Mr Crooner's arms.

We sat at the table talking until they called last orders.

"Do you want me to take you home?" he asked.

"No thanks. I'm going to walk and clear my head. I don't normally drink so I feel a bit heady."

We left the pub together and walked up Low Street. I turned left by Emu to walk to the flats. He was going to the bus station. I suddenly remembered the girlfriend he came in with. When I mentioned her we both realised he had forgotten all about her and burst out laughing.

"Can I see you again?" he asked.

"I told you before that I come with baggage, very precious baggage."

"I know," he said. "You are a single mum. Do you still see his father?" he asked.

"I'm not a single mum. I'm waiting for a divorce, I was married."

He looked gob-smacked. "You don't look old enough," he said.

"Looks can be deceiving. I'm older than you think," I replied.

"Look, I have to go. I'll miss the last bus. I'm living back home at Cross Hills. I'll see you at work. Promise me you'll think about it," he said as he walked away.

Everyone was asleep when I got in. I went straight to bed.

Everything was floating around in my head, what the solicitor had said, what Wilf and me had talked about. At least I knew his name now – it was Wilf Burrows. I wondered as I drifted off to sleep if he was my hero, the man I had been searching for. He certainly had all the qualities I looked for in a man. He was good-looking and romantic. Then, "Hang on a minute," I thought. "He is married with a daughter." Then I thought, "Well, I'm married with a son. Do I want to get involved? I've really got enough problems of my own without taking on someone who is on the rebound from a failed marriage."

I fell asleep undecided. My life was set to change. I was reaching another crossroads. One way led to a forever lover that spanned over four decades. The other road I saw was a working mum, bringing up her son and staying footloose and fancy-free. I was going to be embarking on the journey of a lifetime.

CHAPTER 23: THE BOSS

This must have been one of the strangest weeks of my whole life. On the Monday, as I walked into work, Wilf was just leaving. He looked very smart – jeans, open-necked shirt, new jacket. I wondered where he was off to. Two more fellas joined him. They stood watching me walk past. I felt like a total prawn. I kept my head down and made my way past them. I decided that if he started with the wolf-whistling I was going to smack him one. Well he didn't. As I passed him he started singing, 'Pretty Woman'. I thought, "Right, that's it." I turned round, walked up to him, grabbed his lapels and gave him a long lingering kiss. It was going to be a smack, don't know what happened really. Anyway I let him go and he stood looking very shell-shocked. I carried on into work. His mates were clapping and cheering and also half the office staff were gawping out of the window including Mr Richardson, my boss.

Then, just as I went into the gate a car screeched to a halt and out jumped my friend, Nigel, from the Civil Service. He must have been home visiting his mum. He was very tall, way over six foot. He picked me up, swinging me round, and gave me a big kiss. I thought, "Oh, shit," as Wilf was standing watching all this. Nigel wanted to take me out for a meal that night. He'd something to celebrate.

As he had already checked with Mum about babysitting, after giving her some duty-free for her and Dad, I couldn't really say no. As I got into the office Mr Richardson was waiting to see me.

"My office in ten minutes please, Doreen," he said. He turned to add, "If you can spare me a few minutes in your busy social calendar."

As I made my way to his office one of the girls pulled me to one side to whisper, "Watch yourself with Wilf, the rumour is he's getting back with his wife, she's a bitch. Watch out for her."

"Thanks for the warning," I replied, "but there's nothing going on with us two anyway."

"That's not what it looked like to me," she laughed as I walked away.

When I came out of Mr Richardson's office I was 'gob-smacked'. He'd offered me the Office Manager's job. I couldn't afford to turn down the extra money. The only downside was that I had to have the books ready for the board meeting the following week. I would have to put in some overtime, but not that night as I had something to celebrate as well.

I forgot all about Wilf, he was no longer on my radar. "Shame really," I thought as he was very dishy with 'come-to-bed' eyes.

I didn't get in until late after my night out with Nigel so it was a bleary-eyed Doreen who he dropped off at work. He would be flying out again that day. He had also had a promotion and met a pretty little Spanish girl. I bet that his mum was not too pleased about that! I was waving him off as Wilf walked past on his way to the factory.

"Have you been home yet?" he joked.

I wasn't in the mood. "What's it to you?" I answered, slamming the door as I entered the office block.

I sat in the park at lunchtime eating my sandwich. I'd have to work until seven every night to get the figures out in time for the meeting. Wilf came walking past on his way back from the shop. He sat on my bench. I had never felt less like talking in my whole life.

Before he could say anything, I said, "Glad to hear you are getting back with your wife. Your little girl must miss you."

"I don't know who told you that 'load of bollocks'. I've just started divorce proceedings," he answered. "Look can I take you out one night, or are you hung-up on 'lover boy'?"

"That was just a friend home on leave, not a romantic interest," I replied. "This week is out, I'm afraid. I'm working over every night and Saturday. I've just taken over as Office Manager."

I didn't know if he believed me or not. To be truthful, I didn't want to get involved in his marital mess. I had enough to sort out with my own.

I had an appointment with my 'legal eagle' the following Monday, just for an update. I thought that the sooner I became a 'Miss' again the better. I had already stopped wearing my ring, I had dropped it down a drain with the rest of the 'shit'.

The board meeting went well apart from me nearly walking into the cupboard on my way out. I got the doors mixed up.

"Just checking on stationery supplies?" Mr Wilkinson joked as he walked past.

"Something like that," I said.

My face was bright red. Guess I was more nervous than I thought.

The solicitor's news was not so good. Dudley had started asking about having Paul for some of the holidays. I thought that I needed a 'hit man' to polish him off – I wondered how much they cost! All joking aside, I had decided that Dudley and his family were not getting their hands on Paul for any time, it would be 'over my dead body'. I wondered where my hero was. I could have done with him then to 'stand my corner'.

It was difficult to concentrate on work with all that was on my mind. Also my informer had told me that Wilf's ex-wife was on my case. That was all I needed. I knew that if Dudley got a whisper of that he would use it against me if we got into a custody battle.

It all came to a head later in the week. I dashed out at lunchtime to pick up my boots from the cobblers. I liked to wear them with my jeans and the steel tips on the stiletto heels needed replacing every few weeks. As I walked back along Church Green there were three girls coming towards me. It was obvious that they were talking about me. I didn't know any of them. As they drew level with me the one on the end gave me such a shove that I ended up in the road, narrowly missing being run down by a van. I was livid. They walked away laughing.

I heard one of them say, "She shouldn't mess with married men."

When I got back to work I was still shaking. I stormed into Vernon's office.

"I need to see Wilf now, it's urgent."

"You can see him in his own time, not mine," he replied.

Just then Wilf walked in. I flew at him.

"That bitch you are married to just nearly got me killed on Church Green. She was with two mates."

Wilf never answered.

"Stay the hell away from me," I said. I don't need this hassle. Sort her out or I'll have her arrested."

I slammed out and sat at my desk for the rest of the day, fuming. When I had time to calm down I felt a bit remorseful. Maybe it wasn't his fault but he was becoming a dangerous man to know.

I didn't see Wilf again until the Friday night. He was in town shopping. He stopped to talk and told me that he was shopping for his mum as she had the 'flu.

"Look, I'm sorry about the other day, but I nearly got run over when 'she' or one of her mates shoved me into the road," I said.

"How do you know it was her?" he asked.

"Why, do you have more than one wife?" I sniped back.

"She works at Peter Black's, doesn't she?"

"Yes," he said.

"It was her then. I heard them say 'she shouldn't mess with married men'. As I don't mess with married men it's a sure bet she's married to you."

"Not for much longer," he said.

"Well," I replied, that's your mess. I will leave you to sort it out."

I started to walk away when he called me back. "Doreen," he said, just let me take you to the pictures. You may find you like me."

I don't know what came over me. "Meet you Saturday outside the Essoldo at 7.30 pm," I said as he walked away. I think he was amazed that I had agreed.

Getting ready that Saturday I was in a stupid mood. I had treated Mum to some ciggies and also chocs for babysitting. She didn't mind as her and Dad didn't go out often. I could afford to pay her a decent amount of money since my promotion for watching Paul whilst I worked. Paul and Julia got on well as Julia wasn't much older than him.

A while before Mum had hosted a wig party and I had bought a Dolly Parton wig just for a laugh. I decided to wear it for the pictures. By the time I left the house even Mum didn't recognise me. When I got to the cinema Wilf was standing outside waiting, he did not know it was me.

I walked up behind him and said, "You waiting for me handsome."

He turned and said, "Piss off. I'm waiting for my girlfriend."

He turned away and then did a double take. "It's you," he said.

I laughed. "I guess you don't like blondes then. After what happened the other day I thought I should come in disguise."

We went into the cinema. It was one of many dates. As they say, 'the rest is history'. I thought that I may just have found my hero. However, as we were both Scorpios it was never going to be an easy ride.

CHAPTER 24: THE STALKER

Anyone who has ever been stalked will know how it feels. I was being followed and the fella had been taking pictures. I thought about walking up to the car, lifting my sweater and saying, "Get a good look at these." But all joking aside it was a scary experience. I hadn't said anything to Mum or Dad. I wanted to make sure first that I wasn't getting paranoid. By the end of the week I was sure. I had done the bank run the previous week and was due to do it that Friday as well. My imagination went into overdrive. I had more or less convinced myself there was going to be a wages snatch. As I set off for the bank I had my fingers crossed. In fact, I had everything crossed! I needn't have worried. I didn't see any sign of the car, thank God for that. I thought that whoever it was must have moved on to someone else.

That Saturday I got another big surprise.

Dad came into the kitchen. "Bet you can't guess who I've got in the flat upstairs?" he said.

"Go on, surprise me," I replied.

"It's Kevin's parents. They have had some sort of problem at home, fire or flood, not sure which."

I was very fond of Kevin's parents. I went upstairs with Dad, Paul toddling behind us, just to offer some help and see if there was anything they needed. They were pleased to see me. Kevin's mum was very tearful. A few minutes later Kevin arrived. He was shocked to see me. By now Paul was up on Kevin's dad's lap, he was such a charmer, my son. I was standing back against the wall. Kevin put a hand either side of my head and smiled down at me. I looked into his eyes thinking, "Oh no, not again. I can't fall for him again."

Just then his wife walked in. I wished the floor would swallow me up. I ducked under Kevin's arm and tried to make my getaway. I did feel so sorry for the poor girl, she looked really sad. She went to Kevin's mum and gave her a cuddle. I called Paul to me. Kevin's dad had given him some money for sweets and Paul was giving him his lovely smile and a kiss on the cheek. I sent him back to say 'thank you'. I lifted him onto my hip.

Kevin smiled and said, "That suits you."

To give him credit he did give his wife a cuddle. It was obvious she knew who I was. I made my escape, promising to come again and also asking Kevin's parents to let me know if they needed anything. I felt a proper creep.

I was supposed to meet Wilf and I was going to be very late. I got Paul ready and then we caught the Cross Hills bus. The arrangement was that he was to meet us off the bus and, of course, because we were so late he wasn't there. I knew he lived at Spencer Close so I decided to call on him, just so that he knew I hadn't stood him up. His mother answered the door. I had Paul on my hip with his head on my shoulder. He was getting tired. I realised I had made a big mistake. If looks could kill I would have been pushing up daises. She asked what I wanted and I was just about to answer her when Wilf walked up the road. Paul spotted him, shouting, "Daddy, Daddy," and wriggled to be put down. I put him on his feet before I dropped him. He ran to Wilf who picked him up and put him on his shoulder, that was his favourite mode of transport then. I walked away without giving Wilf's witch of a mother any information, I thought she would be really confused!

"I'm sorry I missed you," I said. "I got held up at the flats. I hope I haven't caused you any problems at home. Don't think your mother likes me."

"Don't worry about it," Wilf replied. "She doesn't like me either."

We walked away, laughing. Paul was giggling away and kept covering Wilf's eyes so that he couldn't see. It was not long before Paul fell asleep. We caught the bus back to Keighley, grabbed some lunch and took Paul to the park. I found out later that Wilf's mum, Alice, was telling everyone that I was a 'slapper' with a little boy in tow. She was convinced that Wilf was Paul's dad. She told all the family that Paul even looked like Wilf. She was to ask several times over the years for the 'truthful answer', but neither of us ever gave her one. She passed into the heavenly world without ever knowing what was what.

After she died I found that she had cut my head off all the photos. Guess she didn't like me then! The feeling was mutual. Wilf got blamed for many things over the years but no-one was ever 100% sure about Paul. Wilf was a sportsman. His father, Bob, always wanted him to be an academic. In Paul, Bob found the academic he had wanted Wilf to be. Bob never supported Wilf in his sports or even watched him play. However, Wilf couldn't have been more proud of Paul if he had played for England.

Paul, in return, loved the only father he had ever known. He was with him when he took his last breath on this earth and it broke his heart. They had a close bond that could only be found between a father and his son. However, I am getting in front of myself with my story and the path before me is bumpy and littered with pot-holes.

CHAPTER 25: SCARBOROUGH

Well, poor old Wilf really got it in the neck about me calling at his house. His mother was not pleased at all. It seemed she had hoped he would get back with his wife. She missed seeing her grand-daughter. She would approach Wilf's ex in town to talk to the little girl, Annette, and tell her she was her grandma. It was sad really. When I first met Wilf he was still attempting to see his daughter at the weekends. After being told on several occasions that the child was unwell or had gone out with one of the family, he gave it up as a bad job. I think Paul filled the empty space in his heart. He told me he had wanted a boy. He also thought that weekend dads just confused children and soon Annette was never mentioned again. Though I dare say that some well intended nosey parker would have informed the child who her father was as she grew older.

Getting back to the story in hand, I had booked a week in Scarborough for Paul and myself. I needed a rest and time to spend with my son. For some reason unknown to me, I asked Wilf if he wanted to join us. I had told Mum and Dad nothing. They were used to me going out with friends. They didn't know that there was anyone special although I think Mum was getting a bit suspicious. She knew it was no good asking me but Paul kept dropping me in it as he was chattering a lot now about Wilf. Nobody picked up on it but I knew that they would as he got better at talking. Also Paul was getting very attached to Wilf. I didn't want him to get hurt. I wasn't sure I wanted to get tied up with any bloke. I still hadn't got rid of the first husband. Anyway the Saturday of our departure to Scarborough arrived. Dad said he would walk with us to the station. I had hoped that Wilf had the sense to stay out of the way. If Paul spotted him the game was up. Well I got onto the train with case and wriggling little excited boy who kept making a dash for freedom. As Dad stood waving us off, Paul spotted Wilf sitting further up the train and launched himself at him. I closed my eyes and said a silent prayer that Dad had not noticed.

Anyway I was going away for a week and with a man, how shameful was that? Well, Wilf's mum had trashed my good name in Keighley so I thought I might as well live up to my new image as a 'slapper of the first degree'. We had a really great time and I took loads of photos. Paul nearly fell in the sea so we bought him some reins. We took him to see the dolphins. Wilf had to sit on the front row and when they flapped their tails we got soaked. Paul thought that was great fun.

We travelled back on the following Saturday. Paul had developed a few spots on his body but, by the time I got him home to the flats, he was covered. He was also running a temperature and sobbing his eyes out. I couldn't keep him quiet. Mum was worried and sent for the doctor who diagnosed measles. But the crying had started when Paul realised that Wilf was going home to Cross Hills and not to the flats with us. Mum told me that Dad knew I had been away with someone. He'd told her that Wilf had just come out of prison. That's the sort of person Dad was. He'd try to blacken anybody's name. I told Mum it was a load of tosh. Wilf had worked at

Ondura a long time. I had arranged to phone Wilf that night at the phone box at Cross Hills. When I told him that Paul was ill and what Dad had said he was angry, to say the least. He said he would call at the flats the following day and meet Mum and Dad to straighten it out and also see Paul, who was still asking for him non-stop.

I was up all night pacing the floor, trying to pacify Paul. He also had a smelly discharge coming from his ear. Mum called the doctor again who sent him to the A & E department at the hospital. I was sitting there for ages with a sobbing child. Mum and Wilf arrived at the hospital in a taxi. Things started to happen then. Within minutes Paul was on Wilf's knee and asleep. I just couldn't believe it. He slept through the doctor checking his ear and finding a piece of bread stuck at the bottom of it which had started to ferment. The doctor removed the bread and sent us home with ear drops to clear up the infection. He also told us that Paul's adenoids were very small and that he might have further problems with his ears and should be monitored. Boy, he wasn't wrong about that. Wilf and I were to spend endless time in the hospital with Paul's ears. I thought we had taken up residence there. Poor Wilf, he couldn't even go to the loo but Paul would be sitting on the floor outside the door waiting for his 'Daddy'. I think Wilf had thought about running for the hills but Paul would have cut him off at the pass.

Things started to get back to normal at last. Mum thought that Wilf was lovely. Dad respected the fact that Wilf had a reputation for talking with his fists. In other words, he was a fighting man, he had to be. I began to wonder if there were any women in his age group who he hadn't dated, slept with or just had a night out with.

There always seemed to be a boyfriend or husband with a grudge against him. I had second thoughts about getting serious with the guy. The trouble was that I was deeply in love with him. Even when I was angry he only had to smile and look at me with those eyes and I was lost. It wasn't a quiet easy-going relationship. It was volatile. We were both Scorpios, not a good match really, we both had a sting in our tails. Wilf was a very sexy guy and ladies did chase him. He found this very amusing. Underneath he was a shy fella with a big chip on his shoulder and I mean *big*. Everything you saw about him was just 'front'. Underneath he needed to be loved. I would have died for him but sometimes I could have killed him.

I never learnt to jive although I could do all the ballroom stuff. Wilf even tried to teach me but I just couldn't get it. The thing was he loved to dance and was really good at it. He also loved to sing rock 'n roll. When we were on an evening out, if there was any live music on someone would shout, "Give us a song Bill." Why they called him Bill I just don't know. I always called him Wilf. I was happy for him to sing. What did annoy me were girls who knew him coming to our table to get him up to jive. He would smile at me, take their hand and off he would go. I hated this. OK, as he said, "I'm with you love, what's your problem." Anyway one particular night he left me three times to dance with someone. I was seriously pissed off. Then, to top it all, one silly bitch came back again.

"You don't mind if I borrow Bill do you?" she simpered at me.

Well, I lost it big time. I don't often swear, well not the

'heavy' stuff anyway but I replied, "As a matter of fact I do. Fuck off bitch."

Wilf's jaw dropped and he looked at me amazed. I stood up and grabbed my coat.

"Help yourself sweetheart," I said. "I'm done here."

As I walked away I looked over my shoulder at them standing there.

"Have a nice life Wilf," I said and ran out. I was devastated. I sat in the town hall square and sobbed my heart out. I thought that I couldn't take any more. He'd hurt me and didn't seem to realise how much he upset me with his 'devil may care' attitude.

When I got home Dad was in bed, drunk as usual. Mum took one look at me and said, "If you stay with him you have to either get him away from Keighley or change the way he acts. It won't be easy girl."

Then there was a knock at the door. It was Wilf. I heard Mum say, "Leave her alone 'till she calms down. You will get nowhere tonight, she's too upset. If you don't watch it lad, you're going to lose her. If she decides to walk she won't come back."

I went to bed. I took Paul into bed with me and cried myself to sleep. I wondered why life was so hard. In hindsight, if I had thought this was hard it was a good job I didn't know what the next few months would be like or I'd have stayed in bed with the covers over my head.

CHAPTER 26: THE GOING GETS TOUGH

I hadn't seen Wilf since I'd walked out on him at the weekend and back at work on the Monday morning I felt like shit. I'd had no sleep. I got called to the despatch office. I was expecting to have some sort of problem to sort out. However, the manager said the problem was the very short skirts my girls were wearing when they brought invoices down from the office. The micro skirt had just taken over from the mini. It was too short for me but a couple of the younger girls were wearing them. The problem seemed to arise if the girls bent over. I could not believe I was hearing this and was getting a bit irate.

"Just what is the problem with my girls?" I asked the manager.

"Well they are showing their lacy knickers and the men are getting distracted from their work."

I could not help it, I burst out laughing. "You can't expect me to tell the girls what to wear," I said.

Wilf then walked into the office. I ignored him.

"OK," I said. "I'll have a word with the girls."

As I was leaving the office, Wilf grabbed my arm, "Doreen, I need to talk to you," he said, looking very miserable.

"Make an appointment," I snapped back at him. "I'm very busy at the moment."

I turned to leave and as I walked past the machines Peter called me over. I talked to him for a few minutes and then made my way back to my office. At lunchtime I took my lunch into the park. Wilf must have been watching for me. As I sat down in my favourite place he joined me. I looked at him.

"I'm not good company today," I said.

He glared at me.

"Don't give me the eyes," I said. "I wasn't the one that left their girlfriend sitting like a prat whilst he did his big Romeo act."

"I have something important to tell you," he said.

"Go ahead." I tried to appear uninterested.

"Have you noticed a guy in a car following you?" he said.

"There was," I replied. "Haven't seen him for a while. He took plenty of photos, another weirdo."

"It's my ex-wife," he said.

"What is?" I asked.

"She's named you as the other woman in my divorce."

I was speechless.

"When you left your wife I was down south, so how is it down to me? If this affects my custody case and causes any problems for me and Paul you and your ex-wife better watch out. No way am I going to be named in your divorce. I'm sure there are plenty out there that fit that bill, but it sure as hell isn't me. See you around."

I walked quickly back to the office.

Mum called me mid-afternoon. My 'legal eagle' wanted to see me after work. My mood got even worse. I wondered what the hell he wanted. I soon found out. After sitting waiting for thirty minutes to see him I learnt that Dudley was pushing boundaries. He wanted visiting rights and all that crap. My solicitor asked if we should try hitting his pocket for back money and support for my son.

"Let me think about it for a day or two. I'll ring you," I said.

"Don't delay too long Doreen or he'll think he's got you on the run and watch out if there's a new man in your life, don't give your ex the upper hand."

"Heard and understood," I replied as I left his office.

I walked to the bus stop in a daze. If I was a drinker I would have gone and got pissed. I was standing waiting for my bus when Wilf appeared.

"We do need to talk. I want to see Paul," he said.

"Don't you start. I've just had about all I can take today." I broke down in tears and ended up sobbing on his shoulder.

"Come on sweetheart. We'll go for a hot drink," he whispered in my ear. I wondered how he could make going for a cup of tea sound like going for a night of passion. It was his voice, his eyes, everything about him. Oh, how I wished I hadn't got involved with him. But it was too late. I was hooked. I just needed to make sure that he didn't know that. I arranged to meet him in town the following day and then we would pick up Paul and take him out somewhere.

When I got home Mum asked what was happening. I didn't tell her too much. I didn't want to until I'd made my mind up about what I was going to do. My head was still spinning. Next morning Mum asked me to pick up some shopping when I went to meet Wilf.

Later on when Wilf and I got back we got a big shock. In Mum's lounge sitting talking to Dad was Dudley plus his parents. I walked into the kitchen to give Mum her shopping. I said quietly, "What the hell's going on, Mum?" She shrugged her shoulders.

I walked back into the lounge, picked up Paul's shoes and gave them to him, saying, "Get Daddy to put your shoes and coat on." I avoided eye contact with anyone.

Paul ran straight to Wilf. "Up Daddy, shoes on," he said.

Wilf picked him up and we left. As we were walking down the road, Paul sitting on Wilf's shoulders as usual, Dudley and his parents passed us. I raised my hand, licked one finger and made a 'one' sign in the air. Dudley was looking straight at me. "This is one to me," I thought. But the cat was really among the pigeons. Now Dudley had got a clear picture of what was going on.

I phoned my solicitor. "Let's hit his pocket," I told him.

"He arrived at my house today with his parents in tow. Unfortunately, I walked in with the new man in my life."

"Oh well," he said. "Let's hope you haven't blown it. I'll see what I can salvage. I'll be in touch."

"We need to sort ourselves out," Wilf told me.

"I don't need sorting out, Wilf," I replied. "Don't get me back on the subject of the other night. The simple facts are that if you ever leave me sitting at the table alone in a pub or club while you dance with some stupid 'bint' that will be it, the finish. There will be no going back. If you're not happy with that, walk away now."

He gave me a silly smile. "I can't go anywhere. Paul won't let me." Paul had fallen asleep on his shoulder. "Let's get this little man home," Wilf said.

We babysat that night whilst Mum and Dad went out. Wilf bathed Paul and tucked him into bed. We were sitting chatting. Wilf got up to go to the loo. When he opened the lounge door he fell over Paul who had been trying to watch TV through the crack in the door.

"Back to bed," Wilf said.

Paul started to protest. Wilf gave him a smack on his bottom and took him back to bed.

When he returned to the lounge I said, "Did you just smack my poor little lad."

"I did," Wilf replied. "He needs to learn that bed time is bed time."

I could see he was trying to judge if I was angry.

"OK," I said. "He is spoilt by me but he's all I've got."

Wilf sat down and took me in his arms. He looked into my eyes.

"You have me baby. I'm always going to be here for you and Paul whatever happens."

That was it. Off I went again. I didn't stand a chance. I just wanted to devour him. We both fell asleep on the sofa. When Mum and Dad returned Mum shook us awake.

"Wilf, get yourself into that spare bed," she said.

"Make sure you stay there," Dad added. "I'll have no nannying in my house."

Wilf looked at me. "What's nannying?" he asked.

I nearly choked laughing.

"Get to your beds," Dad said.

For once we did as we were told. Wilf never really went back to Spencer Close to live after that. He collected his clothes and things. His mother was less than pleased but I thought that was 'tough'. I had enough to worry about without her as well. It was her problem. From then on Wilf was mine.

CHAPTER 27: MANDA AND LITTLE GRAN

Wilf decided to take me and Paul to meet his Aunt Manda and his Little Gran. I didn't know why he called her 'Little Gran', she was quite a strapping lady for her age. The great love and affection he felt for these two ladies was obvious to me. In fact, he had spent most of his childhood with them. His mother would come and drag him home but he would be back as soon as the chance arose. I think Aunt Manda cared for his little girl whilst her mother worked. Wilf used to collect her when he finished work. I wondered how much he was suffering inside. He never saw his daughter and she was growing up without him. I decided that I must try to talk to him about her. We were all sitting having a good laugh when Wilf's mother, Alice, walked in. Everything went quiet. Paul felt the tension in the room and climbed on my knee. He hid his face in my neck. I could not believe what happened next. Alice set into Wilf, saying she had seen Annette in Keighley with her mother, and then went on to ask if he didn't care about his daughter'?

"Look what you have given up for that," she said, pointing at Paul and me. I stood up. I'd had enough of this evil bitch. Wilf made a lunge at her. His aunt stepped between him and his mother but Wilf was determined to give her a slap. Just then Paul started sobbing and shouting for his daddy. Wilf took Paul in his arms to soothe him.

Alice turned to me. "You should take that child back to his father."

Before I could say a word Wilf replied, "He's with his father."

We walked out. Wilf apologised to his aunt for the trouble.

"It's not your fault, Bill. She's a mad bitch. Always was and she's getting worse."

It took Wilf ages to calm down.

I said, "She should be married to my Dad. They would make a good pair."

I was angry that she had upset Paul, but he had forgotten about it already. He was trying to persuade Wilf to get him an ice-cream from the van. He was fascinated by the chimes on the ice-cream van. As soon as he heard them he came running for money. Wilf gave in and got him a cornet. I looked over the road and saw Alice hurrying past. Wilf didn't notice her as he was too busy cleaning the ice-cream off Paul, he'd got it everywhere. Later on, when Paul was asleep in bed, we went for a walk in the woods. Wilf spread his jacket so that we could sit down. I asked him about Annette but he didn't want to answer and when he did I realised that he really had forgotten her. It's as if she was never his.

"It's the best way," he said. "She's young. She will have forgotten me already."

He told me that Pauline, his ex-wife, had young sisters

and now she was living next door to her mother Annette would have playmates.

"Me turning up again would only confuse her," he said.

That was it. I never heard him mention her again. He asked me if I was worried about the custody thing and I replied, "Just a bit." We decided to forget the whole bloody lot and go for some fish and chips.

Laid in bed that night I felt guilty. Had I deprived a little girl of a loving father? But I did not think I had. I believed that her mother had done that long before Wilf ever set eyes on me. I didn't mind taking the blame for things I had done but I was sure as hell not carrying the can for things I had no part in, no matter what Alice said.

The post bought a letter from my solicitor. Dudley had acted true to form. As long as I made no claims on him for support he had no plans to contact Paul again — so much for the devoted father act. It was just a case of waiting for the divorce to go through.

I told Wilf that if he needed a reason for divorce, let his wife name me, unless he wanted to go and find another lady to provide the evidence. He just gave that lop-sided smile that always melted my heart. He was a charmer all right, but would he stay true to me I wondered.

I was outside the flats when the creep with the camera appeared again, taking photos of me and my son. That was one step too far for me. I ran to the car, pulled open the door and grabbed him. Wilf came up behind me and pushed me to one side.

"Get out of the car pervert."

The guy started protesting.

"There is a name for people like you. Why are you taking photos of my girl and my son?"

The guy was trying to show us his business card. I looked at the card.

"Hang on Wilf, he's an investigator," I said.

Wilf asked him, "Who are you working for?"

He named a firm of local solicitors.

"OK," Wilf said. "If you come near her again, I'll kill you, understood?" The guy nodded and drove away.

It was a couple of weeks later before we found out why the guy was tailing us. I got a letter from my solicitor. Dudley was divorcing me on the grounds of adultery – what a bloody cheek. The solicitor was advising me not to contest it.

"If you want out quick just go with the flow. He's given up on your son so it doesn't matter now."

So I got blamed twice. Both times I was not guilty, OK then just a bit guilty. "Oh, stuff them," I thought. I really didn't care what anyone thought about me as long as Paul was left alone and as long as I was single again soon. That was all that mattered. Why the hell I got involved with Dudley I did not know. If Dad hadn't kicked off I would have been married to Kevin and would never have met Wilf. Life is a strange game. Just when you think you've got it all worked out it takes a different road and dumps you on your arse not knowing how, why or what happened. Anyway, on with the show.

Wilf and me were so involved with each other that we didn't much care what was going on around us. We only had eyes for each other.

The next time I went down into Despatch the manager joked, asking me when the wedding was.

"Not for me mate," I said. "I've been married once. That's enough for me."

"You don't look old enough," he answered.

"Looks can be deceiving," I said.

As I walked out of his office he called after me, "Wilf says he's going to marry you."

I just laugh and replied, "In his dreams."

When I met Wilf in the park for lunch I said, "What's this I hear about you?"

"Oh God," he said. "What now?"

I laughed and said, "Arthur from Despatch tells me you're going to get down on one knee."

He gave me the smile again.

"You've got to catch me first Wilfie boy."

"I thought I had."

"Well, we'll see what happens. I'm in no rush to tie the

knot again."

Alice continued to 'bad mouth' me to anyone who would listen. When we called to see Aunt Manda she told me to ignore her, she was just a bitter old woman. I told her I was not bothered what she had to say about me, she was a pussy cat compared to Dad.

Dad had been very quiet, that was a sign that he'd got other fish to fry. I thought that as long as he left me alone to get on with my life he could open a fish shop if he wanted!

I'd been doing a lot of overtime as they were short-staffed at work and no-one had bothered to offer to help out. I had found that you can't be one of the girls and the boss as well. I was not sure if I wanted to be the boss. I thought I might look for another job. Wilf wanted me to stay at Ondura so he could look after me, I did feel pampered.

We decided to have a night out and go to the Mecca at Bradford and to La Ronde for a meal. We had some photos taken in the booth at the dance hall and had a really good night. We got back to Keighley on the bus and then stood waiting for a taxi. Two girls were also waiting, one of them was the one who pushed me into the road on Church Green. I decided to say nothing. I didn't want any trouble. It would just spoil our night. She came over to speak to Wilf and I ignored her.

"How's your little girl these days Bill?" she asked.

I thought, "Oh shit, he'll go mad." He didn't. He looked down at me, gave me a lovely kiss and then turned to her, saying, "This is my little girl." She looked amazed. We got into our taxi. I gave a big sigh of relief and relaxed. She hadn't spoilt our night but I bet that she would relay everything back to his ex-wife.

Why is it when everything is going fine you wonder when the bottom will fall out of your world. I decided to make the most of everything whilst the going was good.

We got a flying visit from Maureen and Billy. I didn't think they were very impressed with us. They did everything by the book and Dad still gave them a hard time whilst Wilf and I flouted every rule in the book and Dad didn't give a damn. I could have told them the answer, it was simply the fact that he never gave a shit about what I did, where I was or with whom. Did it bother me? The answer what that yes it had when I was a kid but then I glimpsed the monster underneath his disguise and this made me very happy I wasn't on his radar. Why he was the way he was about Maureen, who knew?

We all went for a night out together. Billy was taking photos. He had the nerve to ask Wilf to move as he only wanted family in the snap. He was a lucky man that night. Wilf turned to me and said, "Dor, we're leaving," and we did otherwise Billy could have landed flat on his back as Wilf didn't like him a lot.

We headed back to Scarborough for a week. It had become a great favourite of ours. I hoped that Paul wouldn't get anything contagious on this occasion. We had a glorious week and the weather was scorching. We sat by the swimming pool and I got my legs very sunburnt. When we got back to our hotel I was in agony. Wilf had burnt his shoulders as well. At least we had the sense to keep Paul covered up. I went out looking for a chemist to get some after-sun lotion to help. I bumped into Jimmy Saville, who directed me to the nearest chemist. When I got back and told Wilf who I'd met he said, "Did he fix it for us, love?"

"Oh, very bloody funny, I'm sure. Roll over while I put some lotion on your back," I replied, "and I am doing my own legs thank you."

He just laughed. We must have looked a sight. By next morning my legs were still a bit sore but were turning a lovely shade of brown that would save on stockings for a while. Wilf's back, however, was a right mess and starting to peel. I said that he should pop into the A & E department but he wouldn't. He just kept his shirt on for a day or two.

It wasn't long before we were back at work. Isn't it funny that you only have to be back at work an hour and your holiday seems an age ago?

Wilf had a bit of good news. He had sold his house. I didn't even know he'd got one. When he and his wife broke up she took the contents and he got the house.

Clever woman, his ex, Wilf would be lucky if he broke even. He was also paying generous money to support his daughter. That was a joke really. His ex wouldn't let him see her but expected him to support her. I thought that Wilf should try what I did but in reverse. Still it was not any of my business. I decided that if we ever settled down together it might be a concern to me, but only then.

Top left: Doreen on her first bike

Top Right: Doreen with her wild rabbits

Bottom: A very young Doreen at John O'Groats

Top: Doreen 'being mum' to sister, Julia Caroline

Centre: Wilf's parents

Bottom: Doreen's Parents

Top: Doreen with son, Paul, at Scarborough enjoying an ice-cream

Bottom Left: Wilf in Scarborough, hiding from his fans

Bottom Right: Wilf with Paul and the monkey

Top: The Big Day

Centre: Doreen's two boys: Paul and Scott

Bottom: Granddad's princess, Beth

Top: Scott – "like father, like son"

Bottom: Grand-daughter, Beth, all grown up now

CHAPTER 28: THE MONKEY

I hadn't caused any major problems for a while so I thought I was about due to do something stupid – you could always rely on me to cock-up to order.

Wilf and I went to an outdoor market at Bradford. This was a bad idea really due to my previous history with animals. You must remember that this was many years ago when there were no laws in place to protect any animals. You could buy anything at this market – dogs, kittens, chickens geese – and, would you credit it, on the day I go there was a guy trying to offload a small monkey. He had been using this poor creature to entice people to have their photo taken with a monkey sitting on their arm. I went to check out this monkey and dragged Wilf along with me. The poor little thing had a harness on which was far too small and had been rubbing its tummy and legs. They were red and sore but I couldn't see any ulcers. Wilf was about to see me go into rescue mode. I hoped that he could survive the experience. I tackled the guy about the state of his monkey. I flashed my card that I used for ID when I did the wages run. I made sure he only got a glance – it looked official. He seemed impressed. He thought I was someone important. I told him that Wilf was from the market official's office. He then looked a bit worried. He said he had to sell his monkey, he needed money to get home as his mother was dying. I thought he was lying. I asked him how much he wanted for the monkey. He named a ridiculous price. I told him that Wilf had the authority to impound the animal because it had been ill-treated.

Wilf took me to one side and whispered, "You are not going to buy that thing are you?"

But I was determined to rescue it. I told him, "It's in pain. Look at its legs, the harness is cutting into its flesh." I walked back to the guy and said, "I'm not supposed to pay out any money, however, I'm willing to give a small donation to you because of the situation with your mother."

He started to protest.

I said, "My colleague will now ring for police assistance. They will impound your monkey." I started to walk away.

He grabbed my arm. "OK, OK," he said. "I don't want trouble with police."

I opened my wallet and gave him my only £10 note which I was saving for some new handmade Italian shoes. I'd been saving up forever. "Oh, well," I thought, "bang goes the shoes." Five minutes later I walked out of the market with a monkey. Wilf was shell-shocked.

"What the hell are you going to do with it?" he asked.

"I'm going to take it home, remove its harness, treat its sores and then find it a new home," I replied.

"How do you know it won't bite. It's got some bloody big fangs," Wilf said, still looking quite bewildered.

"If it wanted to bite," I said, "it would already have done so."

"You can't take it on the bus," Wilf said.

"I know that, the guy's gone to get its carry box," I replied.

"How do you know he will come back?"

Wilf was getting a bit upset but just then the guy returned with a shoddy looking carry box.

I said, "I need your signature to say you have agreed to give me your pet to be rehomed. As I don't have any receipt book with me you must sign this paper. I will add the details when I get back to my office. Please put your current address and phone number down as I may need to contact you."

"I go back home," he mumbled.

"OK," I said, "but you need to sign this and also tell me what diet you have been feeding this animal."

"She eats what I eat."

I rolled my eyes. I couldn't believe this. He'd probably been feeding it chips, curry, God knows what else. No wonder its coat was so dull. I asked how old she was. He shook his head.

"I go now," he said and started to walk away.

Wilf stepped forward. "Just a minute matey," he said. "The lady asked you a question."

"OK, OK," he said. "I have had her about three years. She was baby when I got her."

Wilf looked at me. I nodded it was OK for the guy to leave. Now was the moment of truth. I wondered what would this monkey do? Also, Wilf seemed to have disappeared.

I called after the guy, "What's her name?" He glared over his shoulder.

"She doesn't have one."

I suddenly felt very sad. I felt the tears form in my eyes. Poor little thing, he didn't even bother to give her a name. I looked down at her. She was clinging onto me for dear life. She hadn't even noticed that her captor had gone. Oh, well I guessed I had now got a monkey. Then Wilf reappeared with two brown paper bags.

"What's in the bags?" I asked.

"Fruit," he said, "Oh, and monkey nuts."

I shook my head, laughing.

"Never mind love," he said. "If we ever get hard-up we can always take the monkey out and take some photos."

"Oh, very funny," I said. "Let's get out of here before we get rumbled."

We made for the park. I had to get the monkey into the carry box without getting savaged. I couldn't take the harness off until we got her home. Poor little thing. Nobody wanted her. I decided to name her, so I called her Mitzi. (I was to have another Mitzi in my life but not until much later on.) She had taken a liking to my scarf. It was a mohair one that Mum had knitted. I took it off and wrapped it round her. The little jumper and pants she was dressed in stank. I bet that they had never been taken off. I was surprised they hadn't become part of her skin. They would be going in the bin. Monkeys in the wild didn't need clothes, nor did this little one. I decided I had better not get too attached as I would not be keeping her. She needed a big cage where she could play and swing on branches. Even that was not ideal but it would be the best I could offer. Wilf gave her some monkey nuts. She didn't know what to do. I opened them for her. She liked the nuts. Wilf asked if he should give her some fruit.

I said, "No, it's not a good idea. If she's been used to human food we could end up with one shitty monkey."

We would have to change her food gradually. I would need to get some advice on how to do that. I put my scarf into her box and she got in herself without any help from me. Amazingly she was very quiet. We did take her home on the bus. She did just one little screech.

A bloke sitting behind us said, "What's in the box?"

"Don't worry mate," Wilf answered. "It's only a gorilla."

"Must be a small bugger," the bloke replied. Wilf just gave a laugh.

We managed to get back to the flats without any mishaps.

"What the hell will your mother and Jock say about this?" Wilf asked.

"Nothing," I replied. "They are used to me. One day I will tell you about my career as an animal rescuer."

He just looked and shook his head in disbelief.

Dad was sitting having his tea. For once he was

reasonably sober.

I thought that he must be hard-up, that would work in my favour. The knack was that you had to know how to play Dad.

"I need your help Dad," I said.

He looked up. "What's up lass?" he asked.

"I've just rescued a female monkey from Bradford Market."

He got up from the table. I'd got his attention. He smelt a money-making opportunity. He could be very cruel where animals were concerned but if an animal was injured by others he would be enraged. I lifted the little monkey out of her box.

"Winnie, just look at this," he shouted through to Mum, who was in the kitchen. "It's time they closed down that fucking market," he spluttered.

I knew that he would get enraged. Mum came out of the kitchen. She stood and looked.

She turned to me and said, "Well our Doreen you have excelled yourself this time."

"How much did you pay for her?" Dad asked

"You did buy her didn't you?" Mum said.

"Yes, I did. I didn't pinch her or kidnap her. I paid a tenner for her," I replied.

"How the hell did you get her for a tenner?" Dad said.

"She's worth a lot more than that."

"Where did you get a tenner from?" Mum asked (you have to remember that a ten pound note was a lot of money in those days.)

"I've been saving for ages. I was going to buy those handmade shoes I wanted."

There was a shoe shop in Cavendish Street that sold handmade Italian shoes, the 'in thing' at that time but very expensive. But, never mind, I would save up again.

Paul had just woken up from his nap. He climbed up on Wilf's knee. He didn't pay any attention to the monkey.

I told him, "Don't touch it, Paul, it might bite."

He hid his face in Wilf's jacket. I thought I had lost my son to that guy. Paul doted on him.

"I need to get that harness off Mitzi and those stinking clothes," I told Mum.

"Where are we going to keep her?" Mum asked Dad.

"I've got that new aviary over in the allotment. I nearly sold it the other day. Can you give me a hand?" Dad asked Wilf.

As they went out Paul made to follow Wilf. "Stay there 'till I get back, then I'll take you for ice-cream," Wilf told him.

I watched in amazement as Paul climbed back on the

chair and waited without any fuss. Wilf certainly knew how to handle kids. By the time they got back Mum had taken off Mitzi's clothes and the harness. Her tummy looked a mess, poor little thing. Mum told Dad that Mitzi needed checking by the vet.

"How much will that cost?" I asked. I was about broke.

The aviary fitted down the long wall in the lounge.

"Do we have to have it in here?" Mum asked.

"It's too cold at the allotment," Dad said.

I was worried about not being able to pay a vet's bill but Dad came up trumps for once.

"I'll pay the vet," he said, "and give you your shoe money back. I'll also find a good home for her when her sores have healed."

I said, "Thanks." It was not often that I'd thanked him for anything in my life. He gave me my tenner there and then. I gasped in amazement.

When I spoke to Mum later she laughed, "He knows when he's onto a good thing. He'll make a lot of money on Mitzi."

"Even so," I said, it was good of him."

I couldn't believe I was sticking up for Dad. What a turn-up for the books.

Paul was sitting on the chair covered in ice-cream. A lot of it was on Wilf's shirt as well. I realised that this was what I wanted for me and Paul, a bloke who really cared about us. But was it what he wanted? I needed to be sure. Paul would be heartbroken if he lost him. I needed to speak to Wilf and ask what his plans were but first I had a monkey to sort out. Mum had given her a biscuit and some chopped-up fruit. She liked her new cage. It had got branches and things to play with. Mum said that I'd lost my scarf, Mitzi wouldn't give it back. She sat cuddling it. Wilf said that I needed to buy her a teddy or soft toy. Julia had lots of soft toys and she gave Mitzi one of her old ones. So then she had a teddy and a scarf. She did look a lot happier.

Dad was true to his word. He sorted the vet out. It seemed that Mitzi was quite healthy but a bit out of condition due to poor diet. The vet gave us a diet sheet and also some powder for her sores. So I guess you could say that Wilf's first animal rescue went well. It was a topic of conversation for months. When Dad heard the full story he thought it was hilarious. Mum said that we had been lucky not to get locked up. Wilf kept looking at me and shaking his head.

"How the hell did we get away with it?" he asked.

Mitzi recovered well and was sold on to a bloke in Leeds who had other exotic animals. How much profit did Dad make? I never knew. I got my shoes so I didn't care. Mitzi got a new home with an experienced owner. The only one who came off badly was poor Paul. Mitzi had become very attached to me. One night I had Paul wrapped in a bath towel on my knee, drying him. Mitzi came over and sat on his shoulder. She had done this lots of times before but for some reason she decided to give him a nip with her teeth. I think she was jealous because Paul was getting all the attention. After that she had to stay in her cage for two days until she moved to her new home. Paul screamed the house down. I'm not sure if it put him off monkeys but it did mean he could get all Wilf's attention and he kept going to show him his scar. Anyway the scar soon faded and he forgot about it. My shoes fitted a treat, very posh they were. For once, Dad got a pat on the back.

With Mitzi gone Wilf no longer had to put up with a monkey sitting on the back of his chair searching through his head of gorgeous black hair for fleas. He was most indignant when Mum told him what Mitzi was doing. I think he was secretly pleased to see the monkey move on. These days animals are no longer sold at Bradford market, thank God.

CHAPTER 29: HOMELESS

I didn't see them coming, but black clouds were gathering above my head. I would be knocked sideways when the storm broke.

Some of you might have thought I'd been very hard on Dad in my previous pages. Well, I hadn't. What he did next proves he was a total bastard and a control freak as well.

I got back home one Saturday lunchtime after working overtime. Maybe if I had been there earlier I could have stepped in and stopped everything kicking off.

Mum was in the kitchen. Paul was on the sofa, asleep.

"What's wrong with Paul?" I asked her as it was unusual for him to sleep at that time of day. "Is he poorly?"

Mum shook her head. "He's upset."

"What about?" I asked.

"Your Dad just threw Wilf out."

I laughed, "Has he got a death wish?"

"Wilf and your dad had a row about something. What, I don't know. He told him to leave."

"Where's Dad?" I asked.

"You better keep out of it our Doreen, the mood your Dad's in he might tell you to go as well."

"He can please himself about that. I've had that bastard right up to here," I said, indicating the top of my head. "Did they have a fight?"

"Well he gave Wilf a couple of shoves and told him to get out and take his stuff with him. I think he was a bit scared of your Dad."

I started laughing. "Are you deranged Mother? Dad couldn't fight his way out of a paper bag these days. Tell him from me that if he sends any of his so called heavy boys to try and sort Wilf out he's wasting his time. Most of them are shit scared of Wilf anyway. If he trys to interfere in my life I swear to God I'll finish the bastard this time. I should have pushed him out the bloody window when I had the chance. Is he throwing his grandson out as well? Why is it, Mother you never ever stand up for any of your kids against the evil pig? Don't you give a shit about us? What about Julia? Will you let him terrorise her and control her life as well?"

I went and got changed, putting on my jeans, jean jacket and my boots. I guessed I was prepared for anything. I needed to find some accommodation quickly for myself and Paul. I was not sure what Wilf was going to do. In fact, I didn't know where the hell he was. I'd never chased after a bloke in my life. I was not going to start then. I decided that he would have to come looking for me. At that moment I was totally pissed off with the male species. Every time any trouble happened it was always a bloke who kicked it off. Well that night I decided I was going to kick off some trouble.

As soon as Mum saw what I was wearing she said, "Doreen, you're not going looking for your Dad are you? Please don't upset him. He'll make my life a misery."

"Well Mother he's been making my life a misery since I was five years old. You did nothing then, you'll do nothing now. If I start talking he won't just be upset, he'll be in jail."

Mum went drip white. "What do you mean?" she gasped.

"What do you know?"

I think you know what I'm talking about Mother." I started to leave, turning to say, "I'll be back for my son as soon as I've sorted out that bastard."

I tracked Dad down in the Market Arms. As soon as I walked in he spotted me. I walked up to his table.

"Sit down lass," he said.

"No thanks," I replied. "What I have to say is best said standing up. I know you have chucked Wilf out but I'll just put you straight on a few things. You don't interfere in my private life. You lost the right to do that a long time ago. What did Wilf do to get up your nose?"

He just sat there. He didn't want me to cause a scene.

"I am sick of the way you cause havoc in people's lives, then sit back and watch the fireworks," I continued. "Well, you better get yourself outside. Wilf wants to see you."

Dad went a very funny colour. "Tell him to come in and have a drink. We can sort this out," he gasped.

"You're in a hole Dad, you better stop digging. Wilf will come in but it won't be to drink."

He reluctantly followed me out. "Where is he then?" he asked.

"I have no idea. I thought you might not want your cronies to hear what I have to say."

He started to get all 'bolshie' again.

"Just stop there Dad. When are you going to realise you have no hold over me. Nothing you can say scares me. In fact, all I see when I look at you is an old man past his prime. You had a very strange hold over Maureen. No doubt we will all find out what that was about. Nothing stays a secret forever. I am going to find some accommodation for myself and Paul. If you upset my son again or touch any of my personal possessions in the meantime I will charge you with assault and wilful damage.

You better listen. I mean every word. Do you understand?"

He just nodded and went back to his beer. I was not sure if his mental state was what it should have been. Maybe the years of abusing alcohol had taken its toll. I had no feelings for this man any more. I didn't think I ever had. As far as I was concerned he didn't exist.

I knew a woman who let rooms and flats. I hoped she was at home. I made my way along Skipton Road. She was not at home but her mother told me that she only let to single men and, as most of those were bus drivers, she wouldn't have kids in her flats – her tenants worked shifts. That was no good for me then. It was going to be harder than I imagined. I had not given Wilf a thought. He would have no problems. He could go home or to his aunt's. I wondered what the hell I was going to do. I decided to see if he was at Aunt Manda's. I felt a total idiot. I didn't want him to think that I was chasing him.

Manda was pleased to see me. "Wilf is taking a bath. You've got trouble at home, Doreen," she said.

"You could say that," I replied. "I've got an arsehole for a father. I don't want Wilf to think I'm chasing him. I won't hang about. Just tell him I'm sorry about the arsehole."

She laughed. "Hang about and speak to him," she said. "He's worried about you and Paul."

"Tell him not to worry. I can take care of myself and Paul. My father ceased to bother me years ago."

She gave me a hug and I made my way to the bus stop. I was just about to board the bus when Wilf called my name. He ran to me and took me in his arms.

"Are you OK?" he asked.

I just nodded. I was not going to cry.

He gave me a kiss and that did it, I went into meltdown.

We sat on the bench at the bus stop whilst I composed myself.

"I hate to see you upset," he said.

"I'm not upset, I'm fucking angry."

"Please don't swear Dor," he said. "It's just not you."

"That arsehole has put me in an awkward position. I need to find somewhere to live and also some childcare for Paul while I'm at work."

"Has he thrown you out as well?" he asked.

"He wouldn't dare. I know too much about him." I was still sobbing.

"Come on sweetheart, let's go to Manda's. We can try and sort something out."

I turned on him. "Don't feel responsible for me and Paul. I'm a big girl. I have taken care of Paul ever since he was born with no help from anyone. You are quite OK to walk away. You don't need this sort of hassle. You have enough of your own."

He didn't answer and lit two cigarettes. He handed one to me. We sat there quietly. I finished my cigarette and stood up.

"I'd better be getting back to Paul. I've already given the arsehole his blessings. I want to get Paul out of his house before he gets back from the boozer. He's already upset the poor little bugger. Paul cried himself to sleep."

"That was my fault," Wilf said. "He wanted to come with me. Your dad wouldn't give me a chance to explain to him."

"You should have decked him," I said.

"I nearly did, but I thought you would be mad at me. I know you don't like fighting."

"Dad thought you were scared of him."

Wilf started laughing. "In his dreams. I might have been twenty years ago. Besides I don't punch old fellas."

I told him to watch his back as Dad had some unsavoury mates who would give you a good kicking for the price of a pint.

I knew I would have to ring in sick on the Monday until I could find some childcare. Then Manda came up with a solution. Wilf's cousin, Maureen, would be happy to watch Paul. She had a lad a little bit older. She could do with the extra cash.

"Well, that's one problem solved already," said Wilf. "I'm just going to solve the other."

He was back a few minutes later. "OK," he said. "Let's go get our lad."

We went and collected Paul. I packed a bag with what we would need for a few days.

"Just give him time to calm down," Mum said. She was upset because I had a go at her. The truth hurts but it had to be said. I was sick of her sitting on the fence doing nothing.

"I don't care how much he calms down Mother. I won't be bringing Paul back here. He's a loony tune. Tell him from me that if he bad-mouths me around the pubs I will bring him down to size. When I've finished telling all I know people will spit on him as he walks past."

As we were leaving the main door I saw Dad stagger off the bus. He really was a joke. I wondered if he knew how many people were laughing behind his back. I decided to put him out of my mind.

I didn't know until much later that Mum had moved all mine and Paul's things into her friend's flat. She was so frightened about what I would do if he damaged anything of mine. She thought I knew a big secret. I knew nothing, but it proved a point, he was ashamed of something, something he didn't want made public. I thought that the truth would out one day and when it did it would leave us all speechless.

We got on a bus to Haworth. Wilf was playing a game, 'Mystery Tour'. He wouldn't tell me where we were going. It all became clear when we got off the bus. He had booked us into the Black Bull at Haworth for the weekend, one last bit of luxury before 'cardboard city'. We had a weekend to remember and Paul behaved himself well. Come Monday it was back to reality.

Monday morning dawned wet and horrible. When sorting Paul's clothes the previous night at the hotel I found a set of keys in his pocket. I asked Wilf if he knew what these keys were. They were his work keys. He was over the moon, he thought he had lost them and would have been in trouble with Vernon if they hadn't turned up. Well that was another problem solved. If we could just find somewhere to live everything would be solved. It had taken Wilf all weekend to convince me that he wanted to be with us and was not just doing this because he felt sorry for us.

After dropping Paul off at Manda's I made my way into work. Wilf had already left a message on my desk. He wanted to see me at lunch-time. I'd also got an appointment at the council offices regarding emergency accommodation. I'd taken an hour off later in the day to cover that.

I met Wilf in the park. It was still dark and dreary but the rain had stopped. It seemed that one of his workmates rented a room on Skipton Road. The house was owned by an Indian lady and her son. It was not ideal as all of us were in one room but it was better than a cardboard box! I wouldn't have put it past Dad to involve Social Services, saying that I'd made Paul homeless. If he had, I thought, he had better start running because he would be dead meat if I got my hands on him.

I had my appointment with the council and explained my situation. The lady was very encouraging. She told me that if I accepted the first offer they gave me we could have a house within weeks. I had told her that we were managing in one room with limited cooking facilities and shared bathroom. She did say that myself and Paul would qualify for bed and breakfast emergency accommodation paid for by the Council but I said I thought it was important for us to stay together. She agreed with me. I left her office with her promise that she would be in touch as soon as possible. It was easier to get houses then than it is now, especially if both of you were working. I didn't tell her that Wilf and I weren't married. I just said that I was waiting for my divorce to come through and she settled on that.

I informed my boss that any overtime for me at that time was out of the question. I thought I had done more than my fair share and he agreed. Some of the others could shoulder the load for the time being.

After work we collected Paul and went to see about a room. Wilf was not happy. He felt that he had let us down and that he should be able to provide better than one room for us.

I thought that all this was Dad's fault and that every time he lost it my life was disrupted in some way. I made myself a silent promise – I would get out of Keighley for good as soon as I could, this town held nothing but trouble for me. I truly believed that if Wilf wanted to make a go of it with me we had to move away. If we didn't, there would be someone interfering or disrupting our home at every turn. If it was not Dad, it would be Alice or some gossip-monger telling tales about Wilf. He had a reputation for being a ladies' man. It was not going to change. There would always be someone ready to drop him in it or some hard man wanting to be the one to knock Wilf Burrows on his arse. I was a bit luckier than him, apart from Kevin, nobody was relating me to Doreen McEwan. I was an unknown quantity. That was why Wilf's ex-wife was so desperate to find out all she could. She didn't want him anymore but she didn't want anybody else to have him either. I thought she had a bloody cheek. Wilf was paying for the upkeep of his daughter but never saw her. His ex-wife thought she could have him on his knees, begging to be allowed to see Annette but since he met me he hadn't bothered.

The room turned out to be quite large and our landlady offered to put in a single bed for Paul and supply bed linen as well. We took the room and paid a month's rent in advance.

We moved in and settled down to a different routine. The weather was getting colder. I was praying for an easy winter. It wouldn't be much fun taking Paul to Bracken Bank every morning if we had a lot of snow.

Paul had not settled very well at Maureen's. He cried every time I left him there. I knew that if he carried on like this I was going to have to make other arrangements. It was not doing him any good crying every day. It upset me to leave him when he clearly was not happy.

Another week dragged by with no change. I had decided to try Paul at the private nursery in Keighley, this meant he wouldn't be out in the cold so long and would have more kids to play with. Also the staff had some childcare qualifications. I was pleased that after his first day there were no tears to cope with. Things were looking up at last.

If I thought about the situation we were in, I knew it wasn't ideal but we had each other. I had furniture in storage so the sooner they found us a house the better. We were lucky that we didn't have to wait too long, but when Wilf read the letter offering us a three-bedroomed house on Guardhouse Estate his face dropped. I didn't know much about the different areas but Wilf said it was one of the roughest areas in Keighley. We would both be out at work during the day so I didn't see what the problem would be. We couldn't pick and choose where we would live and were lucky to be offered anything at all.

The next few months proved to be an eye-opener for me. I was soon branded a snob. The women worked in the mills so I didn't fit in at all as I went out to work dressed for an office job. It didn't bother me. I kept myself to myself.

When Wilf went for a night out with an old mate I stayed home with Paul. At work the following week the rumours were rife. Wilf had been in the Variety Club with a woman sitting on his knee. I said nothing. I just waited to see what happened. Wilf knew something was wrong. When we met for lunch I still said nothing, I sat eating my sandwich.

"Anything wrong?" he asked.

I looked at him. If looks could have killed he would have been dead. "I don't know Wilf," I replied.

Before he could answer I got up and returned to the office. He rang my office twice to try to talk to me but I was in a meeting. He was waiting outside when I finished work. We walked into Keighley and picked Paul up from nursery. I said very little. Wilf got Paul ready for bed. I sat reading. I didn't intend to tackle him about what had happened on his night out. I wanted to see if he would tell me. We were both sitting there saying nothing. Wilf made me a cup of tea and as he put it down he asked, "Have I done something to upset you?"

I shook my head and drank my tea

"Is it something you have been told?"

I still kept quiet.

"If it's about the other night when I went out with Pete I can explain," he said.

I got up and took my cup into the kitchen. He followed.

"Look Dor it was all very stupid."

Before he could say any more I turned on him. "The only stupid thing about it is me. Did I really think you had any intention of telling me before I heard it on the jungle drums?"

"It's not what you think. It was just Pete's idea of a joke."

"Well," I replied, "the joke's on me."

I decided to have an early night. Wilf followed me upstairs. As he got to the bedroom I chucked a pillow and blanket at him and slammed the door in his face.

On my way into work the next morning I bumped into Mum at the bottom of Low Street.

"You've saved me the walk lass. This letter arrived for you. Are you poorly our Doreen? You look terrible."

"Thanks for that, Mum. I didn't sleep too good last night and feel like death warmed up."

"How's the lad doing? We miss seeing him," she said.

"Oh, he's fine," I said but I didn't convince her.

"Doreen you can bring him to me. I'll still look after him." She looked upset.

"I'm sorry Mum. I must dash. I'm going to be late for

work."

I dashed into the main door and collided with Wilf who was on his way out.

"How's my girl this morning?" he said flashing me a smile. I gave him a look that would have frozen hell over and carried on into my office.

I was in a foul mood. I just kept my head down, hoping everyone would leave me alone. Sitting in the park at lunchtime I opened my letter. It contained the news I had been waiting for. I was now a free woman, single again. I thought, "Well, look out world, I'm on the loose again."

My mood had improved. I felt as if a great weight had been lifted from me and then I remembered Wilf, Keighley's answer to Casanova. What was I going to do about him? The answer came to me next day. Pete worked in the factory. I telephoned his manager who I knew very well.

"Send Pete up to my office. There is a query on the loading ticket for the export order on Friday."

I sat in my office waiting for him. I wondered just what I would say to reduce him to a pathetic unimportant little man. I was known to have an evil mouth, it was true, anyone who got on the wrong side of me knew about it. He probably thought I didn't know about the Variety Club farce. He looked a bit nervous as he came through the door.

"You got a problem with a loading ticket," he said.

"Sit down, Pete. There is something I need to discuss with you."

He sat. I looked over my desk at him. He'd rumbled me.

"It's about the other night when me and Bill were out, isn't it?"

"What makes you say that, Pete? Did something happen that night? Let me enlighten you, Pete. I wasn't impressed by what I heard on the jungle drums. You're single, so what you do is your business. If Wilf asked you to fix him up with a bird for the evening, that's between you and him. I'm not fussed either way, but I will not tolerate being laughed at behind my back."

"It was a joke. I didn't know she was bringing a friend," he stuttered.

"So Wilf obliged by offering his knee," I snapped at him.

"Wilf made it clear he wasn't interested. She just plonked herself down on his knee. He dumped her on the floor."

"Really," I said. It's a pity he hadn't got the sense to leave then and come home, isn't it? I guess you will offer him a bed after I kick him out. Close the door on your way out."

I bent my head and started checking my sheet of figures.

"Oh, before you go Pete, your expenses sheet for last month doesn't add up. You are a few receipts short. I'll need them by Friday if you want your money."

He glared at me.

"By Friday, Pete," I said. He slammed the door as he left.

I checked all the expense sheets before passing them to the wages department. Everyone knew that many people claimed a lot more than was due but as long as it wasn't big bucks I just ignored it but Pete had got up my nose so it was his pocket that would be short.

CHAPTER 30: CRIME WAVE

Over the next few months our house was broken into several times. The gas meter was emptied twice. On one occasion they smashed every glass bottle they could find into the bath – shampoo, tomato ketchup, milk – the mess was unbelievable and it took hours to clear up. I thought that this couldn't go on and wondered why these things were happening. It got so bad that I was scared to go to work. The woman who lived next door was convinced that I'd told the police it was her boys who were causing the mayhem. The police had gone next door asking questions as her boys had been in trouble before for breaking and entering. Every morning this woman would be waiting to shout abuse at me as I left for work. Paul couldn't play out with the other kids because of her. Wilf said that we should never have involved the police but what were we supposed to do, just put up with it?

The crunch came one Saturday night when I was in alone.

Someone threw a brick through the window. It just missed me and hit the mirror on the wall which shattered and glass went everywhere. I went out into the back garden. My next-door neighbour and two more 'so called ladies' were watching the fun from their own gardens. I was trying to get all the glass out of my hair and off my clothes. When I went back inside I just didn't know what to do. I knew we couldn't stay there, it was getting ridiculous. The brick could have hit me in the face. I wished then that I had never ever come back to Keighley. These incidents just reinforced the fact that I didn't belong there. I decided that the sooner I got out the better. I drew the curtains and tried to clear up all the glass. I was still at it when Wilf came home.

"What's happened?" he said.

"Someone chucked a brick through the window is what's happened."

I dissolved into tears. He sat down and gave me a cuddle.

"You're not happy are you?" he asked.

"No, Wilf, I'm not happy. I'm going to bed now."

I locked both doors and went to bed. Wilf was up early next day boarding up the window. He also had to work that Sunday. After he left I got Paul ready and took him out. We went to explore Cliffe Castle. It was a big park on Spring Gardens Lane. On a sunny day it was lovely to walk round. We had a sandwich in the cafe. Paul liked the parrots in the aviary. There was a small cave-like hut. I told Paul that there was a witch living there and went on to tell him a story about her and all the spells she had. He listened open-mouthed. He was to ask me many times for a witch story. I wonder if he still remembers Esmeralda, the witch.

When we got home Wilf was already there. He'd just had a bath. Paul jumped on his knee to tell him about the witch.

Later, when there were just the two of us sitting watching

TV, Wilf said, "Pete came to see me about what you said."

"It was nothing to do with you," I said. "He's fiddling his expenses."

"They all do it, a perk of the job," Wilf replied.

"Well Pete overstepped the mark," I said. "I'm responsible for checking the sheets and he was receipts short."

"Oh, come on Dor, it was payback for the bird at the Variety Club. I told you it was a joke."

"I told you, Wilf, the joke was on me. You should have left and come home. If you ever do something like that again I will cut off your balls and serve them up on toast. The other option is that you can leave. The door is always open. If you are with me you don't mess around, joke or not."

He gave me the smile and the eyes.

"I mean it," I said, getting up to go to bed.

"What about Pete's money?" he asked.

"I'll pass it this time. Tell him not to step on my toes again. Well, you leaving or staying."

He grabbed me. "I'm staying sweetheart. I don't want anyone else but you."

Well I thought that was Wilf sorted out, for the time being anyway.

Things calmed down for a while but you know me, there

is always another show-stopper that just waits for me and more often it's bad not good. True to form it came one Friday evening. Wilf was out playing snooker. He was never there when he was needed! Paul had refused his tea. He'd been sick and was now stranded on the toilet. I didn't know which end to see to first. It got worse quite quickly. I needed an ambulance. The phone box was in the next street. I couldn't leave Paul. I called to one of the kids playing outside. It was just my luck it was the youngest of 'her next door'. I asked him to go get his mum. She barged in my door seconds later. I think she expected trouble. I started to explain what the problem was. She was great. She looked after Paul while I phoned for an ambulance. By this time Paul was vomiting blood and was also passing blood and mucus. He was still marooned on the toilet. She also sent her eldest boy with a message for Wilf. It seemed to take ages for the ambulance to arrive. As the ambulance men came in the door, a taxi screeched to a halt and Wilf came running in behind them. We were soon on our way to Airedale General. I left the lady from next door, her name was Edie, in my house finishing her cup of tea.

She said as I left, "Don't worry lass, I'll clean up for you. There will be no more problems with your house, I'll see to that but we never involve the cops, we deal with things ourselves, OK?"

"Thank you. I'll remember that."

She'd never know how relieved I was. We sat waiting in the hospital for hours, well it seemed hours. They had taken Paul into a cubicle, put him on a drip and taken blood. We waited for the results. You weren't encouraged to stay with your child in those days, they just wanted you out of the way so they could do their job. Paul had fallen asleep. He was exhausted. They thought it might be his appendix. I had to sign a consent form to allow them to operate if his condition worsened during the night. We were told to go home and return in the morning. It was the middle of the night. I had no coat and it had started raining. Wilf decided to go to his parents' house as they lived near the hospital. He banged on the door. After a few minutes his father opened it. He stood looking at us as if we were from an alien planet. Wilf explained about Paul. His father never even asked us to go in. He stood there, so pompous.

"I won't let you stay the night, Bill," he said. "I can't condone your sort of behaviour. You're still a married man. You should go back to your wife and child."

Wilf was furious. "It would be a bit crowded, Dad. She's had another bloke since before I left."

Wilf went to grab him as he shut the door. He put his fist straight through the glass panel.

"Oh great," I thought, back to A & E then."

Luckily he only had a few small cuts. Well that explained why their son had a chip as big as Everest on his shoulder. What a cold fish his father was. It's a wonder he didn't catch a chill from the lump of ice that doubled as his heart. We stood in the telephone box by the Junction Pub waiting for a taxi. By the time we got to bed it was time to get up again, Wilf to go to work, me to the hospital.

I left Wilf to pass on my apologies to the girls in the office for leaving them to cope with the end of month's figures without me.

Paul had dysentery, caught at the nursery. The Health Inspector closed them down until they brought their filthy toilets up to an acceptable standard. Within two days both myself and Wilf were floored with it as well. We were confined to home and not able to visit Paul who was now in the isolation ward in a single room being barrier nursed. He was only four. He must have been terrified and wondering where we were. Mum stepped in to take over. She spent very afternoon with him and then went back in the evening to settle him down for the night. Dad even went one night. I thought it was all his fault anyway. If he hadn't kicked off Mum would still have been looking after Paul and he would not be laid in a cot alone in a room on the isolation unit.

Wilf and I were off work for two weeks before we got the all clear and could return. Mum still visited Paul in the afternoon and Wilf and I covered the evenings. Paul was back to normal but remained a carrier so the hospital was reluctant to discharge him. We made an appointment to speak to the doctor. Paul couldn't stay in there indefinitely. He'd caused a big scene at the unit when he got fed up on his own and climbed over the cot sides. The ward staff found him visiting the chap in the next room who had meningitis. He could not be supervised properly unless they stationed a nurse in his room permanently. As we had already suffered with the complaint it was decided that he would be better at home until he got the all clear.

Mum decided that Paul would be better with her whilst I worked.

"After all," she said, he didn't catch anything when I looked after him."

It was decided that Paul could be discharged after the registrar had seen him on the Friday. Mum said she would collect him but they said he would be brought in the ambulance to avoid using public transport. He was no longer infectious, but it was an extra precaution.

Wilf wanted to take me out for the evening whilst we had the chance. I didn't want to bother. It seemed just too much trouble after work but, oh well, I supposed I should make the effort. I had my hair done in the lunch hour and left work early so that I'd be ready in time. Wilf had a shower at work. He was soon suited and booted waiting for me. He looked drop dead gorgeous. His ex must have been mad. He really was a handsome guy but he knew it. He was an outrageous flirt but he knew to behave when he was with me. I had warned him that if I heard any more gossip about what he got up to when he was out without me I would not tolerate any excuses. It would be the end of the road for me and him. I meant every word. If I couldn't trust him there would be no way forward for us.

We went to the Chinese for a meal and then walked up Halifax Road. My heart sank when I realised where he was heading, it was the Vine Pub where Kevin and I had hung out. It seemed a lifetime ago. I had been married and divorced. If you remember, Kevin had already made Paul's acquaintance when we lived at the flats. As far as I knew Kevin was married now with two girls. What I didn't know was that his wife was the landlady's daughter.

We were sitting enjoying our evening when Wilf said, "Do you know the landlady?"

"No, I don't think so, why?" I asked.

"Well, she's been giving you daggers ever since we walked in."

"Guess my reputation must have preceded me," I laughed.

It was true, however, the landlady was giving me some foul looks. I got up and went to the bar for change for the jukebox. As she handed me my money she pointed to a photo behind the bar. "My grand-daughters," she said, "Kevin's girls."

I looked her in the eye and said, "That's nice."

I made my way to the jukebox where Wilf was waiting.

"What's up with her then?" he asked.

"Oh nothing much, just that I was once engaged to her now son-in-law."

"You certainly have packed a lot into your twenty-one years." He sounded annoyed.

"Oh really, well Wilf I heard you've been engaged more times than I've had hot dinners and all with the same ring."

He smiled but I was feeling annoyed. "The ring I buy you will be a new one, my love." He gave me a kiss.

"What makes you think I want a ring? I've been there, done that, don't think I'll bother again, too much hassle."

"You don't want me to get down on one knee then?" He was giving me those eyes again. I didn't know what to say.

I laughed, "I don't think I could survive a lifetime of wondering where you were or what you were doing and with whom."

He looked very sad. "If I'm with you, that's where I want to be. You'd never have to wonder. I could never cheat on you. I couldn't bear to lose you. I'm in love with you so why would I want anybody else?"

I was to remind him of that night several times over the years. The first time was to be quite shortly after that occasion when I got such a shock and then he accused me of stage-managing the outcome.

CHAPTER 31: OH NO!

Six weeks later I took Paul to Mum's as usual. He was pleased to be back there, but missed his little playmates.

I felt very nauseous that morning. I thought I was going to throw up on the bus. Mum took one look at me and said, "You look a bit green round the gills, lass, is it something you ate or have you got a stomach bug."

"I'm not sure. I felt like this yesterday but it wore off during the morning."

"You're not expecting again, our Doreen?" She looked at me waiting for an answer.

"Don't be silly, Mum. I'm on the pill, that's impossible."

Oh God, I wished she hadn't said that. She'd got me racking my brains trying to remember if I missed taking any. I was sure I hadn't. It had been a hectic, worrying time when Paul had been in hospital and also Wilf and myself had been very poorly with the same thing. It suddenly occurred to me that my protection might have been compromised by the fact that I had been sick so much and had bad diarrhoea. I wondered if I was over-reacting. I did hope I was because I really didn't need another pregnancy at that time.

I decided to make a doctor's appointment for that

evening. I said nothing to Wilf. He didn't need to know. Things had been a bit strained between us since the visit to the Vine Pub although he hadn't really said anything about it. I thought the whole thing was stupid. It had been a long time ago, for God's sake. I'd been married since then and had a son. I really didn't know what to do about it all. I felt that if he wouldn't talk to me about what was worrying him then I couldn't help. I didn't think he was jealous of what me and Kevin had. It was all too much for me. I wondered if perhaps Wilf had decided he wanted to leave.

I decided that if that was the case I didn't want anything to stand in his way. I wouldn't be begging him to stay. It wasn't my style. As I'd been on my own against the world before, I believed I could manage it again.

When I emerged from the doctor's office that night, to say I was in shock was an understatement. Well there was no getting away from the fact – I was 'in the club', 'up the duff', 'had a bun in the oven' – or, if you wish to be more genteel about it, I was with child. How did I feel? That was a good question. At that moment my head was still spinning and I had decided to tell no-one. I figured it was my business and had nothing to do with anybody. I was surprised that Dad hadn't had a lot to say about Wilf and me living together. Although the swinging sixties had gone and it was 1970, it was still not an accepted thing to be, as the common people put it, 'living over the brush'. We had both been married, but not to each other, and now I was single again. I had decided that I didn't want to be married again. It hadn't worked out the first time and there would be no guarantee that it would a second time either. I had become very thick-skinned. I didn't 'give a shit' what people thought or said about me. They couldn't refer to Paul as a bastard because I had been married when he was born. It was a good job that I didn't care as Alice had been 'bad mouthing' me to anyone who would listen. The stupid woman still thought Wilf might go back to his wife. I supposed she felt that she had lost her grand-daughter. I thought it was up to her to build bridges and then she might be allowed to see Annette, although I doubted it as she had already been in trouble for making herself known to the child when she was seen out with her other grandma. This was another reason why I wanted out of Keighley but I knew that my plans would have to be put on hold for a while. I wondered how long I could keep people in the dark about my condition. I kept quiet and tried to carry on as normal. The only problem was that I kept being sick in the mornings but so far no-one had noticed.

It was Wilf's weekend off. As I came out of the bathroom, drip white and feeling crap, he asked, "What's up?"

"Something I ate has upset me I think."

He laughed. "That's OK then. For a horrible moment I thought you might say you were pregnant. Thank goodness for the pill, best invention ever."

I didn't comment. He was cooking bacon and the smell was turning my stomach again. I dashed back into the toilet. I felt rotten. I couldn't even stomach a cup of tea. I sat there sipping my water, looking as miserable as sin. I had counted the pills I had left in my pack. They didn't add up. I must have forgotten to take them at least twice. The doctor said it was probably the ones I brought back up when we were both ill that had done the damage. Of course, I couldn't take any more so I threw the rest of the pack in the bin.

I realised that I would have to be careful when I made my future doctor's appointments. I was being sick a lot and had started to lose weight. I was about eight stone at the time but very quickly dropped down to under seven and a half stone and looked very gaunt.

Wilf went out playing darts one night, he was in the local team. On this particular night the match was in one of Dad's favourite haunts. Dad and Wilf had become bosom buddies. I warned Wilf that Dad would lull you into a false sense of security and then drop you 'in the shit' every chance he got. Alas, my words fell on stoney ground. Well, I had warned him. I knew Dad of old and leopards never change their spots.

After the darts match Wilf and Dad sat talking. Dad had added two and two together and made five. "Are you sure our Doreen's not in the club, Wilf?"

I don't know what was said after that because I wasn't there. It was late when Wilf got back. I was already fast asleep, having gone to bed early, feeling exhausted. He disturbed me when he got into bed.

As I turned over, he put his arm over me and whispered in my ear, "When were you going to tell me?"

I felt a chill go right through me. I could smell beer on his breath, it was turning my stomach. I sat up, got my bottle of water and took a sip hoping it would settle my stomach. I muttered sleepily, "What?"

"About the baby," he slurred.

He must have had a lot to drink. He usually managed to appear reasonably sober. He knew the smell of alcohol affected me although I never felt threatened by Wilf. I just didn't know how to reply.

"Did you stage manage this to trap me into marrying you?" he asked.

I didn't lose my temper. I got up, put my slippers and dressing gown on and, without raising my voice, answered, "You are the most vain, arrogant so 'up your own arse' bloke I've ever met. When you pack your bags make sure you leave your key."

I left the bedroom and slept with Paul. It was a bit of a squeeze but we managed. I was up early, not wanting to hold up Mr Wonderful. I thought that he might need to gaze at himself in the mirror to remind himself how wonderful he really was – what an arsehole.

Although he was at home all day I never spoke a word to him. He made several attempts to engage me in conversation but I ignored him. I decided I'd had a lucky escape and thanked God I hadn't married him. He kept himself busy with Paul and then after lunch he got Paul ready to go out.

"I'm going to see Manda, are you coming?" he asked.

I just said, "No." Then I went to lay down. I hadn't slept much the previous night and felt really ill.

Just before he left I shouted to him, "If that evil old witch is there, keep her away from my son."

"Who," he shouted back.

"Your bloody mother. She's barmy, I'm sure she is."

After they left I fell asleep and slept until Wilf woke me after he had put Paul to bed.

"We need to talk," he said.

"I said all I wanted to say last night. I will not marry you or anyone else. I don't intend to marry again."

"Don't be stupid," he replied. "You're pregnant. People will say nasty things about me, don't you care?"

"To be quite truthful, Wilf, I don't give a shit. I shall be leaving Keighley as soon as I can. I should never have come back."

I was sitting in the kitchen with a cup of tea, the first I had enjoyed for ages. Maybe the sickness was over.

"I'm sorry about what I said last night," he did look as though he meant it.

"No you were quite right. I had guessed you were going to jump ship so decided I'd like something to remind me of you or maybe it was the amount of sickness I had when Paul was poorly that made my pills less effective. We shall never know now."

"You were wrong," he said. "I have no intention of leaving, I never had."

"Well, I'm still not remarrying. If you want to hang around that's up to you. The door is always open if you decide I've tricked you."

I curled up on the sofa. I was starting to feel a lot better. He sat down beside me.

"I'm getting used to the idea," he said.

"I sort of got the impression last night that you didn't want to be a Dad again."

"I'm looking forward to this. It's a first for me."

"But what about your daughter?" I asked.

"I didn't get a look in last time. Her mother completely took over. I had been getting ready to tell her it was over when she told me she was pregnant. Then her parents took over. Before I knew what was happening the church was booked. I just had to grin and bear it."

I had seen a wedding photo and he did look totally pissed off. The fact was that their marriage was doomed from the start. It did come as a surprise to hear it was her who did the cheating. Anyway it was water under the bridge. I had to decide what I was going to do.

What did change was the way Wilf treated me. When we were out for the evening he devoted himself to me. One night we were in a pub in Bingley. This was the first time I met Peter Sutcliffe. Wilf spoke to him as we went in and bought him a drink. I was fascinated by him. He was a really good-looking chap and a snappy dresser. His hair and beard were immaculate. I don't particularly like beards but on him it looked good. But I think it was his eyes that made me catch my breath. They were dead, that's the only way I could describe them. There was no depth to them, they showed no expression at all. Wilf went to the loo. A guy who was sitting at the bar suddenly grabbed me in a clinch. I was taken by surprise. He buried his face in my neck. I was trying to fight him off. I looked over his shoulder and saw Peter, who smiled, held up his hand and made a fist, then hit his other hand. I didn't know if he was asking me did I want help or just showing me how Wilf would deal with this guy who was still trying to devour me. The next thing I knew the guy was flat on his back with Wilf standing over him with a face like thunder. He took a ten bob note out of his wallet and threw it at the guy who was trying to get to his feet.

"Ever touch my woman again and I'll kill you. That should pay for your suit cleaning."

Wilf downed his pint in one, apologised to the landlord and we left. I was trembling like a leaf. I had never seen Wilf in this mode before. He took me in his arms.

"Don't worry sweetheart. I'll always be around to protect you."

It was at that moment that I decided to marry him. I knew whatever life threw at me he would always be there for me. The other reason was I loved him so much it hurt. That was never to change. It was challenged many times over the years but he was the love of my life and always would be. I'm not going to pretend it was all sunshine and roses but I'll leave you to be judge and jury.

Three things happened over the next month to give us a boost. Wilf sold his house again, as it had fallen through the first time (we could have moved in there but I wanted a fresh start not somewhere he had lived with his first wife).

Then we got offered a bungalow down Worth village which was much closer to the flats so would make my life much easier. Wilf was over the moon. He didn't want Paul to start school at Guardhouse. He said it was very rough and they would give Paul a hard time. Now he would be able to start nursery at Parkwood Infants.

The third thing, Wilf got his divorce through. He said that he'd never been so pleased to get shut of someone before as he was to get rid of his ex. I think it's sad when a marriage hits the rocks but there was no love lost between Wilf and her, it had turned sour for him before the ink was dry on the marriage certificate.

We decided to tie the knot on my twenty-second birthday. It was 21st November 1970. We had a busy time getting the bungalow ready but it was not finished before we married. We told no-one about what we planned. The only two people at the Registrar's Office were my friend from work, Hilda and her husband. When we came out some of the girls from the office were there to cover us in confetti. I'd had a night out with the girls the previous week. Wilf didn't bother with a stag night. It was to be the last time I ever went out without Wilf. He was none too pleased when I staggered in well after midnight and the worse for wear. I have only been drunk twice in my life and this was one of those times. Wilf was totally disgusted with me. He didn't speak to me all weekend. I could see him holding up a card saying, 'I do' just so he didn't have to speak. I never went out without him again. It just wasn't worth the hassle and, to be truthful, I didn't enjoy myself without him. After the ceremony we went home to get changed. Some of the girls had organised a buffet. I wondered how they had got in but found out later that Wilf had given them a key, so he was in on it. Mum arrived a short while later so Paul could be on the photos. Mum then had him for the weekend and we got two whole days to ourselves. No-one at work knew about the baby until it was nearly time for me to leave. I was still very slim with just a hint of a tummy bulge.

Over the next few weeks we moved into our bungalow. It was cosy but plenty big enough for three people. When I finally left Ondura Wilf bought a push-bike and started coming home for his lunch. He said he didn't like to be all day without seeing me. It certainly broke the day up for me.

Now the whole family knows I don't like lifts. This fear stems from the time Wilf and I got stuck in the one in Leylands House when I was eight months pregnant with Scott. Wilf was convinced I would give birth there and then. We rang the alarm bell and within minutes I heard Mum call up to ask which floor we were on. Dad was the caretaker but, of course, if it was within his drinking hours Mum had to fill in. She climbed several flights of stairs. When she called to me through the lift door she could hardly speak and was gasping for breath. Mum suffered with her chest and had bronchitis every winter. I had told her that the fags would kill her. However, even my warning and a graphic description of a smoker's lung tissue didn't put her off and she carried on puffing until her demise many years later. I was a smoker myself then so really it was a great pity I didn't take my own advice. I did stop for two years when Scott was a baby but when Wilf's health broke down and Scott's epilepsy was unstable my stress levels were off the scale. I know that's no excuse but it's the only one I have. In the wee small hours, trying to sleep in a hospital chair, I found myself reaching for the ciggies. Eventually I did give up completely but that was to be many years in the future.

Anyway, we were still stuck in the lift. I desperately wanted to pee. Then, all at once, the lift started moving upwards. It got to the tenth floor, stopped and then descended really fast. Wilf and I looked at each other. He could see I was terrified. I honestly thought our number was up – goodbye cruel world! The lift then slowed down and shuddered to a halt at the ground floor. Wilf had to carry me into Mum's flat. My legs just gave out, my heart was pounding and I felt physically sick. Mum sent for the GP. My blood pressure was far too high. I felt very unwell. He ordered bed rest so that's what I did for a couple of days. I never have been very good at doing what I'm told but I did take it easy for the weeks before Scott made his entrance into this world.

The week before the baby was due Paul stayed at Mum's just in case I had to leave in a hurry. On 3rd May I had a surge of energy and did all my cleaning, washing and ironing. We had cheese on toast for supper and had been in bed about an hour when I started with very severe stomach pains. Wilf had to run half a mile to ring for an ambulance. He'd just got back as I was getting in the back of it. He wanted to come with me but he had no way of getting back home as he had a six o'clock start the following morning. In those days hospitals didn't encourage husbands to be in the delivery room. I certainly didn't want him there.

I laid in the delivery room in agony waiting for some gas and air that never came. The two midwives on duty were busy trying to quieten the young girl in the room next door who was screaming non-stop. The midwife returned to me just as my son was about to make his entrance into the world. She brought the gas and air cylinder, it was empty. The reason I had so much pain was because I had a dry labour. There was no water to help the baby along, it had slowly seeped away. At 4.00 am precisely Scott Burrows entered this world. He never made a sound – no crying, but was very alert and weighed just 5 lb 4 ozs. The midwife gave me an injection in my leg to encourage my muscles to expel the afterbirth. She dashed away next door and left the syringe stuck in my leg. They took Scott away to take a blood sample as he was slightly jaundiced so they did not tie off the cord until several days later. I was rhesus negative. You were OK with a first baby but a second and any after that might need a complete blood change. Scott was lucky, he got away with it. I had known I might have problems with a second child but they had not told me about a complete blood change. I would have been very distressed if Scott had needed that. Many years ago doctors kept people in the dark about a lot of things. You were given information on a 'need to know' basis. I guess they thought I didn't need to know. I waited until I knew Wilf would be having his breakfast at work and rang his department.

Vernon answered the phone. "Oh, thank God you've rung. He's been in a state ever since he arrived."

I laughed. He bellowed, "Wilf your lady is on the blower."

"Hello love," his voice sounded like velvet.

"Well Wilf," I said. "I'm afraid it's a false alarm."

"Oh God, "he replied. "I can't go through another night like that. I've been worried sick."

I felt so sorry for him. "You've got a son."

There was silence on the other end of the line. "Really," he shouted. I could hear all his workmates clapping and laughing.

"I'm afraid he's very small, only 5 lb 4 ozs." I would tell him about the blood thing and the jaundice when I saw him. I didn't want him stressing out any more than necessary.

When the doctor did his rounds later I got a shock when he ordered blood tests for me. The sister said that they might want to give me some blood. I told her I didn't fancy that idea one bit. She told me that if I could walk to the bathroom and back without assistance I might not have to have any blood. I tried to get out of bed. My legs were like jelly. When I tried to stand up the floor rose up to meet me. I felt so light-headed. I made my way gingerly along the corridor. How I made it back to bed I'll never know. I felt so weak. This was blood loss plus I was anaemic. They started on iron injections plus tablets. My bum was like a pin cushion. I was exhausted. They struggled to get any blood samples. By the time Wilf got to the ward they were seriously worried about me. The doctor had been called back to the ward. My bed was screened off in the four-bedded bay. I thought that Wilf wasn't coming but he'd been collared by the doctor as he arrived. I must have looked a sight. I was propped up on pillows, both my arms were covered with dressings. They were a mess. They ended up taking blood out of my hand and that was swollen up and black with bruises. Wilf was shocked. He took me in his arms.

"How are you my love?" his eyes filled with tears.

"They don't expect me to make it through the night," I tried to joke but I think he took me seriously at first.

The staff nurse came in with more of the obnoxious stuff they were giving me to drink. It tasted like treacle. She waited until I had drunk it. I was hoping I could get Wilf to flush it down the loo, it was dreadful.

"Please bring my son in", I said.

"He's being cared for in the nursery," she replied.

"Well, I would like my husband to see him."

She offered to take Wilf to the nursery. I'd had enough of this claptrap. I started to get out of bed. She quickly ran for the sister who came in with Scott in her arms. She passed him to Wilf. The look on his face was a picture.

"He's so small," Wilf said. "I was only 4 lb when I was born," he told the sister.

"Well this is all your fault then."

He gave her the lop-sided smile that always melted my heart.

"We're feeding him every two hours to get his weight up. Your wife needs complete bed rest as she's refusing blood transfusions."

The sister brought in a cot and Wilf put his very small bundle safely in it.

"I'll leave him with you for a short while. He will want a

feed soon."

When she left Wilf sat looking at his son. There was a look of sheer amazement on his face.

"I can't believe he's ours," he said, looking at me.

"Why, does he look like the milkman?" I joked.

After a while the nurse brought in a bottle and handed it to Wilf. There he was in a black three-piece suit with his mop of black hair and sideburns. He looked so handsome, the typical Teddy boy. I think it was then that I loved him the most. She handed him his son and he gave him his feed.

Later, when the visitors' bell went, I was struggling to keep my eyes open. Wilf looked so lost when he walked out of that ward. He was heading back into Keighley to meet up with his mates to celebrate the birth of his son. I bet there were a few hangovers at work the following day.

I was concerned that Wilf might have wanted a girl but, as far as I was concerned, my family was complete so I thought he would be out of luck. However, he loved Scott from day one and handled him very well. Scott was quite small but that didn't faze Wilf. He was a very hands-on Dad. In fact, he was a perfect husband but the drinking caused me concern and he was a flirt who loved women to pay him attention and he seemed oblivious to the fact that this angered and upset me. But I loved him. He was my world. I could not imagine my life without him in it.

When you look back on your life in later years you realise how much time you have wasted fighting, arguing and saying hurtful things. How I wish I could turn back time. I would use every minute of every day. It is only when you lose something that you realise how much you have lost. The hurt is so great that it is unbearable. Deep down in your soul you feel so destroyed, so alone. You wonder if you really want to go on.

Mum arrived the following afternoon bringing Paul and Julia but they weren't allowed to see Scott. The hospital was being extra-cautious because he was small and kids could be real germ carriers.

Mum went to the nursery to see her new grandson. Paul asked me if he could have a rabbit instead of a baby. I don't think he was very impressed with his new brother. Manda came in to see me. She'd told Alice that she had a grandson. I asked what her reply had been.

Manda shook her head and said, "She's a sad old cow." Guess she wasn't pleased either then. I could not stand that woman. If I'd had my way she would have no place in my boys' lives.

Wilf came to the hospital every night after work. I told him to take a night off. I was on bed rest for six days and then they allowed me to get up. When they weighed me the following day I had lost half a stone. I had no appetite at all. Wilf brought in fruit and chocolates. I had loads of flowers from the girls at work. I'd been really spoilt. Everyone who was in my bay went home and new ones arrived. I was still stuck there. Wilf was missing me and Paul. He looked so miserable when he arrived. It was the Cup Final the following day and I knew that he'd been looking forward to watching it.

"Don't come in tomorrow," I told him before he left. "Watch the footie with your mates."

I had a plan, I collared the doctor when he came on the ward. "Look, I need to go home. My husband is missing me. My mum's got my older son and she needs a rest. I'm due back at work soon."

He looked over the top of his specs at me. "You need a long rest. Were you planning to work full time?"

The outcome was that I got discharged on the condition that I took a break from work. I was still under par and they were worried about my blood pressure which remained quite high.

Wilf came to collect me at lunch-time. When I got home the house was a tip but I couldn't complain. Wilf had been at work every day and then onto the hospital at night. He had to go back to work so I got myself settled. Mum came later bringing Paul home. She soon got the place in order.

The next few days were hard, getting a new routine in place. Scott was a good baby. He slept a lot and never cried. He didn't seem to need attention, it started to worry me. When the health visitor called to check him over she laughed, "Don't moan about having a good baby. Lots of mothers would swap places."

By week two he was sleeping through the night but being sick a lot. I thought that he was not tolerating the milk so by the time the health visitor called again I had put him on goat's milk which we collected daily from a nearby farm. I also introduced rusks to his diet. Needless to say, the health visitor and I crossed swords. I told her that I was coping well so she need not call again. That was it really, apart from taking him to the clinic to be weighed once a fortnight, I was left alone.

It was about this time that Wilf started with health problems. The first problem was soon cleared up. He had a hernia. He was in hospital for two days after his operation and then at home to recuperate. He had been advised to look for an easier job with shorter hours and no heavy lifting so he bid goodbye to Ondura. The district nurse was calling to dress his wound. It looked infected to me but she disagreed and told me to let him have a hot bath. I managed to get him into the bath although it was agony for him to lift his leg high enough to get in. I had filled the bath quite high and the hot water seemed to help a bit. Leaving him to soak, I gave Scott his bottle. Suddenly Wilf gave a sort of half scream/half shout. I dashed into the bathroom. His wound had burst wide open. I couldn't believe the muck and gunge that flowed into the water intermingled with blood and gore. We hadn't got a phone so I ran to a neighbour. She rang for an ambulance. How much easier my life would have been if I had owned a mobile then!

With my help, Wilf got out of the bath. I dressed his wound with what the nurse had left earlier. Off he went to hospital to get sorted. He returned later with boxes of antibiotics, packs of dressings and a very pissed off expression on his face.

"Never mind, love. We'll manage." This was a phrase I was to utter many times over the next few years.

CHAPTER 32: THE HEARTBREAK YEARS

What happened next I would regret for many years to come. Answering the door just after lunch one day I found Alice standing there with a rather portly chap. He introduced himself as Wilf's Uncle George. He had been visiting for a few days, heard that Wilf was ill and decided to call. I shook his hand and welcomed him in, closing the door with Alice left standing outside. Wilf was pleased to see George. Nobody saw Alice sneak in. When I did notice her she was standing over Scott's carrycot. I went to her and took Scott, who was sleeping, out of the room and out of her reach. They didn't stay long. She did not speak to me at all. I just hoped she wouldn't think that this was an open invitation to visit any time because it sure as hell wasn't.

Wilf had got a new job at Goblin as a press operative. He was over-qualified for this but it was a sit-down job. Then he told me it was nights. I was far from pleased. However, he pointed out the advantages. If I got an afternoon job somewhere he could look after the boys instead of bothering Mum. Paul would be starting school soon anyway. I told him he needed to sleep in the daytime. This was something that became a bone of contention between us.

Wilf started his new job and was coping well. I managed to get afternoon work at Keighley Lifts in the accounts department. It was the old pals act as the manager there had worked with me at Ondura. I knew after my first week that it wasn't a long-term thing. This firm was going to the wall, it couldn't pay its suppliers. I hated going into reception and lying to people, telling them that the cheque was in the post. When they came back the next week demanding payment my colleague would attempt to convince them that it was in the post again. Some lucky creditors got paid, it just depended how much money came in the post that day. It appeared that there were no funds in the bank, only enough to cover wages.

Christmas was fast approaching. Wilf developed trouble with his back again and his foot also started to swell up. It was hard for him to bear any weight on it. He still struggled to work, taking large doses of painkillers just to see him through the night. I felt helpless to give him any sort of support. He was waiting for an appointment to see the Orthopaedic Consultant at Airedale Hospital. His use of dangerous levels of painkillers just to enable him to get through his shift had to stop. I believed that he would kill himself as well as the pain. It was a big relief when his appointment arrived. Unfortunately, his tests and X-rays were inconclusive. We were still no wiser. I felt so helpless. Wilf was in pain and becoming very depressed. There was nothing I could do to help him. His consultant was Mr John Cape. The nurses called him the Caped Crusader, but not in his earshot. Over the next few years a friendship formed between John Cape and Wilf. He made it his personal crusade to get Wilf well again. This was to take many years. The first step on this journey was a myelogram . He had to stay overnight. For this procedure dye was injected and this showed up on a special X-ray. The only problem was that Wilf had to stay sitting up all night to allow the dye to drain away or it would have given him serious head pain. He came home the next day. Mr Cape was to send him an appointment to discuss the results. In the meantime he had a cortisone injection into his ankle joint to try to alleviate the pain and allow him to work.

It was nearly Christmas and Wilf was off work on sick leave. We did our best to carry on as normal. I was very worried about Wilf's mental state. It was hard for a young man to accept that he was incapacitated for a while. I uttered my phrase, "Never mind love, we'll manage."

We had each other, nothing else mattered. I changed my job. I needed to be home during the day so I got some school cleaning work. I had to get up at 4.30 am to be at work in Spring Gardens Lane at 6.00 am. It was a grind. I had never done anything as hard as this before. I just wished that someone had told me that Spring Gardens Lane was the 'Flashers' Paradise'. Within a couple of weeks a guy had flashed at me and then chased me. I was petrified. I ran to a private house and they rang for the police. A plain-clothed officer took me round the lanes. It was easy to point the culprit out as he had ice-blue jeans on with a matching jacket. He was charged and released to appear in court later. I put this behind me and carried on. A few weeks passed and I had to work a split shift as it was Parents' Evening. It was after eight o' clock when I finished. Walking down the lane with my brolly it was pitch black and pouring with rain. Halfway down there was a bench. On that night sitting there was a guy in a parka coat with his manhood standing erect for all to see. I started to feel panic but managed to walk past quickly down into Keighley. There I was in the Police Station again reporting a flasher. When they asked me if I could describe him I replied that I only saw his willy and they all look the same. Wilf was worried sick because I was very late home. He told me I'd to pack the job in, it wasn't safe. I couldn't. We desperately needed the money. This made Wilf even more depressed. He felt he couldn't protect his own wife. I promised to look for other work but in the meantime I started carrying a small vegetable knife in my coat pocket. This was to get me in even more trouble.

Two nights later, just as I reached the bottom of the lane, a guy stepped out of the shadows. There was an undertaker's yard there where he had been hiding. I'd had enough. It had been a hard shift. I just snapped. "OK, you pervert bastard. Come one step closer and I'll stick this knife in you."

He did come closer to show me his warrant card. He was a copper. I was lucky that they knew I was scared and just trying to protect myself so let me off with a caution.

I needed to find different work so I started on nights, two nights a week, at a home for the elderly. It was also in Spring Gardens. Wilf insisted I take a taxi into work so that he would know I was safe. It was working out quite well. I enjoyed the work, was at home during the day to keep Wilf company and the money was good. Then one night I really got spooked. I was sitting in the office in the early hours and looked up to see a man standing by the French windows. I ran upstairs and got the Assistant Matron out of bed. She was not pleased. By the time we came back into the office the man had gone. This happened several times but only when I was on duty. Matron called me into the office to speak about it as her deputy had complained about me waking her. I think they thought I was imagining it. I was proved to be right in the end. I was doing supper drinks one night when there was a power cut. The result was that I badly scalded my hand and was sent to A & E and then home. The Assistant Matron had to do my shift. Just after midnight she looked up from her desk to see a man pressed against the French windows. She must have been braver than me. She approached the windows and was going to open them when she spotted something glinting in his hand. She couldn't see what it was, it could have been a knife or a weapon of some sort, so she phoned the police. By the time they got there the man was long gone. The outcome was that they did catch a man some months later but by then I had moved on to pastures new. If I wasn't believed I felt I couldn't work there anymore. I moved on to the Home for the Blind two nights a week. I thought that as it was right next to the police station surely I could work there and feel safe. In those days I cared for forty residents all night with no sleeper in – quite a handful. We always had a police officer call in the early hours and have coffee. They had some really dishy cops but I was well and truly spoken for. Nobody could match up to my Wilf. He owned me body and soul. But he had two definite failings. He had started to drink far too much, every now and then he pressed the self-destruct button. It was a case of stand back and keep well out of his way. He was the man about town. He flirted like crazy but would never admit it. Deep down he was a much different chap, all he wanted was someone to love him for who he was, not what his reputation said about him.

I once asked him, "Why do you act like a prat."

He answered, "That's what people expect me to do."

The amount of times he came home with his knuckles in a mess! You never knew who had got the worst of them. I did put a stop to the stupid women who used to try to latch onto him when he was out. I stood and listened to one of them one night trying to pick him up. He was standing by the bar waiting for me. He could see me over her shoulder. While she was asking him to come back to her flat he kept repeating, "I'm married now." The trouble was that instead of just telling them to 'piss off' he always played the gentleman. I warned him that if it didn't stop I was shipping out. I meant it. I thought I had to leave the town because it was killing me emotionally. I had heard on the grapevine that Kevin had split with his wife. He'd been asking around about me. Wilf was not a man he wanted to tangle with, he would kill him. He already had a thing about what me and Kevin used to have. He just couldn't let go of that.

It was about this time that Wilf tripped up the steps into the kitchen. By the time he sat down his foot had swollen up badly. I wanted him to have it X-rayed but he wouldn't. He was already sick of hospital appointments. Within days an ulcer had formed which was full of puss. It also smelt pretty bad. He knew this was urgent. I took him to his appointment with John Cape. Some swabs were sent away. We waited again for results. While this was going on the pain in his back was getting really bad. I had to send for a locum doctor in the early hours. He gave him a shot of morphine. We sat up in bed all night playing cards as he couldn't sleep. Even the morphine hadn't shifted it. The reason for it all was revealed the following week. Wilf had TB in his bones. It was affecting his arm, foot but more so his spine. He had some more special X-rays done which revealed an abscess on his spine as big as a football. He was rushed into Airedale Hospital once more. I was devastated. The prognosis was not good. His TB drugs were doubled and he was put on steroids to boost their strength. He needed major surgery. I was sitting with him when John Cape told him that he only had a fifty percent chance of walking again if he had the operation.

Without it he would die so he mentally prepared himself for major surgery. I tried to prepare myself for life without him. It was that serious.

The day of the operation dawned. I had been working all night. I'd moved back in with Mum for a few days just in case I had to rush to the hospital. I went home to change and then made my way to Airedale. The surgery involved three surgeons and lasted several hours. I saw Mr Cape after he came out of theatre. He explained what they had done. They had drained the abscess and got two buckets of pus and muck out of it, removed infected bone from his spine and taken bone chips from his hip to replace the bone they had removed. His spine was held together with gold clips. He would be in a full plaster cast for three months. This was to cause big problems for the nursing staff. Mr Cape said he would be kept sedated for the next few days as they'd had to collapse one of his lungs to be able to get where they wanted to be and were slowly inflating it. Because he could not get out of bed they had to put a catheter in. This was to cause Wilf big problems, as soon as he regained consciousness he demanded they remove it. When they put him in the plaster cast they realised they did not have the equipment needed to turn him hourly. After trying to borrow a hoist from everywhere, including the armed services, they rang a bell every hour day and night and designated staff left their wards and came to turn Wilf. It took eight nurses to do this. His morale had taken a nosedive. He hated the cast and could not sleep in it. Very soon he was demanding to be taken out of it. Poor John Cape was at his wits end. He did not know what to do. In the end they decided on a metal corset type thing to immobilise the section of his spine while the bone chips grew. This was much more comfortable for him.

During all this time, even when he was on the danger list, his parents never visited him once. Then one day Alice arrived. She convinced the nursing staff she was his next of kin and the one to contact in an emergency. She also told them he would be coming home to her when he was discharged. As Mr Cape was on holiday the staff just took her at face value and wrote down her phone number and address. Wilf was livid. He was soon on the phone to his father who, of course, didn't want disturbing while he was at work. He told his father to keep her away. His father told him there was nothing he could do about it. When I got to the hospital that day Wilf was in tears. I just didn't know what to do for the best. In the end they moved him to a side room and stuck a 'No Visiting' sign on the door. I told them that his mother had mental health issues and should not be allowed to see him. At home next day I opened my door to Alice who was foaming at the mouth she was so angry, demanding to know what was happening to her son as she had been turned away at visiting time. She lived close by the hospital and had been there afternoon and evening making a nuisance of herself. If was having a detrimental effect on Wilf's recovery. She had waylaid my mum who was taking Paul to see his dad, hoping to tag along with her but the staff

turned her away.

I was at a loss to know what to do. The neighbours were all peering out of their windows, wondering who the mad woman was. I pulled her inside. I felt sorry for her in a way. Wilf's dislike of her was fast turning into hatred. I made her tea, it must be an English thing – in times of trouble we always make tea. Wilf had told me all the problems she had caused for him. He was once engaged to a girl just after he left school. She lived away from Keighley so they were writing to each other. Wilf never got her letters, Alice burnt them. Needless to say, the relationship didn't last long. Wilf had been searching to find love for so long. When he was young he was a keen sportsman. His father never ever bothered to watch him play. His mother was never there for him. She tried to stop him wearing the latest gear. When he got his first drape suit she really blew a gasket. She complained about his hair. Everything about him was wrong. He started hanging around with lads older than him and was drinking in the pubs at fifteen. All the landlords knew him. He was well liked and often sang in the pubs at the weekend to earn extra money. When he married Pauline she let him down by seeing someone else. I can't comment on that because I don't know what he was up to at the time.

I tried to look beneath his hard exterior and find the man within. I thought that if I could get him away from that bloody town he would be able to be himself. Anyway, down to the matter in hand. I was stuck with Alice breathing fire in my kitchen. It really didn't faze me, I grew up with Dad and she wasn't a patch on him. I took my time and explained to her that Wilf did not want her interfering in his life. He was married with two boys and she should just let him get on with his life which was very hard at that time.

"I suppose I'm not going to be allowed to see my grandson either then?" she asked.

I just looked at her. "Why should I bother with you?" I asked her. "You have bad mouthed me all over Keighley. Now you sit in my kitchen asking to see my son. Wilf has two sons. If you can't even accept that you will get nowhere. I think you'd better leave."

She left slamming the door behind her. She told Manda and everyone else that would listen that I had banned her from seeing her son and grandson.

Due to my family circumstances I had to change my job many times. I worked in a toy shop, fish restaurant and then worked in Wilds Cafe and Bakery. Jill of many trades, that was me. I had to turn my hand to any work that would fit the hours I could work.

Someone said to me, "Your life is so hard, how do you manage?"

I laughed and said, "I just do." Had I known what was to happen next I would have been crying and pulling out my hair.

The first thing was Alice again. I had to tell her that Wilf had TB and that both her and her husband needed to be tested. Myself and the boys had been tested. I had an immunity to it which meant I must have been in contact with it when I was a child. Both boys had to have jabs. Anyway she went off on one again. She said that Wilf had been well fed as a child. No way did he have that and she told everyone he had septic arthritis. So when Scott started being ill and he was confirmed as having epilepsy she was enraged, saying it was something from my side of the family. I had given up trying to understand that woman. She would try the patience of a saint. Wilf and I agreed that she should never be left alone with Scott. My Dad was no better. He was convinced that Scott was going to grow out of it. Well, wherever you are Dad, Scott is now forty-four years old and, guess what, he still has epilepsy.

How much can one person cope with? That's a good question. How much more would life chuck at me before I faltered under the weight of it all? It was too much to bear.

I was now visiting two wards – Scott in one and Wilf in the other. Scott sucked his thumb in those days. When he had a fit he would bite nearly through to the bone. It was constantly wrapped up. At least that gave it a bit of protection. It was heart-breaking to watch the poor little soul. What had we done to deserve all this crap?

In the meantime Wilf had another operation, this time it was to remove infected bone from his hand and stiffen his wrist joint so his arm was in a plaster cast. He had bone removed from his foot as well. Metal clips were inserted to hold his foot together. The ulcer appeared to have dried up. His leg was also in a plaster cast. The good news was that they were going to let him come home soon. Scott was also home. I was over the moon. It had been a long time. I didn't know what I would have done without Mum. She had managed to redeem herself a little bit in my eyes.

Wilf was a sorry sight trying to manage on crutches with a steel corset and one arm and leg in plaster. I thought that surely to God we were due a bit of good luck. What a joke. The next disaster was that the bedroom ceiling collapsed on Wilf whilst he was taking his afternoon rest.

I went storming into Dace Son and Hartleys, the estate agents who rented these death traps out. The receptionist laughed. I guess she thought it amusing. She was not so amused when I told her that we would be suing her employers for damages and the injuries to my husband. She soon ushered me into the boss man's office. He was sitting behind his desk looking over his specs at me. I didn't give a shit, the stuck-up excuse for a man didn't faze me one bit. When I mentioned my solicitor's name he started blustering at me. I stood my ground. They said we could move into the bungalow on the next row that had just been renovated. I told him that he could provide the manpower to move us as my husband was now back in Airedale, my sons were with my mother and I was about to go insane. We just got nicely settled in the new place when we got a visit from the Benefits Office. A ponced up little prick who was at school with Wilf said, "We've stopped your husband's sickness benefit as it has been reported to us that he was seen reroofing a house in Silsden."

I don't know how I kept my temper but I did. I answered very quietly, "I think you have been misinformed. My husband is in Airedale. He has been there several months, has had major surgery three times and, as we speak, he is in the isolation unit with a serious infection in his foot which may result in amputation. I hardly think he would be fit to reroof a doll's house, do you?"

Some rotten bastard had reported him. So the vendetta went on. I felt like getting a twelve bore and blowing all their heads off. The post next morning brought a letter. Dear old Pauline wanted more money for her kid so they required Wilf in court the following week. Well that was tough, they would have to go to Airedale to hold their court! Anyway Wilf's solicitor attended on his behalf. The outcome was brilliant. Pauline had been a bit economical with the truth concerning her earnings and savings. She got nothing. The good thing was that a few weeks later Wilf got a letter stating that she did not want any more support for Annette. So there is a God after all.

Wilf was transported to a hospital in Liverpool to be seen by a consultant who had dealt with TB of the bone before. This was the first case they had seen for years. Uncle George came and picked me up on the Sunday and we went to give Wilf some moral support. Wilf stayed in Liverpool for three weeks and returned home with a plan of action. The TB was running riot in his body again. He needed another spinal operation. This one was too tricky for Mr Cape and so he was admitted to Chapel Allerton Hospital in Leeds. It was the old army hospital where I had visited Dad when I was a child.

I stood by the theatre doors looking through the porthole-like windows watching the white-gowned strangers operating on my husband's spine for hour after hour until I could watch no more. I went home exhausted and cried myself to sleep. I feared that Wilf wouldn't walk away this time.

On my way to Leeds my heart was racing. Wilf was now back on the ward. As I walked through the grounds to the visitors' entrance I wondered what I would do if he was not going to be able to walk again, he would not cope with that. I was pleasantly surprised to find Wilf upbeat and cheerful. The patients were all eating lunch. Wilf told me that the food on this ward was really good and they asked if you wanted seconds. That made a change as he usually asked me to bring in ham sandwiches, pork pies and goodies.

Most people on the ward had undergone brain surgery. A poor young lad just lay shouting. He wasn't expected to live. He had been knocked off his bike and dragged by a car which didn't stop. In fact they didn't find the driver. His parents were sitting at his bedside. It is hard to describe the look of sheer agony and sorrow that was etched on their faces. They must have known that if he lived he would be profoundly disabled. However, it was amazing to see the change when I visited a few days later. He was able to form words and was to have an operation to attach a metal cover to his skull where his brain had been exposed. Later, as I left the ward his mother asked how Wilf was doing. I told her 'better than I expected'. He had regained feeling in his feet, before he just had pins and needles sensations. We had been worried that he might not walk again. It would be a long haul but there was light at the end of the tunnel. The young lad's mother told me that her son would be moved to a special unit. He was expected to make a good recovery but his speech, understanding and mobility had been seriously compromised. He would have to try and learn all these things again and only time would tell how successful that would be. The next time I visited his bed was empty. He'd had a brain haemorrhage in the early hours of the morning. The staff couldn't save him. What a total shit life can be. It made me see how lucky I was.

In a special bed next to Wilf there was a university student who had been in a coma for years. His mother came every weekend to sit with him, talk and play music hoping to get some response. It was a long journey for her as she lived in Jersey. He was injured whilst on holiday. I've often wondered, over the years, what happened to him. Did he wake up or pass away? Imagine falling asleep at twenty, waking up years later and finding yourself older, not being able to remember your earlier life. That must be very strange. How would a person come to terms with that?

Wilf had to accept that he wouldn't be able to do a lot of the things he used to. He would be very limited in what sort of job he could get, no heavy lifting or anything like that.

The following day I got a phone call at work. Wilf's dad had left a message to say that he would meet me in the bus station. He was going to see his son – about time too. I thought that he better not give me a hard time. I was not taking any crap from him or Alice. I was doing my best to keep us afloat. I was working double shifts and trying to look after my family and home. I was nearly on my knees sometimes if I had a bad night with Scott. I had felt such a fool the previous week as I had fallen asleep in the hospital waiting area. I was taking Scott to see the epileptic specialist. Scott woke me up by saying, "Mummy the lady is saying my name." God knows that they thought of me. The hospital hadn't been able to get his fits under control. He was taking a lot of medication for such a little boy. It was in syrup form so was putting a lot of weight on him. I feared it would ruin his teeth.

When they were both back in Airedale Wilf's bed was

moved near the window so that he could see Scott playing outside. Scott spotted him one day and refused to go inside, even when it started pouring with rain. The only way the staff could get him indoors was to promise to take him to see his daddy. It was breaking all the rules and regulations but they did it. Paul was missing his dad too. Every time Wilf came home and then had to go back he cried for days. There was no pacifying him. I just wished for all this to be over. Of course, I knew there was no cure for Scott but I knew that if his fits could be brought under control it would give us a fighting chance. I wondered what would happen when he was old enough for school. If I had known how many social workers, local councils, education authorities, in fact half of the whole bloody system we would have to fight battles with regarding Scott I think I would have emigrated or become a recluse. The next few years were to prove an eye-opener!

However, the next step would be to get Wilf home. I felt as if there were half of me missing when he was away.

I met Wilf's father, Robert Burrows, in the bus station as planned. It was sort of like a day's outing with a company director. He talked a lot about his work, what books he liked to read and funny things he remembered about Wilf when he was a boy. He never mentioned Alice once, nor did I. He never enquired how his grandson was. It seemed that they weren't interested in Scott at all. I thought that perhaps it was because he was not perfect. Well, they needed to look at themselves. Scott was special. I always told him that. When he was very small and had his first seizure I was sure he was going to die. I had looked after people with epilepsy before but, when it's your own son, it seems so much worse.

The day passed reasonably well, apart from Bob (he said, 'call me 'Bob'). He was very put out that Wilf's consultant, who was already dressed in his theatre gear, could not spare a few minutes to talk about his son's condition. He told him, "I'm sure his wife will be able to fill you in on all the details."

It was obvious that Bob had expected to see him. I told him that I'd had an hour talking to him and his colleague after Wilf came out of theatre.

We had just been informed that the local buses had gone on strike so we went for a meal and then back for evening visiting which surprised Wilf who thought we had gone home. We had to walk back into Leeds to get a train home. This meant walking through the red light district, which was then the hunting ground of the Yorkshire Ripper. It was very late by the time I got home. I so wished I could take the next day off but I dragged myself to work as usual.

Serving in the coffee bar the next day I looked up and spotted Alice in the queue. I took an early tea-break and disappeared upstairs to devour my free cream cake (perk of the job – it didn't do much for the waistline though). It was good on Saturdays, you got to take home any bread, cakes or other perishables that would not last until the Monday. I filled Mum's freezer with bread and cakes – we never had to buy any.

I thought I had got away in time but the manageress called upstairs, "There's someone wants a word, Doreen." Not wanting to wash my dirty linen in public, I went downstairs to face 'the dragon'.

"I just thought I'd let you know I'm available to babysit my grandson and the other boy while you visit Bill," she said with a big smile on her face. She'd got that much slap on she looked like a clown. The bright red lipstick did nothing for her appearance.

"I've got it covered, thanks." As I walked away, I turned to say, "By the way, the other boy has a name, it's Paul. You would do well to remember that."

I thought what a bitch that woman was. I went over to Hilda, the manageress and whispered to her, "If she asks for me again, tell her I've died."

"You've got my sympathy. If she was my mother-in-law I think I'd get divorced," she laughingly replied.

I got good news when I got home. Wilf had phoned to say that his stitches were coming out on the Saturday and he could come home.

I had an idea to pass by him when I visited that night. It was Mum and Dad's idea really, but I thought it made sense. Wilf thought it was a good idea when I told him the details. There was a vacant flat on the second floor of Mum's block. Dad was confident he could get it for us due to our health issues. Mum and Dad had moved down to the ground floor as Mum was working as a part-time warden. There were several two-storey blocks with one bed flats for the elderly – she looked after those.

It was practical but most people wouldn't give up a two bed bungalow with garden to live in a multi-storey block of flats but there were very good reasons why we would do this. We had asked if we could fence our garden but the landlords refused, saying it had to stay open plan.

This meant that Scott had to be monitored every second he was outside. He had vacant spells connected with his epilepsy and this meant he could walk onto the road and get knocked down. We pleaded our case but the landlords wouldn't reconsider. The main reason we wanted to move though was the next-door neighbours' teenage son. His mother was a disabled person so you would have thought he would have had more consideration for others. This lad had a long-time grudge against Paul, who was several years younger than him. His mother knew this. We had thought it was best ignored unless it got out of hand. Well the previous week it had got out of hand big time. Paul had just gone out to meet his friend. Scott was playing in the sand-pit right outside the kitchen window. I was standing at the sink washing up and keeping an eye on him. Then the mindless cretin from next door grabbed Scott, shouting at him, asking where Paul had gone. At the same time he was stamping on Scott's feet. I flew down the back steps. He spotted me and took off down the road. I shouted, "Run you gutless bastard. Wilf will get you and knock your block off."

Scott was collapsed in the sand shaking and sobbing. It was a good job I needed to stay with Scott or I would have kept lookout and grabbed the little bastard when he returned home. I guessed he would cut across the gardens, not risking the road where he could be spotted. It gave my temper time to cool down. In the afternoon, when Mum called with some shopping (we were preparing for Wilf coming home, I didn't want to leave him while I went to Keighley shopping), I filled her in on what had happened earlier.

"Be careful our Doreen. If you slap her, she's the sort to report you."

Mum thought I should do nothing but I couldn't let this pass. I'd got to sort it. If Wilf got involved he was likely to give the neighbour's son a hiding.

I knew our neighbour was in. I could hear her music. I knocked and she peeped round the door. "He's not in," she said.

I shoved the door open and walked in. "You know what this is about. Because that cretin of yours is a teenager, I intend to involve the police. I will be charging him with assault on an infant." I didn't raise my voice once. "Scott has epilepsy. He could have had a fit and died. Your son is a coward. Just hope that Wilf doesn't get his hands on him. You will be getting a visit from the 'Old Bill'." I walked out. Her face was a picture. I didn't intend to take this further but she would lose sleep waiting for a knock on the door.

A few days later we got a letter offering us the second-floor flat. We accepted it. We were on the move again.

We did have a good laugh about the creep next door. Every time he saw Wilf he turned drip white and ran for cover. It was a long time before he felt safe again.

We soon settled into our new home and Scott loved it. He could play in the playground which was right next to Mum's kitchen window.

Alice started visiting Wilf. Sometimes she visited every day. I was not happy about it but I was at work when she was there. I decided that if she stepped on my toes she would be shown the door.

Dad rented a small allotment next to the flats. Wilf liked to spend time there so Dad suggested that he got a few chickens to keep us in eggs and give him an interest. The pyjama factory at Oakworth, where Maureen used to work, had become a hatchery. I gave them a ring to see if it was possible to buy a dozen chicks. They were really nice and, when I told them about Scott, they said he could have a dozen chicks free but I would have to collect them.

I took Scott to Oakworth to collect his chicks. It brought back a lot of memories seeing my old school and the park where I used to hide when I'd got fed-up with lessons. It seemed a lifetime ago. I took Scott into the park as it was a nice day. He was fascinated with the caves. After we collected our chicks I got him some sweets from the little shop, still there but owned by someone new.

Dad made a box to keep the chicks in and fixed up a lamp to keep them warm. Alice was very surprised to see that we kept chickens in our lounge. We managed to raise every one with no fatalities and very soon they were big enough to go to the allotment. Wilf had also adopted a goose. It flew in one day with an injured wing and decided to stay. Wilf was so pleased to present my mum with half a dozen of his free-range eggs. Dad had planted some vegetables but was annoyed when rabbits ate all his lettuces. He decided to set some snares to catch the 'nibblers'. A few days later Wilf and I were sitting having lunch in our kitchen. We could see the allotment from our window. There was a sudden high pitched screaming noise, it sounded as if Dad had something in his snare. I dashed over and found a young rabbit caught around its neck, the more it struggled the tighter the snare became. I hate to see any creature suffer so I tried to get my hand in to loosen the snare. I managed to do so but the terrified rabbit scratched my arm badly. When I got back to Wilf blood was dripping all over the floor. Wilf bathed my arm and put a dressing on. Later in the day Dad called in.

"I'm sure I caught something in my snares, but they were all empty. You been over there Doreen?" he asked.

"I've better things to do than sit in the allotment all day." I hid my injured arm behind me but I think he knew it was me. He never did manage to grow any lettuces but there were some fat and healthy bunnies running round the fields.

I changed my job again. I was working on a clothes stall in the new covered market and in the fish and chip shop on a Friday and Saturday night. Wilf and Paul used to wait up for me coming in as I would bring them a fish supper. One Saturday I served Kevin's wife. She had a new fella with her so I guessed Kevin's marriage was well and truly over. It was a shame, I always thought he would make a good dad.

Things were going so well for us. I just wished that Scott's health was better. The time for him to start school was fast approaching. A social worker had already been to see us. It was suggested that Scott could attend what was referred to as 'the backward school'. The majority of pupils there were Downs Syndrome although, it was true, some of them did suffer epileptic fits. We told her that was not suitable for Scott. He needed a school that specialised in epilepsy and he also had a mild learning disability. He was tried at a local school for sick children but as he was hyperactive as well the school couldn't cope with him. A school at Bradford that catered for kids who had physical disabilities couldn't cope either. It was then we found out that there were only three schools in the country that specialised in epilepsy, all of these were very expensive. The Education Authority did not like to send children to schools out of their area. They also didn't like to fork out any money. All of these schools were residential. The battle began to get Scott into a school that could cope and where his disability needs could be met. We also had to come to terms with sending our precious little boy away to school. Alice was ranting about it. Dad was none too pleased either. Poor Wilf ended up on the wrong side of the law. Our nice quiet life was about to explode again.

Wilf had got three quails. So he was producing hen eggs, quail eggs and, his goose who Dad swore was a gander, had just laid its first egg. Wilf proudly presented it to Dad, saying, "Here you are, Jock. My first goose egg. It's been laid by the gander. You can have it for your breakfast."

Mum could be heard tittering in the kitchen, "A gamekeeper who doesn't know the difference between a goose and a gander."

Another memory I have of our time in Leylands House is the day my dad was felled by a Christmas tree, which was past its best, the festive season being, by then, just a distant memory. I have to admit that it was my tree that did the damage. But when my dad staggered into my flat with a gash on his head looking dazed and confused, asking for some first aid, I didn't know at first what had happened. Earlier that day I had asked Wilf to take out the tree, which was by then just a pile of fallen pine needles. To avoid making more mess my husband, in his wisdom, decided to toss it out of the kitchen window. You have to remember we were several storeys up. Did he look first? No, of course not. It was Dad's ill fortune to be making his way to his allotment at the same time. I arrived home from shopping just before Dad's dramatic entry so had no knowledge of what Wilf had done.

Dad could have been awarded the coveted statuette for his performance. It went something like this, "Oh, our Doreen help me. I've nearly been killed by some bastard's flying Christmas tree. What pillock would throw a tree out of a window nearly killing innocent folk going about their business?"

At this moment Wilf, who was putting away the shopping, went into meltdown. It was like someone watching tennis – my head looking at Dad, then back to my stupid husband who, by this time, had tears running down his cheeks, trying to disguise his laughter as a choking fit. I couldn't decide which one to shoot first. I got Dad a cold compress for his head, which wasn't bleeding by that time, it looked worse than it was. This gave Wilf a chance to escape from the kitchen and he was fully composed again as he escorted Dad back downstairs. I ran down the steps to remove the flying tree and add it to the bonfire that was in Dad's allotment. I knew that by the time he decided to light it he'd have forgotten all about his encounter. I had a go at Wilf when he returned but every time I said 'tree' he dissolved into helpless laughter. In the end I just gave up.

The following year I bought an artificial tree. For months every time Dad made for his allotment he would look up as he passed the flats just to make sure nothing was going to descend on him.

Talking about flying objects takes me on to the next thing, which was so cruel. Some moron threw a cat from the top floor balcony and that also landed right next to Dad who was sweeping up outside. Still alive, the poor thing was screaming in agony. Dad quickly despatched it to the cattery in the sky. He could hear at least two people laughing on the balcony above. Well, he lost it big time, shouting up to them, threatening what he would do when he caught them. I don't know if he ever did but there were some pretty nervous kids, I bet.

CHAPTER 33: BIG CHANGES

There would be some big changes in our lives over the next few years. The first was that my GP had refused to renew my prescription for the pill. This was because I had been taking it for a few years, I was also a smoker, my blood pressure was elevated (I wonder why!) and they were concerned about the link between the pill and the increased risk of breast cancer. When I told Wilf his first words were, "Oh God, what do we do now?" I thought this was a typical bloke's response. One thing was sure, I did not want an addition to the family. I had more than enough on my plate thank you.

After the boys were in bed that night we discussed the options. Wilf was not too impressed with my suggestions. First one being, 'tie a knot in it' or abstention.

"You're not taking this seriously," he said.

I chucked the leaflets they had given me at him. After glancing through them he sat shaking his head. "I'm not going back to all that palaver." He looked really miserable.

"The only other option is for one of us to have the operation," I said.

We decided to sleep on it. The next thing I knew Wilf had been to the hospital and arranged to have 'the snip'.

"Don't you think you've had enough operations already?"
I asked.

He just smiled. "One more won't make much difference,"
he said. "I'm not taking the chance of you being poorly.
It's a much bigger op for a woman."

That was the sort of man I married. He made me so mad
sometimes but in things that really mattered he always
put me first. If I had needed proof of how much he loved
me it was always there. He'd always told me I was the
love of his life. My whole world centred around him. I
could never see a time when we weren't together. Oh,
we had rows, we shouted, I threw things but we loved
each other, that was all that mattered. I had secret hopes
that one day he would stop drinking. We didn't go out
much together then because the pubs held no interest for
me. In fact, I thought they were the most boring places.
Mum used to say that she wished she could blow them all
up. I was beginning to agree with her. I thought that time
would tell and maybe one day my secret hope would
come true. I never told Wilf about my secret – if you tell
someone it's no longer a secret.

Wilf was walking with a stick then. This was much easier
for him but his stick was to cause him a big problem. He
was returning home one Sunday after a night in the pub.
As he crossed the bridge at the bottom of the road to the
flats a guy jumped him. They ended up fighting in the
road. The police arrived and they were both arrested. I
knew nothing about this. All I knew was that Wilf was
very late. When it got to be 2.00 am I was seriously
worried. I decided I would give it another half an hour
and then I was going to wake Dad to see if he had seen
him. I stood looking out of my lounge window. It

appeared that the whole world was sleeping except me. Then I saw the lights of a car coming up the hill and thought, "Oh, it's only a police car," as they often drove past during the night. But this car stopped and out got my husband. I wondered what the hell he had been up to. I thought, "I will bloody kill him. The older he gets the stupider he becomes." I sat in my chair waiting and wondering what weird and wonderful excuse he would have thought up.

Well, he didn't have any excuse. He didn't know the bloke or why he jumped him. I sat in court and they both stood saying nothing, both ended up being fined. If Wilf knew why this had happened he never ever revealed it. I had warned him that if I ever found out he knew and had never told me he was in big trouble. The police had classed his stick as a weapon. How stupid. I give up on stupid men – they are too much hassle!

Wilf knew when I was annoyed, his life became very difficult but these things just kept happening to him. When he was on crutches he had a voluntary driver who took him to his hospital appointments. When he finally came home with his walking stick he told her that he would be able to manage on the bus. She grabbed him and kissed him before he could get out of her car. Unfortunately, I was on my way to the dustbins and saw the whole thing. I stood by the lift waiting for him. He came through the door laughing, unaware that I had seen what had happened. I smiled and said nothing. I waited to see if he would tell me. After tea we were sitting talking. Mr Cape was still not happy with the state of his foot, the ulcer kept opening up. It looked as though he might have to remove more bone – that would mean another operation. Would this ever end?

"Who was your driver today?" I asked.

"It's always the same woman," he said. "I told her I could manage on the bus now I have a stick."

"It's a good job you can. She was glued to your face when I saw her. You have dropped your standards Wilf, scraping the bottom of the barrel. The irresistible Wilf Burrows in a clinch with a fat old bird."

I laughed as I left the room. He'd made a big mistake. He should have told me. I went to bed and sat reading for a while, he didn't join me. "Oh well," I thought, it is his choice."

Things were very frosty between us for a while. I had said no more to him about it but something had changed. I felt I couldn't trust him anymore.

A few weeks later we took Scott to Airedale for his appointment. Who should be sitting there but 'Roly-Poly'! I took Scott to get a drink. When I returned Wilf was sitting talking to her. I heard him say, "That stunt you pulled has caused a lot of trouble between me and my wife."

That was it as far as I was concerned – just some fat bird who wanted to be kissed by a good-looking bloke, sad old cow. I think it taught Wilf a valuable lesson. If he had told me about it nothing more would have been said. I'm the first to admit I have an evil mouth if someone crosses me, a failing on my part. I think it just shows how insecure I really am. That's Dad's fault as well.

You may have wondered what was going on with Maureen? Well the truth was I had no idea. She and Billy turned up now and again, they had two daughters by this time. I didn't get involved. I had enough problems without worrying about other people's.

Paul was growing up fast. He seemed to be in great demand as far as Alice and Bob were concerned. He rode his bike to Cross Hills most Sundays. I think they saw in Paul what they had wanted in Wilf. I was annoyed about it all, well a bit miffed. After all, at one time they didn't want to know him. Of course Scott was not perfect and Alice wanted everything perfect. Well, I thought that she would just have to accept that Scott was a very poorly lad. He also had a learning disability. It didn't matter how much she pretended it was not true, it had to be faced. Wilf and I made a decision that would be a 'forever thing'. We decided that no matter what happened with Scott we would always care for him and that he would not be going into any type of residential care whilst we were alive. I enquired about a home tutor for Scott but that would have been a pointless effort, he was never well enough for anything like that.

It was about that time that Wilf formed his own opinion about social workers. He thought they were lower than a snake's belly. He didn't trust them. Later in my story Social Services decided to take on Wilf in a fight over what was best for Scott. The result will surprise you. However, a lot of water will flow under the bridge before then.

I went with a social worker and Scott to look around David Lewis School for Children with Epilepsy. It was very impressive and very big. I had to make a decision regarding Scott being placed there. Wilf was not well enough to come with us. Mr Cape was still sorting out the damage TB had done to his bones. His spine was pretty good by that time. However his foot and wrist had suffered damage which needed attention. So I had to make a decision. I said, "I'm happy for Scott to be placed at David Lewis, however, if my husband's not convinced when he is well enough to travel and take a look round, or if we find that Scott does not cope with being away from home, then we must think again."

I was assured that this would be the case. In hindsight I should have got it in writing, in triplicate!

Scott had no early schooling. He had been moved around all the local schools so his first impressions of school were not good. I was frightened that he might become institutionalised. To me, he was still my baby. He was very pleased to come home for school holidays. On one particular holiday the school forgot to send his medication home with him. We had a terrible job getting a doctor to sign a script for his meds. I was livid. Also he was becoming very obese. I thought that we needed to get him off syrup and onto tablets.

In the meantime I was working part-time as a warden for the local council. There was a plan forming in my head to get us out of Keighley and further south where there would be more scope for Scott to get the best care we could find.

However, Wilf had to cope with the loss of two very important people in his life before we waved goodbye to Yorkshire. The first was the lady he loved as a mother – his Aunt Manda. She had bowel cancer which spread through her body at an alarming rate. Wilf went to see her just before she died in the hospice. It was something he never forgot. She was a very special lady.

To catch up on Scott at David Lewis, it didn't work out. Scott became very withdrawn and his epilepsy got much worse. After the big summer holiday we refused to send him back. We knew we had a fight on our hands, trying to prove that his health was suffering. Social Services tried to prove it was the best place for him. It got to the point where they were threatening to take him into care. We didn't back down. Wilf more or less said, "Bring it on."

I never knew why they backed down. I told the social worker who first took me to see the school that she was a lying bitch. She never retaliated. Scott stayed home. He had become very unwell and his fits kept him housebound. He did try to attend a local school for sick children on the days he was well enough but these were few and far between.

After Manda died Wilf's gran who had lived with Manda for years moved in with Wilf's cousin, Maureen. It worked for a while but the lady was in her nineties. She was soon requiring care that Maureen couldn't cope with. Wilf asked me if she could come to us. I said that the decision was his. In the end the old lady went to stay with Alice at Cross Hills, there is no accounting for taste!

Scott was very poorly with his epilepsy and was rushed into St James Hospital at Leeds after a horrific week of non-stop fits. We spent the night there in the waiting room. It got so bad that the hospital had to sedate him to stop the fits. While we waited there we got a message to say that Wilf's gran had died in her sleep. We made a mad dash to Cross Hills and got there just before the undertaker. Wilf was in bits. He went into the bedroom and sat with her until the undertaker arrived to take her away. I think that was the only time in my life that I felt sorry for Alice. She cried like a baby. The truth was that Gran had never got over losing Manda. She went downhill very quickly. She'd been a formidable lady when she was younger and enjoyed watching Keighley play rugby. It had been her wish to have her ashes scattered on the playing field so that she could forever walk the touchline. Wilf carried out her wishes. He went alone. He didn't want anyone with him. It was a very special moment between him and his beloved gran, a final goodbye to his special lady.

I had been very busy behind the scenes scouring 'The Lady' magazine for any warden's jobs that came with accommodation. Wilf and I went down to Littlehampton for an interview but I didn't get the job. I kept on trying. Scott's health had improved after a change of medication. He was much happier at home and we hadn't been hassled by Social Services. His health had been too bad for much schooling anyway so the education people had kept quiet. I had told them that I hoped to be leaving Yorkshire in the near future. I thought that they would be glad to see us go. I did think that Wilf might be reluctant to leave but he seemed to be looking forward to a change of scenery. I was a bit worried that he might always want to return but thought we would just have to wait and see. I knew in my heart that I would never return to Keighley to live. I thought that Wilf and I would stand a much better chance of staying together if we were away from his past life. We had experienced some rocky patches over the last few years. He was still drinking too much for my liking and every now and again he would press the self-destruct button. Our's was never going to be a quiet life, we were too much alike, neither of us prepared to give any ground. Wilf still had a chip on his shoulder as big as Everest but I decided that if we could get away from the gossip, the trouble-makers and Alice we might just have a chance of a life together. When I decided to write my story I didn't want to document every time Wilf and I had a row. I wanted to tell my story, picking out what I thought were the important things, the milestones in our life together. We were both Scorpio's, so not an ideal match. When we were fighting our corner as a couple we were a force to be reckoned with but we could so easily sting each other to death.

Eventually Wilf was fit again and we had two camping holidays in the Yorkshire Dales before we left for good.

We were back-packing so Mr Cape had done his job well.

If he had seen what Wilf had carried in his rucksack I don't think he would have approved. I know that Paul remembers the camping. I didn't find it to be my perfect holiday. I don't think Scott remembered much about it, but Wilf and I laughed at the memories a lot.

Then I got a new title. I was a Deputy Warden, employed by Bradford Metropolitan Council. The only downside was that we had to move into Delph House. At the bottom of my hallway I had an intercom system that bleeped and buzzed most of the time and it made me start to wonder if this was the type of work I really wanted to do. I'd given it such a lot of thought. There was no proper schooling for Scott there and I didn't see any job prospects for Paul, I thought that the town was dying. I just wanted to make sure we got out before it was too late. I did my very best to learn all I could about being a warden. If I had known then how it could rule your life, I think I would have become a bloody road sweeper.

I filled in an application form for a deputy warden's position in Ipswich. I was 'gob-smacked' when I got an interview. Wilf and I stayed overnight. I think we must have picked the noisiest pub in the town. We didn't get much sleep. We were taken to see where we would live if I got the job, it was full-time deputising for the wardens at two sheltered units. One was just across the road from the three-bedroomed house where we would live. The house was OK but I was a bit concerned about the stairs. Scott could easily have had a nasty accident – he had never lived anywhere with stairs. I wondered if I could do the job if I got it. I felt confident that I could, if I struggled with anything, well, I was a good bluffer so thought I would survive. The second unit was across from a playing field, which was behind our house. I met both wardens. Yvonne was a divorcee with two children. The boy was about Paul's age. The girl was older and quite a madam.

It was obvious she was causing a few problems for her mother, who appeared quite pleasant and easy-going. I thought that I could get on OK with her. The other warden was an older woman who obviously thought that she did such a good job that she didn't need a deputy. She had a flat at the top of the two-storey building. She had made herself available to all her residents twenty-four/seven – more fool her. Yvonne's flat was separate and the residents were spread around in a semi-circle in several two-storey blocks. The job entailed visiting everyone at the block you were deputising for on a daily basis. On a good day, with no problems, I thought it would take a couple of hours. From 1.00 pm – 6.00 pm you were free to go about your business. However, if any problems occured and you were on site you had to attend. From 6.00 pm to 8.00 am you were on call for emergencies only. I did know from experience that some elderly people didn't know the difference between an emergency and something that could wait until morning. You had to make sure you didn't become a soft touch or you would be at their beck and call twenty-four hours a day. I wondered if I really wanted this kind of work. In all truth, I would rather have had an office job any day but you did what you had to do and it was the only way I could move to an area where the future prospects looked better for Scott and Paul. Wilf would need a job once he was fully recovered.

The interview went well. One woman on the panel came from Keighley but I wasn't sure that would count for anything. She sat chatting to Wilf about where she used to live and what school she had attended. Wilf could be very charming. I hoped that he would be able to charm her into giving me the job. The other two were men. They were more interested in what experience I'd had and my references. Well I did the best I could and hoped I was in with a chance.

We got back to Keighley, exhausted. My feet hurt like hell – we females must have been mad to totter about on three inch heels. I was half-way through a well-earned cup of tea when the phone rang. I couldn't believe it, they were offering me the job. I didn't know that Wilf had told them that I had been to two other units and was waiting for an offer, they wanted to get in first as apparently I was just what they required. I had a little laugh to myself – I wondered if they would still think that when I had been there for a while.

Well, I had finally done it. I was getting my family out of Keighley. I wondered how Wilf would cope. I had been moving around since I was a baby but, apart from holidays, Wilf had lived all his life in Keighley. He wouldn't admit it, but he loved to walk down town and have people calling out to him. He just loved to be recognised. It was a case of 'I'm Wilf Burrows, come worship at my altar'. I just hoped that he could cope and thought that it would be a big culture shock for him. Just this once he would have to play second fiddle to me. I hadn't worked full-time for ages. I just hoped it would work out for us. One thing was sure, there was no way I would ever return to Keighley. Hell would freeze over before that happened.

Alice was convinced that her son would never leave. I thought that she had a shock coming. That he had agreed to move I supposed proved how much he loved me. He was always right by my shoulder and worshipped his boys. He made a final effort with Bob, telephoning him at work and arranging a night out to have a goodbye drink. I asked if Alice was going too.

"You must be joking," he replied. "The sooner I put distance between me and her, the better."

There was just one last dig at Wilf. It came in the form of a young guy who called at our flat wanting to know why Wilf had been chasing his girlfriend. I shrugged my shoulders.

"News to me," I told him. "I don't know you or your girlfriend."

"We're getting married in a few weeks," he boasted.

"Congratulations. Hope all goes well for you," I said as I closed the door. Did I really want to know the truth? Well, we were leaving in a few days, it wasn't important enough to cause me any grief. I had heard it all before. I just thought, laughingly, "This is what happens when you marry a super star – yeah, right!"

Wilf had bumped into the chap as he was getting out of the lift. "What did he want?" he asked.

"Your autograph," I replied. "Just another of your devoted fans. He wanted to know why you'd been sleeping with his soon to be wife."

"Oh, is that all?" he laughed. We would be having a discussion but then was not the time.

On the day of departure Dad disappeared to the pub without a goodbye. Mum and Julia were there as we loaded a rented truck with all our worldly goods. The council would have paid for a removal firm but the problem was that we had to pay first and then claim it back. We were short on funds. Wilf had been off work for years by then. My part-time work was just enough to keep the kids in shoes and clothes. Well, I thought that everything was going to change. I would be working full-time and the wages were good. We would have free accommodation and our telephone and heating bills were all part of the package. It was the summer of 1981 and things were going to be so different from then on. Wilf and I had been married eleven years. The time had gone by without us noticing. That was 'one in the eye' for Alice and all her cronies!

Wilf said an emotional farewell to John Cape. That man

did so much for us. He even came to see Wilf at home one Sunday before he left for his holidays. Alice never appeared to bid us 'Bon Voyage'. I thought that she would be hiding around a corner somewhere observing us. I only found out recently that she watched us leave the Registrar's Office after our wedding, she hid in a shop doorway across the road. That woman missed so much of her son's life and her grandson's just by being a total arsehole. I thought that maybe she should have married my dad – they would have made a good pair of matching bookends.

Scott and I travelled to Ipswich in the back of the removal truck. Wilf had paid an Irish guy to drive us there and return the truck. Paul and Wilf were in comfort in the front. Stupid thing to do really. We could have been squashed if any of the furniture had shifted. I'm sure we must have broken the law. Scott slept all the way. I got the headache from hell. I'm sure it was caused by lack of oxygen. Paul and Wilf were supposed to swap with us halfway but neither of them could cope with the confined space.

We'd left a tearful Mum and Julia. Mum always said that Dad couldn't cope with goodbyes. That was a load of tosh. He just didn't give a shit. He didn't waste good drinking time on family matters, he never had. If you wanted to talk to him it had to be before or after opening hours. If it was before opening he'd be chomping at the bit, wanting to be away. If it was after closing he'd be too pissed to hold a conversation. I once stood in a pub watching him as it got near closing time. It really opened my eyes. I saw how addicted to alcohol he was. In the last half an hour he would chuck double whiskeys down his throat as fast as he could swallow. Mum ended up doing most of his caretaker's duties. He would be in the pub from late morning until closing at three o'clock. He would catch the bus up to the flats and stagger into his home and sleep it off and was then back out at seven o'clock until ten thirty. I thought that he would be sacked before long or retired early due to ill health. His mental state gave me the opinion that he was in the early stages of dementia. I wondered if maybe he drank to block out the horrible things he'd done during his lifetime. He was never the same after Maureen left. He didn't wreck the house anymore but Mum lived on her nerves, not knowing what he would do next. Julia hated him with a vengeance. I tried never to let my boys get too close to him. He hurt people and screwed up their lives.

During the long ride to Ipswich I reflected on Keighley. What did I hate the most about the time I'd spent there? What if I had never gone back? Well, I wouldn't have had Scott or met the love of my life. Paul would not have had a father who had been so very proud of everything he had achieved.

Wilf loved his sons so much. I believed that I was the only woman in his life that he had ever really loved. It was obvious when I met him that he didn't know the meaning of love. He thought females were a necessary evil, only good for one thing. He'd been so sure of his babe magnet image, it must have come as quite a shock when I responded to his attempts to charm me with indifference. I did turn him down several times and went on dates with other men. I must clarify, when I went out with guys it was just one date, no strings attached. They were lucky if they got a peck on the cheek at the end of the evening. My main reason for living at that time was my son, Paul. Nobody else counted. I found it very hard to split my love between Paul and Wilf. The big question for me was, 'did I believe all the gossip and tales about Wilf and other women'? The quick answer was, 'no, not really'. I had learned to believe only what I had seen or heard myself. Wilf was married to me. He knew what the consequences would be if I ever found him 'playing away from home'.

Deep down he was a very old-fashioned man. Yes, he liked to think he was attractive to the ladies but there was only one lady in his life. However, in the latter years I had to share him with two other important ladies who he loved very much.

CHAPTER 34: IPSWICH AND PEMBURY

Well, I hear you ask, what did you think of Ipswich? If you want the truth, not a lot. The years I spent in Ipswich contained very little that I wanted to remember.

Within a short time we found ourselves on a train to Addenbrooks Hospital with Scott. At his first appointment with his new neurologist it was noted that he was in early puberty, one of the main causes of this could be a brain tumour. I was in bits. Wilf was on auto-pilot. We left Paul in Yvonne's care. I must admit that Ipswich Council were very good. They paid me full wages whilst we were away. It was one of the worst weeks of our lives, waiting for brain scan results. The ward Scott was on was full of very young kids, many of them with their heads shaved, showing scars from brain surgery. I was on my knees praying. I did not know what we would do if we lost our special boy. The worst day was when a child on the ward died on the operating table. His parents were in a state of utter desolation. His body was laid in a side room off the ward. When his parents went to sit with him his mother lost all control. Her anguished sobs could be heard all over the ward. Scott was older than most of the others. He wanted to know why the lady was crying. He'd noticed that the little boy hadn't come back to his bed. He had taken in more of what was happening than we had realised. He asked his dad if the child was dead. Although we had played down the reason Scott was in hospital, he'd guessed it was serious. Wilf took him outside into the garden and explained as best as he could what was going on. It was Friday when we waited in the consultant's office to hear the results of Scott's scans and tests that had been carried out during the previous four days. We left Addenbrooks with our special little boy. He'd got the all clear. There was nothing growing in his brain that shouldn't be there. On the train home to Ipswich Wilf and I were worn out. Scott was full of beans. He was very hyperactive then and Wilf found it hard to manage him whilst I was working.

The following week he was in hospital due to non-stop fits. They were keeping him sedated as his hyperactivity was sparking off his epilepsy. Another big issue was that they hadn't enough staff to cope with him. When we arrived the following day they had moved him to a special unit attached to the hospital which dealt with severely handicapped kids and those with behavioural problems.

In the meantime Paul got into the better of the two schools in our area, which was a relief.

We launched an attack on the Education Department. I told them that they had a legal obligation to provide a suitable school for Scott. Within two weeks we had an appointment at St Elizabeth's School in Much Hadham in Cheshire. In between this time we had removed Scott from the unit after finding him limping badly. He said that a male staff member had stamped on his ankle. I had to peel Wilf off this guy as he intended to sort him out. The state of Scott's foot proved the point, someone had indeed stamped on him. We made a formal complaint. They then had the cheek to ring us to ask if we wanted a psychiatric nurse to travel with us to Scott's interview. Wilf informed them it was a young boy we were talking about, not a wild animal. We had looked after him with no help from anyone for the previous ten years so were quite capable of managing a school interview. Along with everything else, I was coping with working full-time. Looking back now, I don't know how I did it.

Scott loved the school. I'll admit I was very dubious when I learned that it was run by Catholic nuns. My fears were unfounded. They were marvellous. Scott flourished under their care. Attached to the school was a hospital for women with severe epilepsy. Unfortunately, Scott could only stay until he was twelve. Girls stayed on but boys had to move.

Scott had a liking for Elvis and rock n' roll and, along with Sister Veronica, who played guitar, gave a good rendition of 'This Old House' and 'Green Door' at the school concert – like father, like son. I wonder if Scott will ever find a lady to sing love songs to.

I also got promoted to Warden and moved to my own unit, Mallard Court, which housed twenty-four single bedsits for the elderly. We had a two bedroom flat in the middle of the block. The flat was nice but the kitchen was like a small cupboard. Did I enjoy my time in Ipswich? No, not really. I was not cut out to be a warden. You had no privacy, there was always someone knocking on the door or buzzing the intercom.

We had a big surprise when Alice and Bob came to stay for a few days in the summer. Wilf and his dad got on well but there was still the undercurrent between Wilf and Alice. Scott was away at school. Good job he was as Alice was most put out when she learned he was at a Catholic school run by nuns. Thankfully we got through the visit without Wilf strangling his mother. As Bob was there too, she was on her best behaviour.

It wasn't long after their visit that I answered the telephone in the early hours to a very distressed Alice. Bob had died in his sleep – a massive heart attack. He was only fifty-nine. Wilf and I had noticed the blueness around his mouth and fingernails when he was with us but Wilf only found out that he'd already had a small attack the previous year and was on heart pills when he went back to Keighley with Paul to help arrange the funeral. I followed two days later after returning Scott to school. We decided not to take Scott back to Keighley. He was enjoying his time at St Elizabeth's, he didn't need to attend a funeral. I just hoped that Wilf didn't murder Alice before I got there.

I visited my mum and Julia whilst we were there. I never saw Dad. He was in the boozer as usual. He had left a message for me to join him in the pub. Mum begged me to go. "He'll give me a hard time if you don't call and see him," she said.

"Sorry Mum. I remember the hard times he gave me and

Maureen when we were young. I have no desire to spend time in his company."

I left saying that I would ask Wilf to call and have a drink with him just to pacify her. I did ask Wilf but he refused as well.

After the funeral several of Alice's relatives asked where Scott was. Alice glared at me when I told them he was at boarding school. Uncle George took Wilf to one side and asked if it was possible for us to have Alice to live with us.

When Wilf told me I stood transfixed, waiting to hear what he'd said in reply. Of course, he'd told George 'no way'.

"Is George worried about your mother?" I asked Wilf.

He just shook his head. "Don't know. He didn't say anything about being worried."

"He probably doesn't want to be lumbered with her," I said.

She was still a young woman and she would just have to get on with it. She hadn't got Manda and Gran to visit any longer but she used to cause trouble when she went there. She used to steal groceries out of the pantry. It was around this time that Wilf told me that his mother had been in a mental health hospital many years before when Wilf was about eighteen. She'd had an affair with one of the butchers in Keighley. When Bob found out he left and went back to Earith where his family was. He came back after a few months but Alice cracked under the pressure of everyone knowing what she had done. Wilf said that Uncle George went to visit her and signed her out before she was really well. She'd been a bit weird ever since. Oh well then, I thought, it was only fair that Uncle George looked after her. Alice asked me if I would make sure that Wilf attended her funeral when her time came. I'm ashamed to admit what my reply was. I told her I couldn't promise anything. I knew one thing for sure, I wouldn't be attending any more funerals in Yorkshire. I thought that she would outlive us all. 'Only the good die young', that was another of Mum's pearls of wisdom.

Later that year I had to go on a course in Birmingham for a week. Yvonne was supposed to be going with me. Wilf was not too happy but it was part of the job. At the last minute Yvonne's son was rushed to hospital with a burst appendix so she had to cancel and I was told that someone else was going in her place. I didn't find out who it was until a couple of days before I was due to leave. Wilf was livid, it was a bloke from the Elderly Service Team. I knew him by sight and had met him briefly at a monthly team meeting. He was the local scout leader.

Wilf demanded that I refused to go but I couldn't. It was in my contract that I had to attend relevant training courses. Worse still, I would be away on Wilf's birthday. There was nothing I could do. I had to go. It was the longest week of my life. Did I learn anything? Well, yes I did. There were twenty-six wardens on that course and only two of us were still married. The rest were all divorced. I wondered if it was anything to do with the job!

I got a frosty reception when I returned. Although Paul was pleased to see me he sounded as if he hadn't enjoyed the week with his dad. Wilf had made himself a certificate and stuck it on the bedroom wall. I can't remember what was on it. I do know it wasn't very complimentary. It became very clear that he was jealous of me. Well, I thought, I would swap places any time – if he wanted that 'shit job' he could have it.

I had nearly failed on my first week in Ipswich. Remember the older warden who was so efficient she didn't need a deputy? On my first day at the unit deputising for her she was very reluctant to hand over her keys to me. I wondered what she'd got to hide. She also neglected to tell me that there was a resident with mental health issues. I found out later that she never visited this lady. I went in 'blind' and knocked on the lady's door to enquire if she was well. She answered the door with a pair of rubber pants on her head, her fingers done up with sticking plaster and a very large carving knife in her hand. She invited me in. I didn't feel I could refuse, this lady needed extra help.

She spent the next two hours telling me how she lost her only son when he was knocked off his bike and dragged behind a car for quite a distance resulting in serious head trauma. He was eight years old and died a few days later. She had spent her whole life grieving for him. Her husband had left her soon after the boy's death. I told her about the little boy on Scott's ward who had also died in similar circumstances. When I wrote my report I requested that this lady be visited daily. I also referred her to the Mental Health Team. I'm afraid that did not go down well with the warden. She felt that I had overstepped the mark. I just said that I was doing my job. She was scared of this lady and had not visited her for weeks. There was no food in the fridge and she had run out of her medication. The warden thought I would run a mile, she didn't know I'd been brought up with a father who was in 'la la land' most of the time. This lady was a pussycat compared to him. The warden left soon after this. I was offered her job but I declined and later moved to Mallard Court. The gossip was that she resigned before she was pushed and also that she'd had a drink problem. I couldn't comment on that, I didn't know her that well. Although after a few months on the job I could see why someone might be tempted to take refuge in a bottle. It was a demanding job with no privacy. Everyone knew all your business and what they didn't know they made up.

We had a new resident who was in her early sixties. Her husband had recently passed away. She was man-mad and tried to waylay the tradesmen who came in to do repairs. She trapped Wilf in the laundry room and terrified him by touching him in a very inappropriate manner. She was taken into the office where I gave her a 'dressing down'. Wilf avoided her like the plague. She was still a very attractive woman for her age. I was grateful that we had no male residents. Wilf hid if he saw her coming.

Wilf managed to get himself admitted to the chest hospital with a severe chest infection. Bad health seemed to follow him. It was now 1983 and after the holiday Scott was to move to Lingfield Hospital School in Surrey. It was time for us to be on the move again. We needed to move further south to be close to Scott. Paul didn't want to move and begged to stay in Ipswich with his mates. I told him that we moved as a family and that he would make new friends. I was not his favourite person at that time.

I got an interview with The Humanist Housing Association at a place called Pembury near Tunbridge Wells in Kent. I got the job and this time we moved in style. The removal firm did all the packing and we travelled down on the train. Had I known what the Humanists believed I would never have taken the job. They don't believe in God and leave their bodies to science. They avoid paying funeral costs this way. I was sick to my stomach when I found out. We had a ground-floor three bedroom flat with a massive lounge with French doors that opened onto the garden, a kitchen the size of a cupboard and a bathroom not much bigger. But we thought it would have to do for the time being as it was near enough for Scott to come home for weekends.

Paul got himself a job at Curry's delivering appliances. I don't think it did his back any favours. Scott settled into Lingfield very well. Paul was soon to move to Turners Food Manufacturers working in the lab. Wilf also got a job there cleaning the machines. It was shift work but things were looking up. Wilf moved from Turners to work in the kitchens at Pembury Hospital. He was still drinking like a fish. We didn't go out much together. When he was the worse for wear he became very loud. I just couldn't do with it. I thought what a waste it was of a good man, he was doing himself no favours.

Paul found himself a girlfriend. Unfortunately she was from 'Gutterville'. You know what they say, 'you can take the girl out of the gutter but you can't take the gutter out of the girl'. I thought there was no way she was getting my son. I wanted better for him than that. I tried everything to get through to him but, as his dad said, 'at that age their brains are in their trousers'. I allowed her in the flat and tried to make her welcome but it went against the grain.

She was a total slapper. I don't think she'd ever had a job. She was just looking for a meal ticket. In the end I banned her from the building. It made no difference. When it was Paul's birthday we all showed our displeasure by giving him very paltry money gifts. She bought him nothing.

Alice descended on us for a week's holiday and stayed for eight weeks. I wondered if she was ever going to go home. I crossed swords with her many times during her stay. I was at my wits' end. I had no deputy and hadn't had a day off for months. When I eventually got a deputy it was a bloke. That was a big mistake. The ladies in the building would not accept a man. He moved in with his wife who worked in the city. After two weeks I was roused from my bed in the early hours by my deputy's wife who was as pissed as a newt. She couldn't get into the building. I got her husband out of bed and told him to quieten her down. She had woken most of the building and I knew that the complaints would be flooding in by the next day. What a situation. He was sacked a week later and I had no deputy again. I employed one of my cleaners to stand in for me twice a week but even if she was on duty the residents would still come knocking on my door. The ladies there were the worst I have ever worked with. They would call you out in the night for the most stupid things. One wanted her laundry sorting out for the morning, another couldn't get the cork out of her bottle of wine. One day when the deputy was on duty she came running for me as one of the ladies was very unwell. She died in my arms soon after with a massive heart attack.

The strain of working without a break was taking its toll. One night I was called out to the private part of the complex. The people in those flats owned their properties and most of them were just snobs. I found this lady, who was a retired nursing sister, sitting in a bath full of water in all her clothes, holding an electric fire. I stopped at the bathroom door. I knew that if she dropped it she was a 'gonner'. I got a chair and sat by the bath, trying to talk her down, while Wilf called the duty social worker, the police, ambulance and the doctor – it was a farce. I needed two doctors and a social worker to section her under the Mental Health Act. The social worker who arrived was useless. It ended up with me telling him to 'get some balls'. The lady refused to get in the ambulance so we had to get the police to put her in the vehicle by force. It was a shame, when she was well she was a lovely person but that night she was like a 'fishwife', swearing and shouting at everyone and threatening me with the sack. It was daybreak before they took her away. I was exhausted and still had a full day's work ahead. Something had to be done or I would be off sick with exhaustion.

Then I did something I never thought possible. After trying to reason with Paul and getting nowhere, I threw him out. Wilf thought I had made a big mistake. He said Paul would probably move in with 'her'. I thought, well, what would be would be, my little boy had grown up. We had faced the world together when he was a baby. Now I wasn't the most important lady in his life. I prayed to God he would come to his senses before it was too late. I moved his picture and put it away as I got so upset about it all. I began to feel very unwell at times and wondered how much longer I could carry on without a break.

I was pleased to hear that Paul had moved in with a friend from work, sharing his flat. He came round to see us and things slowly returned to normal, whatever normal was. I didn't know it then, but Paul was never to live at home again. My boy had flown the nest for good.

Wilf changed his job again. He started work in a care home in Tunbridge Wells. He'd wanted to get into care work for quite some time. I'm not sure, with his temperament and liking for the ladies, if this mainly female workplace was right for him. I thought it would be like turning a child loose in a sweet shop. At that time we were at loggerheads most of the time. I was seriously thinking of calling it a day. Paul was making his own way in the world and Scott was happy at school. He was growing up fast. I had done what I intended – got my family away from Keighley. Scott was now attending the best school for epilepsy in the country. Wilf and I seemed to grow further apart every day and I thought my marriage was in serious trouble.

When I called at Wilf's workplace to pick him up, as Paul was taking us to Lingfield to bring Scott home for the weekend, I stood talking to the matron for a while and then wandered through to the staffroom. Wilf was sitting with a young girl having coffee. They say wives are the last people to know if their husbands are having an affair. All I know is that when I saw these two sitting 'close and personal' alarm bells went off in my head. Wilf jumped up looking very guilty.

"I hope I'm not interrupting anything," I growled, "but we are going to pick Scott up, that is unless you have more pressing things to attend to." My voice was full of sarcasm.

It appeared it was not only teenage boys whose 'brains were in their trousers'. Silly old fools who ought to know better can't resist trying to pull a young bird either. If there was anything going on with these two Wilf would be left high and dry this time. I wasn't listening to any excuses. I decided to just sit quietly and see what developed. He seemed to forget I could read him like a book. After all, I'd had plenty of practice. I thought he would do well to remember that we were supposed to be a team.

I waited until Scott was back at school before I asked Wilf about his lady friend. He said she was asking his advice. She was going out with a married man. Now, why didn't that surprise me? Wilf thought she had a bit of a crush on him. All the staff went for a drink after work and this 'bint' leaned forward and kissed him in front of everyone. What did the prat I'm married to do in return? He kissed her back. When I asked him why he said it just happened, it was stupid. I would say it was stupid! I thought that if this little minx wanted to play with the big girls she was going to find herself well out of her depth. I was not sure why Wilf told me. He didn't have to. I would never have found out. I thought I must be a fool to believe a word this aging Romeo said. I remembered what mum had told me, "You need to get him out of Keighley or change him." Well I got him out of Keighley but I was never going to change him. He knew he was in a hole and needed a hand to get out. I thought that I was totally pissed off with being treated like a fool, he had better be careful, payback time was not far away.

Things were very quiet for a while and then I started getting phone calls. When I answered the caller would hang up. Then a note was pushed through the letter-box addressed to Wilf. Before you ask, yes, I opened it. Guess who it was from – his little workmate. She wanted to meet him. Could he give her a call? He was in the local pub. I walked in. When he saw my face he knew something was wrong. I was fuming. I'd enough on my plate at that time with work and didn't need a stupid little girl to sort out as well. I was standing next to Wilf when he phoned her and said that he would meet her in Tunbridge Wells after work. I arranged with Paul to take his dad to meet her and bring her back to the flat. Wilf seemed relieved that I was taking this over. At first he had found the attention very flattering, a boost to his ego, but now it was getting out of hand and becoming embarrassing. When they returned the girl looked like a Christian about to enter the arena to be eaten by the lions. I gave her a hard time. She insisted the phone calls weren't down to her. She was lying. I asked her why she was sending notes to my husband when he was off-duty. She couldn't answer that either. I told her in plain English that if she didn't stop making a nuisance of herself I would talk to the matron about her behaviour and then give her a slap. She said she had a boyfriend. I asked if he was someone's husband as well? She admitted that he was and said that he was leaving his wife and young child to be with her. I told her not to grow old waiting, they never leave their wives. I advised her to get herself a single bloke, get married and have a family and told her that then I hoped some stupid young bitch would make a play for her husband and then she would know what it felt like. After she'd gone I told Wilf to get another job or get out. I was not too fussed either way. He knew he was in the doghouse. He'd got some serious grovelling to do. I thought he'd overstepped the mark this time, something just died in my heart.

There was some renovation going on at the private block. We had some big muscley 'Chippendale' look-a-likes erecting scaffolding. I took them cold drinks as it was a scorching hot day. I had to ask them to curb their swearing as some of the old dears were very offended by their colourful language. When I went to collect the empties I stood chatting to one of them. He was telling me about his new baby. After a couple of minutes Wilf shouted to me from the door, "Telephone." You could say he was slightly miffed at me but that would be an understatement. He was very annoyed. I didn't give a shit. I thought that if it was good enough for him it was good enough for me. There was nobody on the phone. He just didn't like me talking to other men – tough, I thought that he could have a bit of what I'd been putting up with for years. I was thirty-eight by then and he was forty-three. You would have thought we were a couple of kids trying to get the better of each other.

"What were you talking to Mr Universe about?" he asked.

"Oh, they are all going for a drink when they finish here. He asked me to join them."

I could see the steam coming out of his ears. I grabbed him before he got out of the door. Mr Universe looked as if he could handle himself but I didn't want him to knock my hot-headed fella on his arse.

"I'll be keeping my eye on you, sweetheart," he said.

I walked into my office chuckling quietly to myself. I thought that he might think twice about flirting in the future.

When the next work outing to the pub came around he asked me to join him there. He was standing at the bar when I walked in.

"Why aren't you sitting with the others?" I asked.

"I didn't want you getting any wrong ideas," he replied.

I had warned him of the pitfalls of working in a mostly female workplace. I thought that he needed to be a bit nasty as far as women were concerned. I advised him to just say, "Piss off."

The following week he arrived home with a woman who had invited me to come round to theirs (where her husband was babysitting) for a drink. I was at a loss, what was this shithead up to now? Perhaps his brain was pickled as well. (He'd started drinking a lot of Bacardi and coke instead of pints.) Intrigued, I decided to play along and followed her back to her house across the road. I realised, quite quickly, that we were being set up, these two were used to swopping partners. I just looked at Wilf. He seemed oblivious to what was going on. I had to believe that he didn't pick up the same vibes as me. I was sober, he was three sheets to the wind. If I hadn't believed that, our relationship would have been over. I turned on my heel and left. Wilf was close behind me. I said nothing that night. In fact, I didn't speak to him for days. Every time I looked at him I felt sick. When we did speak he had the nerve to tell me I had got it wrong.

"I'm a man of the world," he said. "I would have known what she was planning."

I replied, "You were pissed and you put me in danger. Every day I'm beginning to like you less. I said like, I don't even think I love you anymore."

More trouble was brewing. The following week I got a phone call from Maureen to say that both Mum and Dad were in hospital. Mum had been admitted with severe depression, Dad because his health was suffering due to the endless boozing and fags. He couldn't manage to look after himself with Mum laid up. Julia wouldn't look after him. Well I didn't blame her for that. I had often said that I wouldn't piss on him if he was on fire. Sounds hard, I know, but Maureen and I went through hell with him. Maureen said she felt really sorry for him. I thought, "More fool her."

When Wilf heard I was going to Keighley for a few days he decided to join me. The Humanist Housing had to ask a previous deputy, now well over eighty years old, to stand in for me.

When we visited Mum she seemed OK but was smoking non-stop and for someone who suffered from bronchitis every winter that was not recommended. I guess years of putting up with Dad had just caught up with her.

When I went downstairs to visit Dad I walked up the ward twice before I recognised the old chap hunched over in a chair. He was wearing an old nightshirt obviously on loan from hospital supplies. I sent Wilf back into Keighley to buy him some new pyjamas. Dad looked as if he hadn't had a shave for a month. When Wilf returned he shaved and showered him, much against hospital procedure, but, as I explained to the ward sister, my father had been neglected on her ward. Over the next couple of days I noted that he was in his own nightclothes and clean shaven. When we left to return to Kent we promised to come back and visit. I didn't know then but that was to be the last time I saw either of them.

Mum was discharged home but had a brain bleed a few days later and had to be resuscitated by the paramedics and was readmitted in a coma to the Intensive Care Unit.

I knew nothing about this until a friend rang me. Mum remained in a coma for a week and then passed away with Julia, Maureen and Dad by her bedside. I didn't go back for the funeral. Mum was gone. There was nothing I could do for her anymore. Julia disappeared off my radar.

She did tell Maureen to let her know when Dad died, that was if she could find her, as she wanted to 'dance on his grave'. Dad struggled on for another year with Maureen and Billy doing everything they could for him. He then had a stroke in hospital followed by a massive heart attack. He was sixty-five years old. Mum had been sixty-three — not a long life but a hard one. I did not go to either funerals. On Dad's flowers I wrote, 'Remembering a Scottish soldier who lost his way'. Mum's flowers read, 'Until we meet again'. Dad died with just a priest at his bedside. I always predicted he would die a lonely old man who nobody wanted. Maureen and Billy were to regret having him for Christmas. He kept them awake all night calling out for Maureen and used their front garden as a urinal, his brain destroyed by alcohol abuse or the nasty secrets that he took to the grave. Many years later when Maureen spoke out the 'shit really hit the fan'.

So I was an orphan then but, to be truthful, I had disowned my parents when I was five years old so I thought that I'd been an orphan all my life. My memories of Mum were to be tarnished by what was revealed, not because of what she had done but because of what she failed to do.

Wilf got a new job working for the Leonard Cheshire Foundation, but he was to lose it when my health broke down and I resigned as a warden. But before that I must bring you up-to-date with what happened next.

CHAPTER 35: REBECCA

When this young lady entered our lives I remember thinking, "Oh, that's a biblical name." Was this young lady indeed an angel? Becky became a very important member of our family. She supported me through the most terrible time of my life. Without her I would have crumbled. When I stumbled she helped me up and I carried on. When Paul met Becky I was in the 'nobody is good enough for my son' phase of my life. I'm sure a lot of mums can relate to that. Wilf gave her a hard time too with his wicked sense of humour. He got a shock. She gave as good as she got and he respected her for that, they made an amazing team. Becky helped me a lot by doing some hours to let me have a break.

Wilf started having a lot of pain in his foot. I prayed that the TB bone hadn't come back. He went to Pembury Hospital for an X-ray and they found one of the screws that Mr Cape had used to hold his foot together had broken loose. It was causing swelling and pain. As the bone grafting had become solid by that time the screw had to come out. Wilf was devastated. He hated hospitals. He'd vowed never to go into hospital again. I'm afraid that over the next few years he would be hospitalised many times. He went into Pembury to have this screw removed. He should have stayed several days but hatched a plan with Becky helping him. She had worked at the local newspaper office but, after her spell as a relief warden, she decided to try care work and got a job in a care home in Tunbridge Wells. She was in uniform when we all went to the hospital to visit. I didn't know that Wilf had convinced the ward staff that he was fit to go home. Becky nicked a wheelchair from somewhere. Wilf was in it double quick. He'd forced his foot into his slipper and off we all went with Becky doing her Florence Nightingale bit.

Wilf regretted coming home too soon. When Becky took his slipper off it was full of blood. I had warned him. If he had stayed in hospital they would have been able to control his pain. I had nothing in the house strong enough to even take the edge off it. I wanted to get the doctor in to give him some morphine but Wilf wouldn't let me. He struggled through the night. As he had to go back to the hospital to have it checked the following day they gave him some Oramorph which really zonked him out. As per usual he got over it and went back to work. He hadn't been back very long when I collapsed in the office one morning whilst taking rent payments. When I came to I refused to go to A&E and just got myself to bed. By the time Wilf came home I was much worse and running a high temperature. He called the doctor. I had glandular fever. I'd have thought I was too old to get that but it made me very poorly. Wilf rang Head Office and told my boss I was off sick. He also told them that it was due to the pressure they had put me under – no time off and my workload. They told him to employ some temporary workers to cover my hours. I was never to return to work as a warden again. My mental health deteriorated and I was on 'get happy quick pills'. I still can't remember those six months of my life. Something took over. I tendered my resignation. I was sent a letter asking me to quit the premises. We contacted the council who told me to stay put until they found us a house. The Humanist Housing Association made it very uncomfortable for us to stay put. However Tunbridge Wells Council came down on them like a ton of bricks, they were breaking the law by turning the phone off and other things so they pulled in their horns and left us in peace. After about six weeks we were given the keys to a bungalow in Cranbrook. We took it but Wilf was unable to get to work from there as the bus service was crap. Even our move didn't go smoothly. It was now 1987. On the Thursday, as we were due to move on the Saturday, there was the famous hurricane. A tree came right through our bedroom window. Due to my medication, I never heard a thing. Next morning I couldn't understand why the electricity was off until I looked outside. The road was blocked with fallen trees. Paul, now working at BT, was on the road non-stop night and day trying to restore the telephone network. He called in to check on us. Poor lad, he looked worn out but he brought a big flask of tea from Becky's mum as they had a gas cooker and could boil water. I had never tasted anything so good. I hadn't had a cup of tea for days, I swear I was having withdrawal symptoms.

Before we left Wilf bought me a Yorkie puppy. She was so tiny. No, I didn't call her Trixie. I called her Twinkle or Twinkie for short. She was the first in a long line of Yorkshire Terriers, I loved the breed. Cranbrook was a small town really, bigger than a village but not big enough to be a town. It also had a lot of small-minded people living there. I was used to that sort of thing due to the time I had spent in Lumsden. I warned Wilf of all the pitfalls. Did he take any notice? No, of course he didn't!

The first time we went out the pub barman told Wilf he

didn't serve Yorkshire men as his wife had run off with one. I thought, "Oh boy, here we go again."

Wilf got a job in an old people's home, Hartley House. He soon gained a reputation as an excellent care assistant and got to NVQ3 level very quickly. Then he made a sideways move and went to work at Hillside. This was a home for young adults with learning disabilities. He was a glutton for punishment.

Scott was to leave Lingfield soon and would be coming home for good. He was so pleased about it – no more boarding school – so Wilf would have it at home and at work. He proved himself again, taking the drug training and all the other courses. He already had a good knowledge of epilepsy, having dealt with Scott since he was born. He went on nights and became Senior Night Care Manager. I went to work in the community for Social Services. Things were looking up again. There was also the very good news that Paul and Becky were getting married. Wilf was concerned that he was too young, but Paul had made his mind up. Scott had returned home to live and was attending a centre for adults with learning disabilities in Tunbridge Wells.

Paul and Becky married on 17th September 1988. Paul was twenty-two. Becky was a lovely girl. She was very caring and always took the time to listen to Scott. Becky's parents were good with him too. They always sent him his own Christmas card instead of including him on ours. He loved this as he never got much post.

It was a beautiful wedding. Becky looked so lovely and very slim in her dress. Scott ended up getting drunk by accident. He kept getting glasses of what he thought was orange juice but it was Bucks Fizz. Wilf looked over to him and saw him slip under the table. It was quite funny but Scott wasn't allowed any alcohol, not with his medication. Wilf had to take him outside in the fresh air to try to sober him up. All in all, though, it was a great day. I had a good feeling about Paul and Becky. They were going to be OK – perfect for each other.

Wilf was settled in his job. The only fly in the ointment was Wilf's drinking. He had tried many times to quit but his heart wasn't in it. He had to want to stop for himself, that was the only way it would work. He started having a few problems with his deputy manager. She was divorced and man hungry. She went out of her way to get him on his own and offered sexy invitations about going out for a drink then back to her place. I told him that a man of his age should be able to put one stupid old slag in her place. Everything came to a head when she cornered him in the kitchen, standing behind him and rubbing herself up and down against him. He pushed her out of the way and went into the office to do his report before he went off duty.

I could see that he was in a mood when he came home. However, the situation sorted itself out when he was off work with 'flu. I went in to collect his wages. I didn't know this sex starved slapper but, when I saw the painted nails and the cleavage on display, I guessed it was her. I knocked on the office door and went in. She was making such a big thing about how good Wilf was at his job and how he was a much valued member of staff. I commented that I thought he would be moving on soon as he was not happy in the workplace. When she asked what was wrong

I acted dumb and said, "Oh, some sex starved older woman has been sexually harassing him, making him feel uncomfortable."

I looked straight at her and continued by quoting Wilf. "Why would he want a cheap burger when he's got fillet steak at home?"

She coloured up. I thanked her for his wages and left. Guess she got the message. She steered clear of him from then on.

We had no more trouble from her. When Wilf got to work a few nights later he spotted one of the female residents running down the road into the village totally naked. He had to run after her and escort her back to the building. He took off his jacket and put it around her shoulders but it didn't cover her bare bottom. The local bus passed them and Wilf was the talk of the village, seen with a naked woman in broad daylight. It is a good job I had a sense of humour or I would have killed him. For all of his blustering and his 'man of the world' act anything like that embarrassed him. He was always moaning and groaning about work but he really loved that job. He was very well thought of by the management.

Our life became a bit more peaceful and settled. In June 1992 Paul and Becky presented us with our first grandchild – a boy they named Pip. I loved this little person from day one. He was a treasure. As he started to toddle about and speak a few words he just captured Wilf's heart. He made a complete fool of his grandad one day on the playing field by convincing Wilf that he knew all the different names given to the ways you could throw a Frisbee. Wilf was most put out when Paul and Becky told him that Pip had got one over on him.

Pip was a very pretty baby – too pretty to be a boy really.

He was to grow into an amazing adult, a really well balanced, well-grounded young man destined to go into the world and strive to reach his goal in life. But, let us give him time to enjoy his childhood first. He was joined in April 1994 by our grand-daughter who was a young madam with attitude. She became her grandad's princess instantly. I thought that I would pity any boyfriends in the future. I think Wilf had her matched up to marry Prince William in Lincoln Cathedral. William spoilt his plans by marrying Catherine.

Poor Beth was a bit of a winger as a baby. Wilf told Paul and Becky, "Take this child home and don't bring her back until she's eighteen." But she grew into a beautiful, caring, but sometimes dippy adult. As soon as Beth got to the toddler stage she would make for Uncle Scott's bedroom. They spent hours in there, colouring and watching DVDS.

Scott would read her stories. We all thought that she would lose interest when she became a teenager but she never did. Both my grandchildren have respect for people with disabilities. I remember Paul telling one of his friends, "If Scott's disability upsets you, don't bother coming round anymore."

In 1998 Paul moved to Switzerland with his family. We all missed them very much. They surprised us one Boxing Day when they turned up to visit without letting us know. It made our Christmas very special.

It was 2000 and that year proved something I had told

Wilf many years ago which he didn't believe to be true.

We began to get phone calls from Alice which were very strange. She had visited Paul and Becky before they went abroad but she only visited our bungalow once during her stay. She had only been with us a couple of minutes when Wilf ordered her out. She hadn't changed one bit. She'd brought him news regarding Annette – a subject Wilf hadn't mentioned for years. Why did she do that? It only made him detest her more. Anyway, I got a couple of calls from the warden at the flats where she was then living.

She expressed concerns about her mental health and the possibility that she could be in the early stages of dementia. She also asked if Wilf would be able to visit. I told her, 'no' on the visit as it was very unlikely that Alice would open the door to him. It got to the point where she wouldn't open the door to anyone. They had to force an entry, saying that they could smell gas. I had to give permission for her gas to be turned off for safety. She lived in a block of four flats and could have blown everyone up. Staff were also told not to buy any more cigarettes for her in case she set the place on fire. I contacted her GP with a view to getting her moved for her own safety. She had no means to cook food and no heating but the GP refused to help. Things came to a head that night when Alice was found wandering in the early hours in only her nightdress in the pouring rain in very cold weather. She was admitted to hospital with a chest infection and hypothermia. She died a few days later from pneumonia. Wilf's cousin, Maureen, was with her when she died. She had been rambling in her mind since she was admitted, believing herself to be a child again. Three strange things came to light when Uncle

George entered her flat to empty the property. Wilf had refused to go back to Keighley so asked George to get it cleared. They found she had no clothes at all in the flat. There were about thirty packets of cigarettes, all opened with one or two cigarettes taken out. There was no edible food in the fridge, everything was rotten and mouldy. All the photographs in the house had my head cut off. I'd told Wilf years ago that she was a 'looney tune', a 'bunny boiler'. Wilf refused to go to the funeral. I'd never had any intention of going. Paul and Becky, who had been home, visiting, were flying out to Zimbabwe with the children to visit members of Becky's family. So Alice had no immediate family members to see her off on her final journey. Did I feel sorry for her? The answer was 'No – she brought it on herself, her chickens had come home to roost'. She had just about enough insurance to pay for her funeral, only a few pounds in her bank account even though she had sold her own house before she moved into the sheltered flat. Where had all those thousands gone? Who knows? All I know is her only son didn't get any of it. She gave Paul and Scott a few pounds when she visited us. The only people who know where her money went are the ones who spent it. The reason she had no clothes in her flat was because she had become incontinent. Her rubbish bin was found to contain some very smelly soiled clothes. I hear you asking, 'how could this happen?" In the later years I tried to encourage Wilf to be more tolerant towards his mother but she knew the buttons to press and kept on doing just that. There was no love lost between me and Alice. I cut her a bit of slack due to her strange ideas and actions but it became very clear to me that her mental health had needed attention for quite a long time, but everyone just humoured her. She had been that way for years. Bob was the person who should have addressed this issue a long time ago but it suited him to ignore it and get on with his life – the stone just kept rolling until it reached its destination. Did I feel I could have done more to help her? The answer was 'yes'. However, she became an interfering old witch and caused trouble wherever she went. She must have known that people detested what she did. Over time everyone went out of their way to avoid her. When Manda died she lost her only friend. Years later, when Wilf and I were looking through old photo albums, we both said what an attractive woman she had been. She'd worked as manageress at the Co-op dry cleaners in Keighley. Her clothes were always smart and fashionable. Even in later years she still wore her heels but her make-up was like a circus clown. She used bright red lipstick and plastered it on. Her hatred of me was understandable. I had taken her only son, the person she'd treasured most. I would have gladly shared him with her had she acted like a human being, not a despot. Well, Alice was no more and we moved on with our lives. Every year we got a Christmas card from Uncle George with cash in it for Scott. Then, suddenly, they stopped. He had joined Alice in wherever you go when you die.

Paul and Becky returned from Switzerland in 2000 but decided to sell their house which they had been renting out. They moved to Colne near Ramsey. I don't know if Paul realised that he was just a few miles from where he was born, chances were that his biological father still lived in the area. He had been Paul Burrows since he was a toddler. He had no intention of trying to track down a man he never knew. Wilf was frightened that he would. I spoke to Paul. He hadn't even given that a thought. Wilf had always been his daddy, ever since he first sat him on his shoulders all those years ago. Paul was moving up the ranks in BT and completed an Open University degree course. Wilf boasted to me, "There you are. I told you he had a brain. He takes after me." We were so proud of what he had achieved. He had done his studying at the most difficult time when his children were small. Becky had supported him in everything that he did.

Pip wanted a Yorkie so, with Paul's permission, we bought him one for his birthday. He named him Leo.

In Cranbrook we had three dogs, two Persian cats and Tigger, she was a feral who we had adopted. Wilf's opinion was that it was like living in a menagerie with 'Dr bloody Dolittle'. We lived in Kent for twenty-three years. The biggest mistake we ever made. We should have moved back to the north when Scott finished school. The trap we fell into was that we both had reasonable jobs and were earning good money. Wilf was never truly happy in Cranbrook. The last time we were in Yorkshire was just before my mum died. Wilf was shocked by the fact that his old mates had to be reminded who he was. When he bought several rounds of drinks in a pub we were in he overheard people calling him 'a flash bastard from down south'. He didn't take into account that most of those blokes were out of work and he was 'flashing the cash'.

I said to him, "Well they should have got on their bikes like we did and looked for work elsewhere." The majority of them had never been out of Keighley and had worked at the same firm since they left school. One by one these firms went to the wall. The unemployment was high. All the textile companies were gone and the engineering ones were quick to follow. I did bump into David who had worked for Dad on the moor (if you recall he was the small lad that Dad had employed to help with the shoot along with Ray who was the brainy one). He was driving the bus we caught when visiting Mum and Dad in Airedale hospital. He looked at me. He was trying to figure out who I was. When I asked him for two return tickets it suddenly clicked.

"You're Doreen from the Moor. Well you grew up nicely."

I laughed and thanked him for the compliment.

"How about meeting me later for a drink. We can talk about old times," he said.

"I don't think my husband would like that, do you?" I replied.

"Well, I won't tell him if you don't." He was quite the charmer now was David.

"I think you already did. He's stood behind me."

He took one look at Wilf and blustered, "No offence, mate, no offence."

When we were sitting down Wilf commented, "Now I know why we left Keighley, it's full of arseholes."

I don't think he liked the fact that I was still attractive to men. I had stayed slim and tried to dress to suit me, not just what was in fashion. I still looked 'tasty' in my jeans and boots.

"That's one in the eye for you, Wilfie baby," I thought, chuckling to myself. "The girl still has what it takes."

CHAPTER 36: THE EARLY CRANBROOK YEARS

It was my turn to have a health scare. On a routine visit to my GP my blood pressure was off the scale. My cholesterol was 5.4 and my GP wanted it under 5 so I went on a special diet. Then she found a lump in my stomach which she thought might be something serious. She told me I was in 'the change'. I'd got night sweats, palpitations and mood swings. Then I started having panic attacks. I wondered what I was changing into. I hoped it was something good after all I was having to put up with! All joking aside, if you have never experienced a panic attack you can't know how terrifying it can be. I came back one day from shopping feeling very unwell. Wilf rang the GP. She sent me to Pembury Hospital as she thought I might be having a heart attack but it turned out to be acid reflux which attacked muscles in my chest area. The hospital wanted to do an endoscopy but I decided to go home instead with various capsules and what not to keep my stomach acid where it belonged. When my appointment arrived for my scan I feared the worst. I was convinced that I had cancer. This did nothing to help my blood pressure. I was fed up with the whole thing. How Wilf endured years of bad health I'll never know. It was my Dad's fault. He always said that sickness was just an excuse for lazy people. If I'm not well I always apologise to everyone for being a nuisance (old habits die hard).

Anyway I came home with a clean bill of health, scare over.

Wilf was now Training Manager. He had a new recruit on nights who soon started to annoy me. She rang Wilf sometimes daily for advice on the job, or so he said. I did hope he was not being stupid again. I decided that if he was he could get himself out of the shit. I told him that if I answered the phone once more to this woman she would get a 'mouthful'. She was married with young kids. I wondered what her husband thought about it all.

One evening there was a disco at Hillside. I decided, after Wilf had gone to work, that I would take Scott along to it as he knew most of the residents, they all attended the centre in Rusthall. I got quite a shock when I saw this new member of staff – a 'looker' who dressed very inappropriately for work. I thought, "Let's hope she doesn't bend over or we will all see what she's had for breakfast."

Wilf was busy in the office so he didn't notice us. I watched this woman walk into the office, bend over and whisper in Wilf's ear. He looked up at her and laughed.

"Right, that's it," I thought. I walked in and asked, "Can I share the joke?"

Wilf went drip white. The woman didn't know who I was and tried to shepherd me out of the office saying, "I'm sorry. Guests are not allowed in the office."

I smiled at her and replied, "I'm sorry. If you drape yourself over my husband again I'm going to seriously rearrange your face."

Wilf joined in. "There's no need for that Doreen." He sounded annoyed.

I didn't care about that. I thought that he could 'get stuffed', I was totally sick of his behaviour. "I've just had her husband on the phone asking what's going on with you and Dolly Parton here."

She looked really scared. "What did you tell him?" she asked.

"That's on a need to know basis and you don't need to know. I think he's making his way over here. You can tell him yourself"

She looked near to tears. "Oh God, I hope he doesn't come here and make a scene."

I thought I would let her sweat a bit. Her husband hadn't rung me. I was being evil. She left the office and Wilf closed the door. I moved to leave.

"Just a minute. I want a word," he said. "There's nothing going on between me and her."

"Tell someone who gives a shit, Wilf. I thought we had got away from all that crap. Did you think I was stupid? But that's it. This time you've pushed the boundaries once too often. As my mum used to say, 'it won't always be dark at seven'.

"What's that supposed to mean?" he asked.

"I think it means the kids are grown-up now so what's good for you is good for me. See Scott gets a taxi home. OK, I'm, leaving." I slammed out of the office and went into the grounds where 'Dolly' was sitting having a cigarette. It was obvious she'd been crying.

"Please don't tell my husband," she sobbed. "Wilf wasn't interested in me. He talked about you all the time. I did fancy him but, as he said, he's a happily married man."

"Tell someone who's interested. I'm not. I'm done here."

I went back inside and waited around for Scott. Wilf tried to talk to me but I cold-shouldered him. To say it was icy in our house when he arrived home next day was an understatement. It took me quite a while to be civil with him. For some reason I felt he had really let me down this time. However, we were about to be hit by a tornado.

First of all Hillside and Wilf parted company. He didn't move far, just next door. It was a much bigger home called The Castle. Many years previously it had been a Dr Barnardo children's home. It was thought to be haunted.

It was time for Wilf to prove himself yet again. He soon settled into a new routine. I continued to work in the community but not for Social Services. I worked for a private agency. I had now achieved NVQ Level 4 so negotiated my own hourly rate and worked the hours I wanted. This suited me much better. I also did some private work. It was around this time that I got a phone call from Maureen's eldest girl. The only contact I'd had from Maureen over the years was the cards she sent at Christmas. The 'shit was about to hit the fan' big time. Maureen was in hospital on a locked ward. Her mental health had broken down again. The gist of the phone call was that Maureen had claimed that Dad had been sexually abusing her since she'd been small. I ran to the bathroom to vomit, my head felt as if it would explode. How stupid had I been? Everything became crystal clear – such as the endless trips to our room. He had been the reason she never smiled. That had been the reason he beat up any guys who had shown interest in her. That had been what she'd tried to protect me from. Why hadn't she spoken out? If it had been happening to me I would have shouted out to anyone who would have listened. I wished now that we had buried 'the bastard' instead of cremating the evil pig. Why hadn't Mum done anything? She must have known. If we had buried him we could have all pissed on his grave. With Mum it had always been least said soonest mended. "Well, Mother dear, how do you intend to mend this?" I thought. What he had done had impacted on Maureen's whole life. I was so mad I couldn't contain it. I sat down and wrote a long letter to Maureen. What I put in that letter was between two sisters, I would never disclose it. The thing that really puzzled me was the way she had let Mum and Dad look after her two girls whilst she visited Scotland with Billy. After Mum passed away why did she bother to do so much for Dad? I'm sure there was a psychological answer to that. I'd had the other answer many times, especially when he'd been sitting on the windowsill at the flats five floors up. I'd had the chance to put an end to him. I'd chickened out. What would that have made me? A murderess or an avenging angel? Well an angel I never was. It had taken me a long time to figure it out but I remember Wilf saying to me years ago that how Dad acted around Maureen was not what you would expect from a father. As I sit writing this, casting my mind back, I remember that we never had many fun times with him. There was always an undercurrent. Mum was always walking on egg-shells. I found it hard then to think of

Mum in a good light. The questions kept arising. Did she know? I think she must have. How long had she known? Well, I'm pretty sure now that she knew something was going on when we lived on the moor. Look at the way he reacted when he found out that Maureen had flown the coop. He'd camped out on Gran's lawn in Horncastle and been picked up by the police. Why, oh why had Maureen not spoken out then? He was dead and gone and wouldn't face any retribution, unless, of course, he'd faced the wrath of God. But if there really was a God, why had he let it happen in the first place? I knew now why Maureen hadn't found the incident with the knickers funny. I would never be able to laugh at that memory again. I just thought she was being silly, boiling her underwear every week. She'd been trying to make herself feel clean again. He'd been cruel, evil, a pervert. How could Mum have carried on sharing a bed with him? How could Mum have said nothing when she found out? Why hadn't she walked out and taken us with her? I will never be able to answer these questions.

I never spoke to Maureen about this. I figured that if she'd wanted to talk it through she would have. When I think back she had given many clues. She'd dropped hints, I just hadn't been old enough to recognise what she'd been hinting about. This must have been the big secret that Dad thought I knew about. So, in a way, Maureen had kept me safe.

The next thing that happened was the close of The Castle. The management had kept it 'hush hush'. It all happened in a couple of weeks. They moved the residents out one by one and then put a notice of the closure in the local paper. What a way to tell your staff that they are all out of work! The owner had applied for permission to turn the building into luxury flats. He got a big shock when the application was turned down. The building was still boarded up and derelict when we left Kent. Some years later reports indicated that the rumour of the building being haunted was true. Wilf had spoken to me about several cold spots in the building and that it was difficult to get a signal from his mobile. Two long-serving night staff, both ladies, left at a moment's notice after encountering a small girl running down a corridor towards them, bouncing a ball. Wilf never saw a little girl but did say that there were parts of the building that the night staff avoided unless there were two of them.

Wilf took this opportunity to drop his working hours to part-time. He worked at the local school as part of the cleaning team. He'd become totally disillusioned with care work, in particular the way the homes were being allowed to flout the rules and regulations and that people were turning a blind eye. This just reinforced our decision that Social Services would never get Scott into one of these places whilst we had breath left in our bodies. Over the next few years several things were to happen which would affect our lives, but, before that happened, Wilf and Scott went to see Paul and Becky for a few days. Pip was with me, keeping me company. He must have watched an awful lot of DVDs that week. I discovered half my plates, mugs and other items under his bed. Well, that was one way of avoiding the washing up.

Don't quote me, but I had reason to believe that two certain people took themselves off one lunchtime to the local pub. No, it wasn't Paul and his dad, it was Becky and her drinking buddy, Wilf. I have it on record that both of them returned to Paul's home much, much later the worse for wear. After being politely asked to leave, as the public house in question did not stay open all day, Wilf and Becky remained bosom buddies for the foreseeable future, both denying any knowledge of what happened that day.

Paul came to visit us to celebrate his dad's sixtieth birthday. I warned Wilf before they went out not to return 'three sheets to the wind'. For once he did what I asked, he was relatively sober. Paul, however, was as pissed as a newt. He sat on the sofa under Wilf's arm singing to him and telling us all how much he loved his dad. Wilf put him to bed, just as he had all those years ago. Next morning I made as much noise as I could whilst making Paul bacon butties. He didn't even have a bad head.

It was the following year that Wilf started having a few problems. One morning he was so embarrassed when he wet the bed because he couldn't get to the toilet in time. I made a doctor's appointment without even asking him. If I had given him a choice he wouldn't have gone. The doctor sent him straight to the hospital. She just said that she had a strange feeling about him. She didn't bother with the usual treatment (which was a course of strong antibiotics in case he had an infection). I knew what she was thinking. He had a blood test to measure the level of PSA in his blood. It needed to be less than 4. Wilf's was over 10 and rising. He was booked in for a biopsy. He didn't know what to expect. I already knew but didn't tell him. I didn't want to put the fear of God in him – it's not a very pleasant procedure. Wilf thought that they would take one biopsy but, in fact, they took ten. He didn't feel any pain, just heard the distinctive click as each sample was taken. He was sent home with some extra strength antibiotics to make sure he didn't have an infection and also to prevent him getting one. We waited for the results. We waited two weeks for his appointment. I wanted to go with him but he said he needed to do this alone. I had given up smoking the previous year. The doctor had said that it would help to lower my blood pressure. It didn't but I did feel much better without cigarettes. At times, when you are under stress, you feel that you really need a cigarette to calm your nerves, but, as I had stopped for nearly a year, I didn't intend starting again. I knew when Wilf walked in that the news was bad. I just didn't know how bad. My lovely man had prostrate cancer Gleason 7 – not the most aggressive but still a cancer which would grow at a moderate rate. Cancer kills people, I couldn't get this into my head. I thought it was not fair. He'd had his fair share of illness. I didn't feel we could go through this. I couldn't bear it. We talked about the options that the consultant had given him. There were three. Firstly, they could monitor it to see how fast it was growing.

Secondly, he could take hormones to try and control it. Thirdly, he could have a radical operation to remove his prostrate. He had already made his mind up, I could tell by the look on his face. I asked what his consultant thought was best, he thought it was the operation. He'd said that Wilf was still young and that he thought the only way forward was to remove his prostrate, he would try to spare as many of the nerves as he could. Wilf had reluctantly chosen the operation. It was the only sure way of clearing the cancer from his body. We just had to pray to God that it hadn't spread to the lymph nodes. If it had, well, I didn't know what would happen. After a biopsy they had to wait eight weeks before they could operate. They asked Wilf which hospital he would like his operation to take place in. He opted for Maidstone and it was scheduled for early December. He went to see the special nurse who was to explain all about the operation and what he would need to do after the surgery. She gave him some pelvic floor exercises to do, this was to help prevent incontinence and leakage – he didn't want to spend the rest of his life in pads and rubber pants. He knew then that he would leave hospital with a catheter which would stay in for three weeks – that meant it would be taken out on Christmas Eve. The nurse also explained the difference it would make to his ability to have a normal sex life. My husband had always been a very sexual man so he was devastated to learn that he wouldn't be able to have any sex life at all without the help of medication. This was the worst thing that could have happened to a man like Wilf. He decided that he would be better off dead. He was intending to cancel his surgery. His mental health was poor and he soon became depressed. I begged him to see the GP for something to lift his mood but he refused. He became verbally abusive to me and that upset me a lot. I loved my husband very much but there is a point of no return. This is when you can't take any more. I didn't know how to help him. I spoke to Paul on the phone. He asked me to get his dad to the doctor but, short of tying him up and dragging him there against his will, I could do nothing. I sat and waited, hoping that his common sense would make him do the right thing.

To bring you up to date with what was happening to Scott at the time, well, he was doing well. He had been on TV and in all the newspapers due to a leisure centre in Tunbridge Wells refusing to allow him and some friends, accompanied by two staff members, the use of their sauna. First, they said the party was too large. But, when the staff offered to split them into two groups, they changed tack, saying, "Well, they're not normal are they? Our regular members might be upset by them. Could you bring them back after dark?" When Scott returned home to tell his tale, within two hours I had the local TV reporters, complete with cameras, at my door and a newspaper reporter followed close on their heels. I made a quick exit and left for work. At this moment I was working the afternoon shift in the kitchens at a private boys' school. I thought that Wilf would handle the situation so much better than me. Anyway, the media also went to a local firm where Scott was doing work experience. This row rumbled on for weeks. I spoke to the Leisure Centre Manager. There was no problem getting through to him, his name was Paul Burrows and the switchboard operator thought I was his mother. He started blustering as soon as he realised who I was.

"I'm recording this conversation," he spluttered.

"Good idea," I replied. "We can use it as evidence when we take your company to court on charges of discrimination."

His manner changed at once. He went into 'damage limitation' mode. "Surely we can settle this dispute amicably."

"I doubt that very much Mr Burrows. Letters have been sent to the Prime Minister. The Head of Social Services will be on TV tonight discussing this issue. You are in a hole and you should stop digging. My son has used your facility before. Your staff never questioned him. Perhaps he looked more normal, did he? I don't think so. You are up the creek without a paddle, so to speak." I put the phone down and left him to stew in his own juice.

Wilf had the Head of Social Services on the phone asking him to 'put a lid' on the matter. Wilf told him that it was a matter of principle. They tried to say that Scott and his friends had medical issues. This was true, however, they had trained members of staff with them so that shouldn't have been a problem. The row rumbled on. Scott got a letter from Sir Patrick Mayhew. Basically, he said it was regrettable that this had happened but thought it was a case of 'crossed wires' rather than discrimination. I didn't agree. They wanted us to 'button it' then. Scott received a letter of apology along with a year's free pass. When he realised that this offer did not extend to his friends he told Mr Burrows to 'stick his free pass where the sun don't shine' or, as Scott said, "He can shove it up his arse, I'm not interested." When Wilf telephoned Mr Burrows to relay Scott's message he did put it more politely. I'm afraid that was not enough for me. I went to the leisure centre and asked to see the manageress of the sauna. She trotted out of her office. I had met her type before, looking very smart in a two-piece suit, hair perfectly set and so much 'slap' on her face (it must have been inches thick – bet she used a paint scraper to get it off at bedtime). Oh dear, sounds like I was discriminating against her the same way that she had discriminated against Scott. Was I wrong? I'll let you be the judge of that!

I asked for a price list. It was only at the end of our conversation, when she'd finished trying to sell me a year's membership, that I told her who I was. She was standing right next to the pool. Oh, I so wanted to shove her in after giving her a good slap, but I knew I would be arrested so had to be content with watching her make a dash for the safety of her office. I left with a smile on my face, job done – another one sorted out, would it ever end?

Scott had a lady friend at Rusthall Centre. I was not well pleased. She was twelve years older than him. Her mother tended to dress her as an old lady. They decided to get engaged, more her mother's idea I thought. She had three daughters and was trying to marry them all off. It was a novelty to Scott at first but that soon wore off. On holiday with her and other family members she showed her true colours when she started trying to boss him around. When Scott arrived home he didn't say much really but later on that evening he asked me to read through a letter he had written to Susan, his lady friend. It was very brief and to the point. He might as well have written, 'You're dumped'. It was after reading that letter that I had my first hint that he might be autistic. It had never been so obvious before. Paul had commented that he was rude at times. I defended him as always, "He's not rude, just very to the point," I said. Wilf just shook his head. He was always telling me off for sticking up for my boys when they were younger. By that time Paul was a parent himself but I still defended Scott against all comers. I said, "I'm a mother, that's what mothers do."

Scott had given up on the day centre. He always felt he didn't fit in. He had also had his medication changed. When Wilf took him to see his neurologist she was on maternity leave. He saw a locum who decided to take him off Epilim, saying it was an old outdated drug. In his wisdom he put Scott on Lamotrigine. I just hoped he knew what he was doing. Wilf wasn't convinced and decided to monitor the situation very carefully. Scott was given an appointment to see a psychiatrist at Tunbridge, a man who was supposed to be used to seeing people with a learning disability. I thought he was an 'arsehole'. There was a slight suspicion that Scott was showing signs of schizophrenia. This idiot lent over the desk and, staring into Scott's face, said, "If you were schizophrenic we would take over your life."

Wilf couldn't believe what he'd said. "Are you trying to frighten my son, you idiot? Does the NHS pay you a salary for terrifying your patients?" He removed Scott from this, 'so called' psychiatrist's office. We arranged a private appointment for him so that we had a report at hand if anyone started making waves for us. Not one of these 'professionals' identified that he was, in fact, autistic.

That brings you up-to-date with Scott. Now what about Maureen? I wasn't sure what was going on with her. I dropped her a line saying that Wilf had cancer and was waiting to be operated on. I never expected to hear from her but she phoned me saying how sorry she was and offered me her support if I needed it.

Paul arrived to stay whilst his Dad was in hospital. It became a pattern with Paul, if Wilf was unwell, Paul was never far away. The day of his admission dawned. He was due to go into the hospital after lunch. My stomach had been doing somersaults for days. I felt permanently nauseated. Wilf hated saying goodbye. He left me very tearful. He would not let Paul take him onto the ward. They said goodbye outside the hospital. Wilf was to regret this as he then spent most of the afternoon sitting in the dayroom waiting for his bed to become free. If Paul had been there at least he would have had someone to chat to. He had told Paul that he did not want me to visit as he was only going to be in a short while. He wanted me at home with Scott. I found this hurtful. It felt as if he didn't want me anymore. He thought this would spare me from all the stress but it didn't, not being able to see him just made it worse. Anyway, I did as he asked and stayed at home with Scott. I rang the hospital in the afternoon the next day when I thought he should be back on the ward. The ward sister was not sure where he was and asked me to call back later. I did but she still did not have any idea where he was. My 'stress bucket' overflowed.

"Have you lost my husband?" I asked, "or has he died on the table. Perhaps he's left the hospital and is on his way home and has decided he won't have the op after all. How the hell can you say you don't know where he is? I will be ringing back in thirty minutes. Please make sure you have an answer by then." I slammed down the phone and wept.

I was coming apart at the seams.

Paul was working at the exchange in Tunbridge Wells. I rang him and asked him to come home. When he got home he rang the ward. Wilf had reappeared as if by magic. Paul managed to speak to the doctor on duty. When he got off the phone he looked worried. Wilf was back from theatre but having breathing problems so they were giving him oxygen. Paul wanted to go to see him but visiting would be over by the time he got to the hospital so he got on with what he had decided to do in our bedroom.

He wanted to re-decorate it and put laminate flooring down to make it nice for when his dad came home. We were expecting Wilf to be in hospital over the weekend so were surprised to get a call on the Friday to say that he was being discharged. This caught Paul 'on the hop'. He was working all night to try to finish the bedroom in time, he nearly managed it. Paul picked his dad up after he finished work. He had visited every night. I stayed away as that was what Wilf wanted. I couldn't understand why. I had always visited him in hospital and he had always wanted to see me before. What had changed? I guess Wilf had changed – the cancer had affected him, it had changed everything about him. I just didn't recognise my husband any more. I was never to get Wilf back again, not my Wilf, not the man I married. When I met Wilf he gave me his heart unconditionally. That's why I never worried too much that he would ever get seriously involved with anyone else or that he would leave me. His heart was mine forever.

I was so pleased to see him walk up the garden path. He was crying. I gave him a big hug. I was overjoyed to have him back. He didn't go to bed that night. He was finding it hard to lay down. The hospital had put in staples instead of stitches this time. As the wound was closing it felt very tight and was causing some discomfort. I had warned him against sitting upright all night. I thought that he should get his feet up or he could have very swollen ankles and legs by the morning. I curled up on the sofa. I needed to be close in case he needed me. By morning his ankles were badly swollen. I ordered him to bed and propped him up with as many pillows and cushions as I could find. The District Nurse was due that day to check his wound and catheter. I knew most of the district nurses. I had worked with them in the community. I had also done a course on catheter care. I knew how to change the bags, unblock a catheter and change dressings. I still thought it might have been a better idea if he'd agreed to have the nurses help with managing his catheter but he'd been adamant.

"My wife can do all that. She's had the training."

If he could have got away with me taking out his staples, he would have. It made me remember some stitches that Dad had in his head many years ago. He should have gone back to the doctor's to have them taken out but he'd got Maureen to take them out for him. Mum told him he'd get an infection so he'd sprinkled some powder he'd got from the vet on his head just in case. If the dogs needed stitches, Dad did them himself. This powder was to sprinkle on the wound. The things he got away with were unbelievable. Anybody else would have contacted MRSA or whatever the equivalent was many years ago. One of Mum's pearls of wisdom came to mind 'The Devil looks after his own'. Guess that was true then.

The first time I had to put a new bag on for Wilf my hands were shaking so much. I'd done this on a daily basis for years but when your husband is the patient it changes everything. He'd asked me to help him in the shower. Well, the air in the bathroom had turned blue with all the swearing he'd done. I'd looked after some grumpy old sods in my time but he took the biscuit.

He asked, "Am I the worst patient you've ever nursed?"

I'd replied, "Without a doubt, but if they had sworn at me like you did I'd have refused to help them again."

"I'm sorry, love. I just hate all this palaver. It makes me

wish I'd not bothered with that bloody operation." He was very upset and crying. I'd tried to comfort him but he thought I was pitying him. It didn't matter what I did, I ended up in his bad books. I tried to understand how he felt. He was a proud man. Having people messing with his personal bits made him very angry. I was the nearest person so he took it out on me. I bit my lip and carried on. I'd hurt my back a couple of years before and then I'd needed his help to get dressed. I couldn't even put my own knickers on. I remember being as mad as hell about it. I had to attend the hospital twice a week for months of intensive physiotherapy. That's what you get for working in the care industry.

When the time came for the staples to be removed the corner of the wound was infected and very angry looking. The nurse came back later with a broad spectrum antibiotic for him to take. I was very surprised that she hadn't taken a swab.

"I think you need to take a swab before he starts taking antibiotics, don't you?"

She looked at me as if I'd got two heads. "I don't have a kit with me. I'm sure these antibiotics will do the trick," she replied.

I just repeated what I'd said again and added, "With my husband's record of infections in wounds I'm not prepared to take that risk. Perhaps you can call back later on."

She flounced out of the door. I didn't know that nurse, she must have been new.

Wilf glared at me. "Why do you have to upset people?" he asked.

I just gave him the look that said 'don't push me any further'. As I left the room I turned to say, "If that's MRSA in there we need to know sooner rather than later."

When the nurse returned she left me a pile of dressings.

"I'm very busy this weekend. I'm sure you can manage. Someone will be in on Monday. If his catheter blocks ring this number." She handed me a card.

I took the card. "I've done the training. Unless it's something major I know how to unblock a catheter."

"Bully for you," she said as she slammed the gate behind her.

OK, what did I do wrong? I just wanted to make sure there was nothing nasty hiding in his wound. Was that wrong? I don't think it was. When I got up the next day Wilf was still in a foul mood. I just tried to avoid confronting him about anything. His chest was very wheezy. When he first came home from hospital he wasn't smoking but by the state of his ashtray I could see he had started again. I managed to get through to the Monday without any disasters. I knew the nurse who came that day very well. I'd worked with her on a few occasions. She confirmed that the antibiotics would clear up his infection. I heard her say to Wilf as she left, "You don't really need us, Wilf. Your wife is more than capable of looking after you."

When I let her out she whispered to me, "Watch his mood. Don't let him get depressed." Short of dressing up as a clown, red nose and all, I really didn't know how to stop that from happening.

It was his check-up at the hospital the following day and I wanted to go with him to give a bit of support but that meant that Scott would have to come along too so Wilf would say 'no'. If he'd allowed me to get some respite care for Scott we would have had some time just for us. My husband was so stubborn sometimes. I thought it would do Scott good to have some time away from us as he must have been sick of the arguments as well. I'd made my mind up I was going to talk to Social Services in the new year about some respite care. Mind you, I'm stupid. Instead of putting my feet up when I could I started cleaning the house. I must have wasted half my life cleaning the house.

The results at the hospital had been good. The cancer had not spread to the lymph nodes. Wilf's prostrate gland had been 75% cancerous which was worse than they had first thought. If he had taken the 'wait and see' option he'd have been pushing up daisies by then as it would have quickly spread to his vital organs. From then on he would have a series of blood tests (which could last up to ten years) to make sure the PSA level in his blood stayed unreadable. Looking back now, he'd been very lucky. A lot of family members on his mother's side had lost their lives to cancer. On his Dad's side it was heart attacks and other heart issues. None of his family were very healthy. Mind you, both my parents had been in their sixties when they died so I knew I might have some health issues to face as well. I'd already had the same problems as my mum had with her teeth. I'd got a full denture on top and a partial one on the bottom. As there wasn't an NHS dentist in Cranbrook it had cost me a lot of money. Scott had to go into East Grinstead Hospital to have his wisdom teeth removed. No dentist was prepared to do it due to his epilepsy. He was there for two days. I wondered how many parents had encountered the problems we had. It didn't matter which hospital or where the hospital was, they couldn't cope with learning disability kids or young adults. They couldn't cope with autistic kids or young adults.

So if your son or daughter had both you didn't stand much of a chance. We'd spent more nights sleeping in hospitals to care for Scott than I'd like to remember. I'm afraid the situation hasn't improved over time.

CHAPTER 37: CRANBROOK DESCENDS INTO MISERY

I was beginning to suspect more and more that Scott might be on the autistic spectrum but it was no good voicing my opinion. Nobody was interested. The opinion appeared to be that, as he had a learning disability, what did it matter what else he had got. Well, I'm sorry but it sure as hell mattered to Scott. It would also explain a lot of the things he said and did. This would be a battle we fought but not at this time. I'd already got a battle on my hands and I could only cope with one at once. Well, I thought I had better soon learn to multi-task as battles didn't wait until you were ready to fight. They creep up and attack when you're not expecting it.

Wilf had his catheter out on Christmas Eve. He had been worried sick that he wouldn't be able to pee when they took it out. He knew that if that happened he would have to have another catheter put in and couldn't bear that. I told him not to stress out, just drink plenty of water. Anyway the Christmas miracle happened. His catheter came out and his bladder acted as it should. His exercises had paid off. He never leaked or became incontinent. He made me promise that if he ever became ill never to allow a catheter to be put in. I passed that promise on to Paul and Becky. We all kept it.

Many times over the next few years Wilf had regretted having the operation. It devastated him when he realised how restricted he would be and how the operation had affected him. Something he had taken for granted since he was a young lad was no longer there without the help of medication. He felt a total failure and wouldn't discuss anything with me. He locked himself away from us all. He soon became very depressed. On his last visit to the hospital he was given some phone numbers of men who had previously had the same procedure. I thought to myself what a waste of time, he won't talk to his family so why would he ring total strangers. I was wrong. The first chap told him that he had been incontinent ever since his catheter had been removed. I wish he hadn't bothered with the next chap. He'd told him that because he was no longer any good in the bedroom department his wife had walked out and never returned. I was livid. You would have thought the hospital would have been more careful and checked people out before handing out phone number to men who'd recently had surgery. My God, if he wasn't depressed before he sure as hell would be then.

I told Wilf, "You did all the exercises so it's unlikely that you'll develop incontinence problems. As for the other idiot, his wife may have left for many reasons." Both these men were a lot older than Wilf so none of it was relevant.

I was watching every word I said. He wasn't very pleased because Scott and I had been going to the library twice a week to try and learn how to use a computer. Scott spending a lot of time alone in his room hearing me and his dad arguing all the time can't have been very pleasant for him either. I contacted Social Services, asking if a social worker would come out to see us. I had to call back later and cancel this request as Scott's epilepsy started to become unstable. He started having seizures one afternoon. We couldn't stop them and had to call the paramedics. We had given him two lots of rectal diazepam which had no effect whatsoever. An ambulance arrived with two technicians. They might as well have sent Postman Pat as technicians are not allowed to administer medication. Next to arrive was a paramedic who had heard the urgent request. He was off duty. Without the help given by this paramedic Scott would have died on the bedroom floor. When he was stable again he was taken by ambulance to A & E. It was during the journey that Scott had the most horrific fit ever. He'd been laid on the stretcher with two straps across him. Somehow he managed to get tangled up in them and one was tight round his neck leaving him gasping for air, blue in the face and choking. Wilf tried to reach him but the technician was standing in the way, his mouth open, transfixed. Wilf found out later that he had no experience of epilepsy.

Wilf shouted at him, "Get the fucking strap undone, he's choking."

As they got the strap from round his neck Scott suddenly lurched forward in a massive fit and his shoulder hit a metal pole with force. He had two more fits before they reached the hospital. I dread to think what the outcome would have been if Wilf hadn't been there to take over.

Scott arrived home the next morning. He'd been on a diazepam drip to keep him sedated. When I tried to take off his jacket he screamed in pain. We looked at his shoulder which was swollen and black with bruising. By the next day he was in worse agony so I sent for the GP.

His diagnosis was severe bruising. He left us with a script for strong pain relief. But before we had time to get the tablets we were on our way to hospital again as Scott was suffering with prolonged epileptic seizures. By the time we reached A & E I felt very nauseated. I'm like good wine, I don't travel well. As they pushed Scott into a cubicle he started fitting again. I flung back the curtain, shouting, "Can we have some help in here," just like they do on the telly, but this was no pretence it was for real. I was pushed out of the way by the two doctors who rushed in followed by a nurse. I couldn't take any more and collapsed into Wilf's arms sobbing. What the hell had Scott done to deserve this? I looked up to the heavens silently cursing God to hell and back. Later Wilf spoke to the doctor about Scott's shoulder. By now we were convinced that he'd done some real damage. The staff had experienced problems getting a cannula in Scott's arm. There was blood all over him, the doctor and the floor. The nurse had to cut his tee-shirt off. I remember, stupidly, thinking that Scott would be so cross as it was his favourite shirt. When we got to X-ray there was so much bruising and swelling that they immobilised his arm and gave him an appointment for the fracture clinic the following week. I drew the short straw so took him to the clinic. When the X-rays were done we went in to see the doctor, who was Spanish. He looked at the pictures, shaking his head. Turning to me he asked why we had left Scott in pain without seeking help. Holding on to my temper with both hands I explained about the GP's diagnosis.

He shook his head in amazement. "This is a classic

epilepsy injury. How could he miss that?"

I stood quietly fuming, wondering who I was going to sue first. We had to sit and wait to see the consultant for his opinion. Scott was hungry so I took him to get a sandwich. As we returned to the waiting area the staff nurse lost her cool with me, it went something like this.

"Do you think the consultant has got all day to wait around for you?"

Well that was it. I took a step forward, and, glaring at her, I replied, "Oh, I'm so bloody sorry we've kept you waiting but my son has been fitting for two days and hasn't eaten. He was hungry."

She came back at me with, "There's no need for bad language."

"Just be grateful I had the courtesy not to use some heavy-duty words after the forty-eight hours I've just lived through," I replied as I swept past her into the consultant's office. He was really nice. He chatted to Scott and then sent Miss Snooty to get me a cup of tea.

He explained to me that Scott's shoulder joint was smashed beyond repair. In fact, he said, it was one of the worst injuries he had dealt with. The operation to replace his shoulder joint would be long and very complicated and because his epilepsy was so unstable it would also be extremely dangerous. He was not prepared to take the risks involved so it was decided to let nature take its course and allow the injury to heal naturally. We went back several times to check how it was doing. After a few months the joint had fused itself. Scott had restricted movement in that arm for years but now he can hold his arm above his head without any problems.

Our lives rumbled on. The relationship between me and Wilf was deteriorating. Each day was a struggle and I was always glad when it was bedtime. We had been sleeping apart ever since it had been necessary for Wilf to get up several times to use the toilet. He said that he didn't want to disturb me. I saw it as an excuse and thought that he didn't want to be near me. Wilf had never had a jealous nature but now I couldn't leave the house without facing an interrogation when I returned. In the end I stopped going anywhere without him. It just wasn't worth all the hassle. Some days I would have given anything just to sit quietly somewhere all on my own. What a change. In the early days we had both loved being together and did everything together. I really couldn't see any way forward for us. I thought this was the beginning of the end. When we were a team we had taken on all comers, nothing fazed us. But now we seemed to be systematically destroying each other. Wilf had convinced himself that I was having an affair. This had to be because he had no confidence in himself any more. He was very depressed but refused to seek medical help. Paul rang me to say, "You need to get Dad to the doctors." I knew this but there was no way that Wilf would agree to see our GP.

He really was in a sorry state. He would burst into tears and curse and swear at me for no reason. He had isolated himself from me and Scott. He would sit in his chair in the corner and didn't want to eat or converse with me for days on end. When he did talk it was to accuse me of everything under the sun. How I could be blamed for anything when I never left the house was beyond my comprehension. Something had to give. The more I tried to get things back on track the worse it got. I gave myself a makeover. I went back to wearing skirts and stockings and bought myself some new underwear. This just seemed to give him ammunition. He got even more abusive. I went back to my jeans and boots. Sod him. I decided to stop answering back, kept very quiet and smiled a lot. I think he thought I had finally flipped. It took him by surprise. Whatever he said I just ignored and carried on with normal conversation. I didn't try to defend myself as I had been doing. It is very hard to have a row with someone who won't fight back. The crunch came one night when he insisted I get up and look for a mobile he was convinced I had. He said that he had heard it ring. It's hard to search for something that doesn't exist. I was so incensed. I dumped everything on top of my bed. "Search yourself, bloody fool," I yelled, grabbing my duvet and pillow I stormed out into the lounge, slamming the door behind me. I lay on the sofa with the latest Trixie who was a whippet cross. She slept at the bottom of my bed. Wilf wasn't too pleased about that either. "Well, stuff him," I thought. He'd got me really pissed off by then, he'd better watch his step. I had been awake all night and was just nodding off when I heard him clattering about in the kitchen. The door slowly opened and in he walked with a mug of tea.

"I've made you some tea my love," he whispered.

I was still livid. "Stick your tea," I hissed, pulling the duvet over my head. Trixie opened one eye and growled.

"I'll just leave it here love," he said as he left the room, closing the door behind him. I sat up. No point in wasting good tea.

I lay quietly considering my options. The problem was that I still loved him with a passion. He had always worshipped me. I knew I was the love of his life so why was all this shit happening. No matter what he said the truth always shone from his eyes. I was convinced now that he'd had a nervous breakdown and thought that without treatment the stone would carry on rolling until it reached its destination. I just hoped and prayed that it wouldn't end in tragedy.

The whole thing came to a head one Friday outside the supermarket. A young chap who worked in one of the many charity shops had been looking for a flat. It just so happened that someone I had done work for had rooms to let so I phoned her and he got the room. This had been some time ago but the lad remembered. He put his arm around my shoulder and bent his head to thank me. He was about six foot four inches so I was a midget at the side of him. Wilf stormed out of the store. I saw him coming, his face like thunder. I excused myself and hoped that the lad would make himself scarce. Wilf was an old man at that time but he had been a street fighter. The young fella wouldn't have stood a chance. When we got home the air was blue. Wilf called me every name he could think of – some I'd never heard before. I just stood and took it. I wondered if he was bloody thick or what. This young man was just a kid, late teens or early twenties. What could he possibly see in an old bird like me? I was beginning to feel like a loony tune.

A couple of days later Chris, a chap who used to drive Scott's minibus, did the same thing, but he hugged me.

Wilfie boy never said a thing. He already knew I didn't like Chris very much because he was a heavy drinker and he stunk of beer that day, it just turned my stomach. My nerves were very frayed, my blood pressure off the scale. I was suffering a really bad headache and just felt like shit. As I lay in bed that night I realised that I was beginning to hate Wilf. He had become cruel and nasty. We were now sharing a double bed again. I had hoped the ice inside him would melt and we could be together as we used to be but, oh no, that just wasn't going to happen. He kept repeating over and over, "Admit what you have done, we can put it behind us and start again."

I wasn't prepared to admit to anything, even if he drove me insane. I thought that Wilf had a nerve. How many times had I got him out of the shit? He always was just a little bit guilty. He would flirt, fool around and then shout, 'help' and like an idiot I would sort it out. He was still a good-looking fella but all his attention was centred on me.

Then things changed again. He got up one morning with a face like thunder. My first thought was, "Oh shit what have I done now?" I felt that the best thing to do was just carry on as normal. I did this for most of the day but the looks he was giving me started to grate on my nerves.

"OK," I shouted. ""what the hell have I done now to offend you?"

He then tried to convince me that I had started talking in my sleep. The things he told me I had said were crude, vulgar and I didn't even know what some of it meant! Well, that was it for me – the worm turned.

"Right, I've had enough. You are driving me round the bend. I never thought I would ever say this but you and I are finished. I can't carry on any longer." I locked myself in the bedroom and sobbed for hours. I'd considered making something up, hoping he would leave me in peace. I had got to a point where I thought I was going insane.

Then he changed in an instant. Over the next few days he bought all new rings for me – wedding and eternity. It was as if he had to clear the decks and start again. He got down on one knee and asked me to marry him again. I wondered what would have happened if I'd said 'no'. But, of course, I said 'yes'. You see I loved him, always had. He was my world. I couldn't live without him.

Things calmed down and began to improve. We talked about leaving Kent and moving back to Yorkshire. Paul kept telling him, "You have to make sure you are moving for the right reasons." All I wanted was our life back as it used to be.

I had stopped smoking the previous year. I did it without any help from patches or other aids. Wilf was persuaded to follow suit. When I had to call out the emergency doctor in the early hours because he was very blue and couldn't breathe, the doctor gave him some steroids to help him. He was advised to give up the cigs or he would be dead by Christmas. His own doctor gave him two inhalers and told him that he had COPD caused by smoking. It was then that I realised he was no longer drinking either. The thing I had wished for all our married life had happened but with all the hassle that had been going on it went unnoticed. Wilf had often given up drinking for short periods just to pacify me but it never lasted. Somehow I knew this time that it would. It brought home to me that he was starting to feel his age.

He still tried to do everything around the house and garden but I was watching him, like a hawk. I believed that if I wasn't careful I would lose my man, not to another woman, but to God. That was something I thought I would never be able to accept. Wilf was taking control of my life. I never left home without him. I stopped carrying cash and just let him take over, it seemed easier that way. I just wanted a peaceful life.

Scott had an appointment to attend King's Hospital in London. It was decided he should be admitted and that his epilepsy be monitored to try and stabilise his condition. Because Scott had a learning disability he would need an escort. It was decided that I should accompany him. We were to be away for five days. On the morning we were due to travel Wilf changed all the plans. I stayed home and Wilf went to King's. It was a bad decision. He was in no fit state mentally to cope. He phoned me day and night asking if I had been out. At one point he said he could hear someone talking in the background, "Who did I have in the house?" It was a nightmare. When they got back he questioned me non-stop for hours. Had I been into Cranbrook? Who did I talk to? Who was in the house when he rang me? Then he noticed a tee-shirt in the pile of ironing I was doing. "Where did that tee-shirt come from?" he wanted to know.

"It's one of yours," I replied.

Well he wasn't having that. He ranted on and on, insisting that someone had been staying at the house whilst he was away and had left their tee-shirt. Poor Scott just shut himself in his bedroom. He must have been totally sick of it all. If I didn't answer Wilf just got more and more irate. The stay in London had done his brain no favours. He had spent the whole time imagining what I was up to. Scott told me later that his dad had been no help to him really and had been very upset at times, crying in the bathroom.

The whole episode had been a waste of time. They didn't capture any epileptic activity at all, but within a few hours back at home Scott started fitting again.

I was very worried about Wilf. Thinking about cancer, a lot of his relatives on his mother's side had died from that disease. His Auntie Manda was very young when she passed away and his Uncle Douglas had also died in his sixties from cancer. I was not too sure about Uncle George as we had lost contact with Keighley after Alice died. Wilf's father had died from a ruptured aorta at fifty-nine – none of them long livers. Both my parents died in their sixties, it gave me the shivers just thinking about it.

Wilf had a strange dream about his parents which upset him. He thought it could be a premonition of his own early death. I told him that it was just a dream and that lots of people had strange dreams that they didn't understand.

He dreamt he had walked into the lounge and seen his dad sitting in one of the armchairs. He had sat himself on the arm of that chair and as he looked at his dad he changed into his mother. Wilf had said to her, "Oh no, you haven't come for me?" She'd replied, "Not now but it won't be long." I know this bothered him for quite a long time and then he seemed to forget it.

We had been in Kent for twenty-three years. When we

first moved there we had planned to return northwards when Scott finished school but, in the meantime, Paul had married a local girl and we had our grandchildren so everything got put on hold. To be fair to Wilf he had never really liked living in the south. His father had been from Earith in Kent so he had extended family there but he'd lost touch with them years before. I had never met any of them.

The time had come to think about making a move before we were both too old to be bothered. To be truthful, I was none too keen to move. I just didn't want all the hassle and mess it involved. It just felt a step too far at that time.

When you think about moving on it makes you cast your mind back to the things you remember from those twenty-three years. You remember for two reasons. One, because you really enjoyed what happened and two, because you hated every minute.

Most of the happy times were with Pip and Beth. Pip was very soft-hearted with animals. He came rushing in one day shouting that the cat had a mouse which she was tormenting as cats do. Wilf was terrified of mice so I dashed out with gloves on. It was Supergran to the rescue. Well, our cat, Tiggy, took off at speed when she saw me. The poor mouse was crawling around half dead. Looking at Pip's tear-stained face I just couldn't tell him it would die anyway. So I gathered it up and we walked to the nearby playing field. When I put it down in the long grass it seemed to recover and dashed into the hedge. Pip had a big smile on his face and told everyone how he had saved the mouse. I hope it survived but somehow I doubt it.

Pip thought his grandad could fix everything. One day he brought in a dead baby bird. He thought his granddad could make it better. There was no way round that one. Pip sat on his grandad's knee whilst Wilf explained why dead creatures could not be made better. Thankfully, the ice-cream van took Pip's attention and the incident was soon forgotten.

Now, Beth was a different kettle of fish. She had picked up my Persian cats and tried to carry them around so many times. The cats' ears would go flat to their heads when they heard her voice. One would hide under my bed, the other in the airing cupboard. Only when they were sure she had gone home would they emerge from hiding. This carried on until she was a lot older, then they forgave her and would come to be stroked.

When Paul first went to work in Switzerland Becky would take the kids over to see him some weekends. This was when Pip had a nasty accident getting off the train. A stupid woman, who was dashing off, slammed the door on Pip's hand, nearly severing one of his fingers. She saw what she had done but didn't even bother to wait to see if Becky needed help. Poor Becky was there with a suitcase and two screaming kids, one bleeding badly. Pip was rushed to East Grinstead where they re-attached his finger. Paul had to get the first available flight home to be with his family. I knew I wouldn't have coped very well but Becky is a cool customer. She didn't panic and got on with what needed doing. I wish I could be like that but I'm a panic person. Wilf, however, keeps his cool and carries on.

Another sad memory around this time was for Paul who

was shocked to hear that his best man, Russell, had been killed in a motorcycle accident. Pip stayed with us whilst Paul and Becky attended the funeral. It was so sad that a young man was cut down in his prime. Young people don't die, do they? Well, I'm afraid sometimes they do. The shock was evident on Paul's face when he returned.

It was a reminder of his own mortality. When the page turns and your name is written there it doesn't matter what age you are – it's check-out time, the world can be so cruel.

A much happier memory was when the children travelled alone to the UK to spend time with both sets of grandparents. Wilf was working the early part of that week so my friend, Patience and I took them to the hop farm at Paddock Wood. Patience was a retired nanny – they soon renamed her Mary Poppins. She lived up to the title. She had a cold box in the car boot containing all sorts of treats, an emergency first aid kit and everything needed to keep young kids happy. Poor Patience lost her favourite hat when it blew away and got stuck on the roof of an outbuilding. However, a young fella climbed up and rescued it. We had some lunch and the kids went to play in a ball pool. Beth managed to bang heads with one of the other kids so it was Patience's chance to do her first aid bit. We then walked around an exhibition showing where all our water came from and what we used it for. We were busy explaining some of the displays to Pip and didn't notice that Beth wasn't there. I started looking frantically around the displays. It was Pip who spotted her sitting on one of the display toilets having a wee. It was a working model so no harm was done. It brought a smile to the faces of a lot of mums. I just stood red-faced. Patience, however, was in stitches. We beat a hasty retreat and went to look at the animals. Pip just had to tell Grandad, who also thought it was hilarious.

Later in the week Wilf and I took them to Tenterden to the play area. Then we went into Waitrose to do some shopping. Beth had a nasty habit of hanging onto the side of the trolley. Wilf warned her several times that she could tip it over and, of course she did. What a hullabaloo there was – shopping all over, broken eggs. Beth had hurt her knee and it was swelling up fast. Wilf stuck a bag of king prawns on it. We had both kids sitting crying – Beth with her king prawns poultice and Pip because, as Beth was crying, he decided to join in. I thought, "I wish I had a camera to take a quick snap titled 'a fun day out with the grandparents'." Beth had her granddad wrapped round her little finger. He spent the rest of the day carrying her, either on his shoulders or in his arms. She had a large bruise to show Colin and Jill when they came to collect them. I bought both kids a present before they left. Beth picked a Minnie Mouse. Pip, however, picked a ginormous brown bear which was a lot bigger than him. Poor Jill had to get it aboard the plane home and then off at the other end. Paul and Becky must have wondered who it was carrying this bear as it was so big that you couldn't see Pip at all. Knowing Pip he probably still has it now – good old Bruno.

Wilf took Scott to Disneyland in Paris. Even that turned into a farce. It was the hottest day ever. Scott nearly passed out. All the staff there were on strike and the hotel they stayed the night in was on the busiest road. They were going to go into Paris in the evening but it had been such a shit day they couldn't be bothered. It was such a shame because Scott had been looking forward to it for ages.

In 2001 when Paul and Becky returned from Switzerland they sold their house and moved to Colne in Cambridgeshire. This put Paul in the area where I met his biological father. In fact he probably still lives there. Wilf was concerned that Paul might start looking for him. It was worrying him so much that I spoke to Becky. She said it hadn't even crossed his mind. Wilf was the only father he ever knew and they were devoted to each other.

In 2004 Becky started her own dog grooming business. It really took off. She was so busy.

In 2006 I took Scott to Colne to stay for the weekend. I intended to visit Maureen. I knew she lived close by as did her girls. The trouble that this ended up causing, I wish I hadn't bothered. Wilf did warn me to leave it alone but I wanted to see her. We were both getting older. I wanted to see her before I joined the heavenly choir. Well, it was a big mistake. I haven't anything to say about that visit apart from the fact that I found Maureen very changed. It was obvious that she'd suffered some health problems.

When I returned home I didn't hear from her. When her birthday came around I still sent a card. About a week later I got some post. I was pleased, I thought she had written to me. What a shock when I opened the envelope to find that she had torn the card into small pieces and sent it back with a note accusing me of all sorts of misdemeanours. It was clear she was very unwell. I did speak to Billy on the phone and told him what I thought.

However, it fell on deaf ears. I drew a line under the whole sorry business. I wouldn't be bothering that family again, ever.

CHAPTER 38: GOODBYE, GOOD RIDDANCE

I needed to find a way to get us out of Kent. By this time I didn't have the option of getting work. We lived in council property so I thought the best way would be to get someone to exchange with us. I hated Kent with a vengeance. Wilf told me that some of our neighbours had said various things about me that weren't true. Was I going to do anything about it? No I didn't think I would bother. I'd had enough of small-minded people whose lives were so dull and drab that they had to poke their noses into other people's to spice up their day. I believed I owed them nothing. In fact, at one time or another, most of them had come to me for advice about their own personal problems. Wilf was also convinced that people were whispering behind his back. I knew that I needed to move us out whilst we still had some sanity left.

I decided to put us on Home Swapper. As we were in rental accommodation it seemed the only option. Initially Wilf had me checking every day to see if we had received any replies but soon began to lose interest.

I was spending a lot of time with Scott on the internet. We had joined a site called Able Here. It was a free site run by disabled people and was the brainchild of a young man with cerebral palsy called Karl Dean. He was an amazing individual. What he had achieved by this stage in his life was unbelievable. He championed the cause of the disabled at every opportunity. Some of the high jinks he got up to must have terrified his poor mother. He always had a group of very dependable people around him. Karl showed me a new side to disability and the challenges that disabled people faced every day. He was also partial to a drop of the amber nectar. In fact, one year his Christmas tree was made completely from lager cans. I remember thinking, "Good God, he couldn't have drunk all those." He came across as a happy, well-balanced young chap who lived every moment of every day. I hope that one day he finds the lady of his dreams, the one who can see the man, not the disability.

Amanda from Able Here also played a part in my life. She was always there with words of comfort. When I felt down she always managed to lift my mood. We still speak now several times a week. I hope I'll be able to visit her soon to present her with her copy of 'The Gamekeeper's Other Daughter'.

Wilf soon got the hump about how much time I was spending online. He thought emails were a very secretive way of communicating. God help me if I got one from a member of the opposite sex. My husband couldn't believe it was possible to get a message from someone you didn't know. He also thought it was possible for me to delete Facebook from Scott's computer. Before long he was standing, looking over my shoulder, every time I went online. It spoilt any enjoyment, so I began spending less and less time on the internet. It got so bad that I only logged on to order our shopping and this was with Wilf sitting at the side of me. I had to check every day to see if anyone had left a message on Home Swapper about our bungalow. I really didn't think we stood much of a chance. I wondered who would want to move to Cranbrook, we couldn't wait to leave it.

As each day passed the chances of leaving Kent seemed to get more and more uncertain. But one day I was sitting drinking my morning cuppa when the phone rang. It was a woman from a place called Leverton which is just outside Boston in Lincolnshire. I knew some of the places in the locality. If you remember, I had stayed with Uncle Eddie in Louth. I had also stayed with my grandmother in Horncastle. She hadn't liked me very much. Maureen had always been her favourite. Maureen had been very fond of the old girl, whilst I couldn't stand her. She thought I was too much like Dad. She was wrong about that, very wrong.

Anyway the woman who rang had a son who lived near Cranbrook. Her daughter-in-law worked at the hospital in Tunbridge Wells. I had secretly hoped it would never happen, not because I wanted to remain in Kent but I felt so low, physically and mentally, that I did not think I could cope with another move. Wilf was over the moon. He told me not to worry, he would cope with all that needed doing. Paul took photographs of our bungalow. The plan was that he would go and have a look at this woman's bungalow and take some photos to send to us. He would also show her the pictures of our place. Everything moved very quickly and a moving date was set. We could never have managed it without the help Paul and Becky gave us. They did a lot of the packing and helped us meet the costs of the move.

On 4th July I left Kent for the last time, taking with me Scott, two Persian cats and two dogs. We travelled in Becky's car. I was being sick before we got to Maidstone. It was a long drive. I just don't travel well. Wilf, Paul and Pip were left loading furniture into a hired van. By the time we got to Paul & Becky's I felt like death warmed up.

I did honestly believe that this move would kill me. We spent the night at their place and then set off on the Sunday for Leverton. I got a shock when we got there. The bungalow only had two bedrooms but it was massive compared to the one we had left. The garden at the back was more like a field, it went on forever. The lounge looked out onto the fields. We could sit and watch the cabbages grow. After everyone had left I had to lie down. I felt sick to my stomach. Wilf was still full of nervous energy. He spent the evening sorting the kitchen cupboards. Scott was desperately trying to get his bedroom, all his music and DVDs in order. He wasn't doing very well. Although he wanted to live nearer his brother, the reality was that he couldn't cope with change. He was trying to remember what order he had his music in and it was obvious that his anxiety levels were very high. He got worse as the days passed. I wasn't much help to him. I just felt so ill. I couldn't sleep, didn't want to eat and just wanted to pull the blankets over my head and pretend I was somewhere else. As the days passed we managed to achieve a degree of normality. Scott was driving himself bonkers re-arranging his CDs over and over again. I felt sure he would be fitting before long.

We had to go out to register with a GP. That was one thing we had to sort in case Scott needed to see the doctor. Did I like the place? To be honest, I didn't take much notice. I kept myself to myself and just got on. For the first couple of weeks things were good between myself and Wilf. I was just thanking God it was all over. Then when Wilf asked me one morning if I was keeping contact with anyone from Cranbrook, I couldn't believe my ears. My heart sank down into my boots. I thought,

"Oh God, here we go again." I had moved for him and nearly killed myself doing it and he still wasn't going to let go of his stupid notions. I just looked at him, tears running down my face. "Oh, please Wilf, not again. I can't take it any more."

He just shook his head and walked away. I thought, "The torture goes on then."

I never knew how the days would be but one look at Wilf's face soon put me straight. I decided not to argue with him about anything. He went with me to get my hair cut. He told me that my hair grew forward and told me to get it cut so it combed forward. I just obeyed orders. I hated my hair forward. Then I realised what he was doing, he was making me into an old woman. I always wore jeans, he wanted me in polyester trousers. I just did as I was told. I got a shock when I went to the doctors for a check-up. I was nearly a stone overweight. I felt a total frump and decided to go on a diet. I lost a stone very quickly and was back to a size 12. I just couldn't understand Wilf. He had always been a snappy dresser but in those days he slouched about in joggers. His self-esteem was rock-bottom. Well he wasn't the only one.

By late August 2010 Scott was fitting again. He had also started having non-epileptic attack disorder as well. He was on the go twenty-four hours a day. We were nearly on our knees. He was admitted to a special unit in Lincoln. We thought they would be monitoring his epilepsy. We couldn't have been more wrong. We were not well pleased to learn that they had been trying to control the non-epileptic movements using behavioural management – a very Draconian and outdated method.

Scott was in the unit nine and a half weeks and appeared to be enjoying the day centre and being with the other residents at first. I then learnt that this unit trained people to go and live in residential accommodation. I was livid. They actively discouraged contact with home. I had to ring and demand to speak to Scott. It came to a head one night when Scott phoned and said he was being abused by staff. I had never known Scott to tell an outright lie so I phoned the unit and questioned them regarding what Scott had said and also warned them that I would have 'their guts for garters' if any of them laid hands on him. They denied it. We decided that Scott needed to come home. I rang him later that night. When we finished talking he forgot to turn his phone off. I could hear a female member of staff shouting and swearing at him. That was it! Wilf had to stop me ringing a taxi and going to Lincoln to remove him. I must admit Wilf's way was the correct way. We contacted Scott's psychiatrist and said we would be taking him home at the end of the week. He was surprised. He thought we meant for the weekend. He didn't know what to reply when I told him, "No, to live. Scott lives with us. We don't want him placed anywhere. We never asked for anything but a few weeks' respite."

On the Friday we went to pick him up. I had been warned by all the family to keep my mouth shut and my hands in my pockets. I was fiercely protective of Scott. At that moment in time I would have killed anyone who hurt him. Scott is forty-three years old now but will always be my little boy. I will always look after him for as long as he needs me or until I die, whichever comes first.

During this time Wilf and I had got on really well, just like old times. We always were good together when we were fighting the world. Whilst Scott had been in this unit he'd been seeing a psychologist. She carried on seeing Scott, but at home. This lady was Dr Liz Boyd. She soon became a valuable member of the team and our family. Liz was a wonderful, caring person. She didn't just treat Scott, she helped the whole family come to terms with the fact that Scott was autistic and had been all his life.

I knew I was right. What I couldn't understand was why it had come to the fore so much at that point. Some days he would sit with his head covered and refuse to eat, drink, take medication, wash or shower. Things started to go downhill fast. It was hard to tell which of the movements were epilepsy and which were non-epileptic. Wilf was convinced these non-epileptic movements were done on purpose just to get up our noses. Liz and the neurologist told us, 'no', he had no control over them at all. He got a lot thinner and started hearing voices in his head. Sometimes he would be thrown onto the floor from a chair or sofa by the movements. I was really worried. He was also fitting. There were days and nights when he walked backwards and forwards around the bungalow. We had to lock both doors and hide the keys in case he got out and wandered off. We also hid all the kitchen knives when he told me that a voice had told him to kill his parents and then go to the top of the garden where he would be changed into another person whilst his dead body was still laid in the bungalow. A specialist was sent from Pilgrim Hospital to examine him at home as it was impossible to get him dressed and to the hospital. He was given anti-psychotic medication. This appeared to make him worse and caused more fits. Whilst all this had been going on Scott had told his social worker about his experiences in the unit at Lincoln. She, in turn, told her boss and then a full scale investigation was put in motion. The outcome of this was inconclusive. The people who Scott named had it noted on their records that a complaint had been made against them. I know who I believed but it was a case of not enough evidence against them.

Scott continued to go downhill. He became very secretive. I woke up one night to find him standing over my bed.

Apart from it nearly giving me a heart attack, I felt so sorry for him. He was 'out on his feet' but couldn't sleep, nor could anyone else. Pills were prescribed to slow him down and also pills to make him sleep. We just couldn't get the happy medium, he was either knocked out or climbing the walls.

We woke up one morning to him screaming in the bathroom. When we managed to get the door open he was in the corner terrified and sobbing. When we got him calm enough to talk he told us that a demon had pushed him against the wall and tried to strangle him. The red marks were evident on his neck. I wondered what the hell was going on. Had he tried to strangle himself? To consider the demon theory was pure insanity. Liz was due to see him the next day so we plodded on hoping that she would have a magic pill to put it all right. As night fell I was unnerved. He had not eaten all day although we had managed to get some bottles of water down him. We decided to take it in turns to watch him. He had started to talk to and answer himself, or that is what we thought was happening. It would have scared us to death had we known who he was talking to – it would have freaked us out completely.

Wilf had fallen asleep on the sofa. I was standing outside Scott's door trying to hear what he was saying. All was quiet so we went to bed, hoping he would do the same. I hadn't been asleep long when I was blasted out of bed by Elvis singing 'Blue Suede Shoes'. I was really angry and went storming into his bedroom, or tried to. He had locked the door. I shouted to him, "Open this door or I shall call the police to kick it down."

All went quiet. I heard him say, "No, I don't want to kill Izzie." Izzie was his little Chihuahua who had been his constant companion for years.

By this time Wilf was also standing by the door. Wilf shouted him to unlock the door or he would shoulder it open. All went quiet and the door slowly opened. There

stood Scott with an idiotic grin on his face. The room was in utter chaos, the floor littered with DVDs, CDs, empty cases, pens and rubbish. The curtains and rail were dragged down and his handprints could clearly be seen on the windows. When I asked what had been happening, he replied, "I needed to get into the garden to dance with the devil."

He stood there totally naked. My poor little boy had gone completely mad. As I started to clear up I remembered Izzie. I could see his little bed with his blanket over the top. I peeled the blanket back and there lay little Izzie fast asleep and snoring. I thanked God for that. I picked him up and removed him from the room but when I next looked he was back with Scott – a very loyal dog. He lay on the floor looking up at his master, now in bed, trying to sleep. Wilf spent the night in the chair by his bed. At 6.30 am next morning I sent a message to Liz asking her to bring a doctor with her, someone to prescribe something to help Scott. By the time Liz arrived Scott was much worse. Not only was he talking to other people, he could see them as well. He was what they call a 'responder'. The doctor said he would have to be taken to hospital and the only available bed was in Lincoln County Hospital. As, by this time, he lived in Lincoln, Paul waited on the ward with Becky for Scott to arrive. Wilf walked him out to the ambulance. I felt in my heart that I would not get Scott back, not the Scott I knew. Epilepsy I could cope with but this was a whole different ball game.

Paul and Becky met Scott on the ward. When they rang us later they were both in tears. Wilf and I didn't sleep at all that night. When we rang and spoke to the nurse in charge she confirmed that Scott was very ill. He'd been put on anti-psychotic medication again. I stressed his epilepsy. I wanted to make sure that the staff would watch him. I told them that we would visit later in the day.

I was shocked when she replied, "His brother is visiting each evening so we would prefer if you left it until his condition improves."

Well that was the first time in Scott's life that one of us hadn't been sitting at his bedside looking after him. I blamed myself and Wilf and all our arguments whilst we were in Cranbrook. Scott had known that all was still not well between us. The main factor was, I think, his autism.

It is not unusual for people with autism to get worse as

they get older. Before we left Cranbrook Scott had to get rid of some things, mainly videos and tapes. This is another thing about autistic people, they collect things. This is called 'special interests'. First it was records, then tapes, followed by videos, DVDs and CDs. It gets to be an obsession. At this moment in time we have more than six hundred and eighty DVDs, hundreds of CDs and Scott has spent over a thousand pounds downloading music to his computer. Still, I suppose it could be worse. I read about one boy who collected cat poo. His father's garage was full of black bags containing poo. If they tried to get rid of it, he would go into meltdown. At least what Scott collects is socially acceptable.

I was having an early morning cup of tea. It was before 7.00 am and the phone rang. My first thought was that it was about Scott, that he'd had a bad fit and had died. Wilf picked up the phone and then handed it to me. It was Maureen's eldest girl. What she told me froze my blood. My sister had died the previous day. No-one had bothered to let me know. I didn't even know that she was in hospital, let alone the fact that she was near death. I was upset but also very angry. She was my sister before she was anyone's wife or mother. I felt cheated. I never even got to say goodbye. We went through a lot together. Well she was at peace or so I hoped. I decided to stay away from the funeral. I always thought that Maureen wanted to be buried but she was cremated so I guess she changed her mind. I wondered where Dad ended up. Was there a special place for people like him, evil perverted people who prey on the minds of their family and have a life-long effect? He did not have a life-long effect on me. I had enough shit of my own going on to be troubled by memories of him. I made my mind up then to write about me, 'The Gamekeeper's Other Daughter', the one who spent the first few years of her life believing she was invisible, then the next few years wishing she was. Me, who fought my own corner from being five years old, me who survived everything Jockyboy threw at her. I stopped being scared or even caring before I was a teenager. My husband used to say to me, "You are hard, Doreen. You keep a piece of yourself back so no-one can ever have all of you." I don't know if that was true or not but I remember a small child inside me crying and no-one hearing so that's when I grew up and faced the world with my mask of 'who gives a shit'. Not many people saw the real Doreen. I'll leave it up to you to decide who was the real me.

Time moved along. Soon Scott was well enough to come home. On the day he was discharged his consultant shook my hand. "It's been a pleasure to have Scott on my ward," he said. He also warned me, "Try not to let him travel this road again. He may not be so lucky next time."

I knew there were strong signs of schizophrenia in the way his psychotic episode presented itself. There was a strong religious content to his delusional thinking, the feeling that he was possessed by evil spirits. I was also warned to keep him out of churches and not let him spend too much time in his own company.

A short time after Scott returned home we found something else had returned with him. Scott came home with his 'Beings'. He explained them as people. Some were created in heaven whilst Scott was in hospital. When he first came home there were two of them 'Lisa and Cara'. Scott said two beings were not enough so God decided to bring in a ghost to help slow down his movements. This ghost was called Tracey. She had lived on this earth and was a friend of his who had died in hospital after a heart operation. Things didn't improve so God created Princess Tracey who didn't live in Scott's body but was nearby watching over him. Then came Maria, Quara and Stacey, interestingly, they were all female. Liz tells me that this is Scott's coping strategy.

When he finds himself in a situation he can't cope with or his body freezes and he is unable to move he will summon one of his beings to take over. His voice will change a little, it will become quieter and more polite. I'll ask him who he is and he will say one of their names. His support workers are now also getting used to the different voices.

Scott is now forty-four years old. He still has his movements on a daily basis. He still looks for ways to stop them. However, nothing works for more than a day or so. His beings are also with us, part of everyday living for our family. Scott is not encouraged to talk to strangers about his beings. He knows they will not understand and will shy away, thinking he is mad. So our life goes on.

Scott started attending a day centre in Boston. This was just a stop-gap really. We knew that when he got back to his normal self it would be too boring to hold his interest. It was about this time that a support worker called Caroline Miller entered our lives. It became clear that Caroline understood what Scott was all about. She didn't find him strange or scary, could read his body language and knew when to offer help and sympathy and when to distract and encourage him to do something new and exciting to get his mind away from thinking about his movements, which, on bad days, drive him to despair. Caroline was to become my right-hand. I trusted her with my home, my money and with my most precious possession, my son, Scott. Over the next three years she would support me through the worst part of my life, when my heart was broken into a thousand pieces and life became not worth living. She would hold me when I cried, listen to me in my hours of despair and anger and wipe away my tears.

Without her I would not have coped.

CHAPTER 39: PLEASE DON'T FORGET ME

We all went to Boston to see the Christmas panto, 'Peter Pan'. Scott loves Peter Pan.

The next morning I came out of the shower to find Wilf looking very unwell, sitting on the sofa. He had chest pains, was blue around his mouth and very breathless. I put six aspirin under his tongue and rang 999. He was having a heart attack. I couldn't believe it and wondered how much more our family could take. He was in Pilgrim Hospital for ten days and then taken to Nottingham to assess if he needed any surgery. He was discharged the week before Christmas. He still intended to cook the Christmas lunch for us all. I asked the butcher to cook the turkey and the ham for us to make it easier for him. He was a stubborn man, he always bounced back again. The cardiac nurse told him it had been a mild heart attack but that he needed to take it easy for the next three months. He said 'OK' and then carried on as normal. Because he'd had a heart attack the GP told him that he couldn't have any more pills to help him in the sexual department. So he was not well pleased about that. But to be fair, what his surgeon told him after the prostate removal was coming to fruition. A lot of what he had lost was coming back, so he could strut around like a stud again.

It was good to see him get some of his confidence back but he still had good and bad days. I was not always flavour of the month. I just had to take the good with the bad and keep quiet. Life was easier that way. I'd become a 'yes' person. Everything he told me to do I just said 'yes' and got on with it.

I went to the doctors for a routine blood test with my 'escort' as usual. A few days passed and then I got a call from my GP, I needed to make an appointment to see her. Off I trotted, along with Paul on this occasion. My blood test results showed that I was very anaemic. I was not too worried. I told her my diet was not perfect and blamed that but she didn't agree. I knew what she was thinking. She booked me in for an endoscopy. For anyone who doesn't know, this is when they get you to swallow a small camera so they can have a look at your stomach. She was checking for stomach cancer. I said nothing to Scott as I knew he would only worry. Wilf kept telling me, "You'll be fine, love. Only the good die young." For once I didn't panic, I decided 'what will be will be'.

The day dawned and I thought I would be nervous. I was not. I was having the procedure done after lunch. I even got to eat my Weetabix and had a cup of tea at eleven o'clock. I had to take someone with me so Wilf tagged along. I refused the anaesthetic. I just agreed to have my throat sprayed. After all the horror stories, it really wasn't that bad. I didn't have a sore throat afterwards either. The reason I refused to be put to sleep was that I like to be in control of what's happening to me. The other reason was that if Wilf was sitting with me until I came round he could say I had been talking and then make up what I supposedly had been saying. I didn't know why he had to do things like that. They decided to take biopsies. I could hear the click every time they took some stomach tissue. They also took a sample of fluid to see if any nasty bugs were lurking there. I waited for two weeks for the results. It seemed I had a hiatus hernia, it was very common for people of my age. "Well, "I thought, "That's one thing. I never was common."

I breathed a sigh of relief as this was the second time I'd been given the 'all clear'. They wanted to do a colonoscopy but this was a step too far for me. I didn't mind them sticking a camera down my throat but they were not sticking it anywhere else. Besides I was already doing a bowel cancer trial for Nottingham Hospital. I had no symptoms so just didn't see the need. I took the horrible iron tablets until my blood tests came back OK. Then I just forgot the whole episode. I didn't have time to be ill.

It was Scott's forty-first birthday and the whole clan were coming for lunch on the Sunday, including Beth's fella. About an hour before they were due to arrive Wilf came out of the kitchen. I could tell by the look on his face that the 'black mist' had descended again. I thought, "Oh great, this is all I need when everyone is coming for lunch."

"Why don't you just admit what you have done, then we can draw a line under it and move on. I can't carry on like this," Wilf said.

He then told me that he intended to go back to Lincoln with Paul and find a flat unless I admitted that I'd had an affair with this young fella in Cranbrook. I was between a rock and a hard place. It was Scott's birthday, he would be so upset. It would ruin the day for him. For the only time ever in my life I admitted to something I had not done. I had a false face on all day. I really could have killed Wilf. He was messing with my head. I just waited for the day to end. When everyone was in bed, including Wilf, I sat drinking my final cup of tea. I didn't want to go to bed with him. I sat in the chair by Scott's bed for a while and then got a pillow and cover and fell asleep on the sofa. I was so angry. Wilf had played a rotten trick but the question was what did I intend to do? I really didn't want to live like that. I waited until Scott had gone out for the day with Caroline then I confronted my husband.

"What you did yesterday was despicable. You have a bloody cheek, all the women you have been involved with over the years and you have the nerve to accuse me of cheating. Well Mr Wonderful, unlike you, I haven't cheated. I don't give a shit now if you believe me or not."

He turned on me then. "I've never cheated on you. I admit I was a flirt, I got close to it a few times but I never did."

"Well, Wilf," I said. "There is the difference between us. I never even got close. I only ever wanted you."

I thought over the years the amount of times I'd thought he'd been playing away from home. I even found a pair of knickers in his jacket pocket. I knew that had been set up. I knew it was one of his mate's idea of a joke but it had caused me a lot of heartache. If I ever asked Wilf face-to-face what he'd been up to he would just give his stupid grin. He never said 'yes' or 'no'. Deep down I knew he'd never been untrue. I would have known. If he had I would have left him without a backward glance. I wondered why he was doing this when we were both in our sixties.

We had a heart-to-heart and he admitted he'd been 'down'. We agreed to try harder to make our marriage work as the only people getting hurt were us. We plodded on together, this was the best we had been in years.

Wilf put in a claim for PPI. We had forgotten all about it until we checked our bank statement. Wilf was 'gob smacked'. It was a lot more than he thought he'd get. This was a bit of luck for us. Our life got easier overnight. We had struggled with money most of our married life and now we had some to spare. It was a nice feeling.

We went through to Lincoln one Saturday. Wilf treated everyone to lunch at Stokes. It was a lovely day. We then had a family outing to Mablethorpe. Paul hired an extra car. We had a great day – went to the fair and just enjoyed the day. Wilf, for once, seemed happy, more like his old self. Once again, I saw the love he felt for me shine from his eyes. We were a couple again. We had survived everything the world had chucked at us. Despite all the people who had tried to split us up, there we were forty-two years later, still together.

I never thought in my younger years that I would ever be sixty-five but the following year I would be and Wilf would be seventy. I wondered where all those years had gone and why we wasted so much time bickering at each other.

2012 had been a good year for us. I wondered what 2013 would bring. Had I known then what was round the corner, I would have given 2013 a wide berth. There was a storm brewing that would knock me sideways. Would I be able to survive what 2013 had in store?

In March 2013 Wilf started to tell us all 'no seventy years birthday cards'. "I'm not going to be seventy, an old man", he said. He was still young at heart. He then told me he wouldn't see his seventieth birthday.

"Don't be stupid," I said. "The amount of ill health you have suffered, you've had all the serious things."

It was April when it all started to go wrong. I was ill with a stomach bug so Wilf went into Boston to pay some bills. When he got back he said he didn't feel right. He'd had a funny turn in the taxi on the way to Boston. I tried to determine what sort of turn but he was having trouble trying to explain what he meant. As the day progressed he got much worse. He couldn't seem to get the words out, couldn't find the right words. It was very strange. I was getting concerned. Alarm bells were ringing in my head. I did the usual checks. I was pretty sure he hadn't had a stroke. I rang the GP's. They really didn't like sending doctors out.

"Can you bring him to the surgery?" the receptionist asked.

I made it crystal clear to her. "My husband is feeling very unwell. I have my son with me who has complex health issues. Are you suggesting I bring him along as well because he can't be left alone."

She said she would ring me back. After about ten minutes the phone rang. The receptionist informed me that one of the doctors would be out to see us before evening surgery. When he did arrive he did all the checks I had already done, then said, "I'm not happy. I want him to go to A & E to be checked out. He may have had a small bleed." He left saying that he would arrange for an ambulance. We sat waiting. After two hours it still hadn't arrived. I rang the surgery to be told that it had been requested but 'you'll just have to wait'. Another hour passed. I'd had enough, I thought, "Sod this." I rang 999 and requested an ambulance. When they arrived they also checked Wilf out. I told them the GP had been and thought that he may have had a bleed. I left Scott in Caroline's capable hands. I thanked God for Caroline, I don't know how I managed before she came into our lives. One of the ambulance men commented that Wilf 'looked OK now'. I put him straight.

"My husband has been feeling unwell since this morning and he has got more and more distressed sitting about waiting for an ambulance. As my husband had a heart attack last year, I'm taking no chances."

He then informed me that Wilf's stats were normal. I replied, "My husband's doctor wants him checked out so that's what is going to happen."

What a joke. There were four ambulance crews waiting to offload patients, we made it five. A & E was 'chock a block'', all the cubicles were full. It was just general chaos. A member of staff was trying to release some of the crews. She looked at Wilf, "You'll be OK sat on a chair," she said as she walked past. Then a nurse came with a chair for him. I was desperate for the loo. When I returned he was on the floor. I helped him up and spent most of the time hanging onto him to stop him falling again. After what seemed an eternity, we were moved into a cubicle. There was no trolley, not even a chair for him. A health care assistant came to take blood. By now I was starting to get angry. Wilf was very unstable. At last someone with a brain brought in a trolley. He got his bloods done. Then they decided to send him for a chest X-ray and CT scan. A doctor examined him but could find nothing obvious.

They decided to keep him overnight. I needed to go home to relieve Caroline. Before I left I stressed to the staff that Wilf was not his normal self, he was confused. I told them that when he was ready to come home I would collect him.

I didn't want him wandering about on his own. Alas, it all fell on stoney ground. He was discharged the next morning. He wandered about outside the hospital until he was spotted by our usual taxi driver who brought him home. I was livid. He could have walked under a bus. The two doctors who discharged him told him to see his own GP. By then he was convinced that it was panic attacks that were making him feel poorly. I didn't agree. I'd suffered from panic attacks for two years. I'd had none of the symptoms that Wilf was now experiencing. I had a gut feeling, even then, that this was something serious. I didn't want to spook Wilf as he already thought he would die before he was seventy.

Sitting around in hospitals gave you time for reminiscing. I had a little chuckle to myself. Do you remember the Elvis lookalike in Lumsden who did all the first footing? Well, Wilf was near enough his double, or had been when he was younger, when I first met him. When he decided to chase me around asking me to go out with him I turned him down every time. I went into a pub with live music whilst on the office night out – the rest is history. He was singing with a rock group, serenaded me with a love song. I melted, he won my heart, my body and my soul forever. It suddenly hit me. I thought, "This is the time when illness will win and he'll be taken from me." Could I cope with this? No way, I was not letting that happen.

During the next few months he was back and forward to GP appointments. He was tested for dementia and passed that. During this time he had two chest infections and was given steroids and whilst on these was more or less his old self. When the steroids finished he was back to struggling to remember words and his speech was getting worse. The doctors still thought he was suffering from panic attacks and depression was added to their diagnosis. They gave him more pills for this. During a good period in June he decided to do a roast dinner. He hadn't done this since his heart attack. All the family arrived. The lunch was delicious. That was to be the last lunch he ever cooked.

July 2013 started out OK but by the end of the month he was much worse. On 9th August we were in Boston shopping when he became very unwell. I got him home in a taxi. He was having a lot of shaking attacks and tremors. He fell to the floor in the kitchen during one of these attacks. I sat on the kitchen floor with him, holding him in my arms. My husband was frightened. I had never seen him like that before. He kept asking me what was wrong, what was happening to him? I held him close.

"Don't worry my love," I told him. "I'm getting this sorted today. I'll make sure we find out what's wrong."

I again rang the GP's surgery. I didn't ask for a doctor, I demanded a qualified doctor get there, examine him and get him another scan. My husband was seriously ill. By this time I knew that. I didn't want a trainee who had never seen him before. I wasn't taking any more 'crap'.

He was examined and sent into A & E as an emergency. I waited at home, pacing the floor, waiting for Paul to arrive to care for Scott whilst I got to the hospital. As I walked into the department that evening my heart was beating so loud I'm surprised everyone couldn't hear it. As I walked into the cubicle Wilf was sitting on a chair. There was a trolley there but the junior doctor attending him couldn't get him to lay on it. It was unbelievable. His face was redder than I had ever seen it. He had shoved all his medication, which was in a plastic bag, into his fleece pockets. I was desperately trying to find his inhalers as his breathing was very bad.

The junior doctor returned with a copy of the scan report in his hand. His command of English was not good but I could understand him. It was unheard of at that time to get an English doctor in the Emergency Department.

He finished reading and asked me, "Are you the wife?"

I just looked back. "Sorry," I said.

"Are you this man's wife?" he asked again.

I replied that I was.

"Well," he said. "There is no nice way to tell you this. Your husband has an inoperable brain tumour. It is quite large. He has maybe six months to live. It's a follow-on from the prostate cancer he had before.

I lost it big time. "Don't talk bollocks," I said. "Can it be removed?"

He replied that it was too deep in the brain to try and remove any of it.

All this time Wilf was in 'Noddyland', sitting on his chair, grinning like a fool. Thankfully, he hadn't taken in anything this medic had said.

"We will admit him to CDU and then transfer him to Queens at Nottingham as soon as they confirm they have a bed for him. It was at this point that my husband should have been given steroids to relieve the pressure on his brain. This wasn't done but you will learn about that a bit further into the farce that night was turning into.

I walked out of the cubicle and phoned Paul. "You better get here and bring Scott. Your Dad has an inoperable brain tumour, he's going to die quite soon." As I said those words, tears streaming down my face my Scorpio brain was already planning my revenge. They had said that he was having panic attacks back in April, now they were saying ' brain tumour', but he presented with the same symptoms both times so who had cocked up? Someone must have. It would cost my man his life. Someone was going to pay for this with blood. I was so angry. When Paul arrived after he had seen his dad he started talking to doctors, making notes and taking names.

I think he was on the same track as me. We followed Wilf up to CDU but even that didn't go smoothly.

By this time I was being physically sick. I had to get a

vomit bowl from the nurses' station. The Staff Nurse asked, "Is Mr Burrows vomiting?"

"No," I replied. "I find attending the A & E in Boston seriously affects your health."

She gave me her, 'I'm not amused' look as I walked away.

Time moved on. No-one had been to see Wilf, a critically ill man – disgusting. Everyone agreed that I should go home and take Scott with me. I kept breaking down in tears. I just couldn't cope with what I had been told, my brain wouldn't let me. Scott didn't appear to pick up how serious his Dad's condition was, which was a blessing at that time. By this time Wilf couldn't speak any words that were understandable, he couldn't make up any sensible words. We didn't know what he wanted to say and this was making him more distressed and angry.

Paul ordered a taxi for us and we made our way home. Scott was quite tired and was soon on the sofa, asleep. With time on my hands, my mind went into overdrive. Had I just kissed my husband for the last time? Would he be in a coffin the next time I saw his face? This was destroying me. Somehow I had to get a handle on it. I would have to care for Scott 24/7 from then on. I would also have to care for Wilf. How much would he be able to manage for himself? The future stretched in front of me like an endless tunnel with no end in sight.

The little Yorkie that Wilf had bought for my birthday was nearly a year old by that time. He didn't like to see me cry and jumped on my knee to try to lick all the tears away.

The phone ringing shook me out of my dreamlike state. Every time I'd answer the phone I would dread the news it could bring. Many years previously Wilf and I had made our plan of action. Scott had to be cared for no matter what and kept to his routine as much as possible but I knew, deep in my heart, that if it had been me laying in that hospital bed Wilf would have been at my side holding me in his arms no matter what. The problem was Scott was not easy to handle. Leaving him with anyone but Caroline at that time was not an option and she was on a much deserved holiday, after working long shifts for me over the previous few days before she went away. She had been my rock. Without her I would never have survived the weeks that lay ahead. She was there to catch me when I stumbled. She listened to me rant, rave and swear at God, the world, all the doctors and even myself.

I wondered why me and Wilf had wasted so much time bickering at each other, having rows and not talking for days. All that had paled into insignificance. Scott was to spend the next few weeks praying for a miracle. Paul never left his father's side. From the moment he knew that he had a serious condition he slept in whichever hospital his dad was in. He worked on his PC by the side of Wilf's bed or in the dayroom, anywhere he could get an internet connection. That was how much his dad meant to him. Paul was a toddler when Wilf first met him. He had put him on his shoulders and that's where he stayed right to the end. Wilf had a special place in his heart for each of us. First it was just me and then Wilf gave all his love to Paul. He lost contact with his young daughter around the time he met me so Paul filled that place in Wilf's heart. He didn't agree with 'weekend dads'. He thought it confused young kids. His ex-wife made it very difficult for him. Wilf knew that my long-term plans did not include living forever in Yorkshire and that if he came along on my life's journey it didn't include a long distance relationship with his daughter from a previous marriage. I just couldn't imagine his ex-wife letting Annette spend some of her school holidays with us.

I spent a lot of the long evenings, whilst Wilf was in Nottingham, thinking back over what Wilf had told me about his childhood years. I soon understood how the chip on his shoulder became a huge boulder that he carried for most of his life. It made me understand why every so often he would push the self-destruct button and for those few hours he didn't 'give a shit' about anyone, not even me. As we got older he had told me much more about Alice and how she had changed from a fun-loving young woman to a trouble-causing old witch. I had got a taste of how this felt when Paul met Becky. I knew I had met my match and soon realised that I would have to learn how to share Paul or lose him.

Wilf had felt no affection for his mother in later life. Bob, his father, was a very cold fish. When Wilf excelled at sport Bob lost interest in his only son. He wanted an academic. He would have been pleased to know that both Paul and Paul's son, Pip, graduated with Masters degrees – Paul in business management, Pip as an interior architect. None of this mattered to Wilf. He was proud of both his boys and his grandchildren. That would not have changed no matter what their career choices had been. Becky also earned her special place in his heart. She was the only woman I would have shared him with. She supported Paul from the day she met him. She was at his side when his Dad took his last breath on this earth and his world fell apart.

In 2013 Jill and Colin, Becky's parents, moved to Lincoln. Wilf was to say how much he admired them as Jill was coping with health problems too. They both attended Wilf's funeral. He would have been touched to see them there.

Wilf had told me about his childhood in Shipley. How he came home from school to an empty house. Alice always spent the day in Keighley at Manda's and only returned in time to cook an evening meal for Bob. He told me about the time he'd had a fight with a boy at school, like young kids did. Anyway, the lad's mother came over to complain to Alice about the trouble. Alice wasn't there so the lad's mother gave Wilf a smack in the mouth for hitting her son.

Of course, Alice went storming over when she got home and had her say but it was too late, her son had been scared and she'd let him down. She let him down again when Wilf fell down the cellar steps, trying to bring up some coal to light the fire before his mum got home. He was hurt and had to be taken to hospital, but he suffered and bled until Alice got back. When he was a teenager and started smoking he came home after drinking and set his bed on fire. Bob had to throw his mattress out of the bedroom window. His parents made Wilf sleep on just the springs until he had saved up enough money to buy a new mattress, tough punishment indeed. After all, he was under eighteen, the legal age to buy a pint, had they tried to stop his drinking then he wouldn't have been a heavy drinker by the age of twenty-one. I think it would have been fair to say that they were a bit embarrassed by Wilf's behaviour. He knew this and soon learnt to spend as much time as he could at his aunt's house, where he knew he was loved. He wasn't very kind to girlfriends in his teenage years. It wasn't unknown for young ladies to wait for him outside his house and ask him to walk them home after he returned from the Saturday dance at the Mecca in Bradford. I'm not sure if all these young women were 'legal'. He got a shock one Monday when the girl he'd walked home on the previous Saturday night came into Driver's Milk Bar in her school uniform. They remembered him but he had long forgotten their names. He was a 'one night stand' fella in those days. I think that's why he was so shocked when I wasn't interested in dating him – he'd never had any trouble pulling the girls. But I'm afraid he met his match in me. I didn't make it an easy ride for him.

In the last few weeks of his life he shared lots of his hopes, regrets and dreams with me and these words stick in my memory and carry me through when sadness overcomes me. "You can console yourself with the fact you were the only woman I ever loved. You were the love of my life. I would have died for you."

At that moment in time he laid in Queens Hospital in Nottingham waiting to go to theatre yet again, this time for a biopsy on his brain. After he returned home I found his notebook where he had been writing about his family, even the dogs. He was so frightened that he would not remember us after they had messed his brain around.

I spoke to Wilf daily on the phone. He was often crying, telling me he loved me. Then he said the thing that broke me in bits, "Promise you won't forget me."

I was still sobbing when Paul called later. "He's getting things back to front," Paul said. "He's frightened he will forget everything when he has the biopsy."

If you could see what he wrote in his notebook, it was so sad. Paul took me to visit the day before Wilf's biopsy. One chap tried to get in Wilf's bed. He was so good with him.

"Come on mate. Your bed is next door," he said, leading him gently to his own bed.

When we were sitting close together Wilf asked me, "Is there a life after death?"

I shook my head. "That's the six million dollar question," I replied.

What he said next had me in stitches. "If there is nothing after you die I'm going to be seriously pissed off."

"Well, you wouldn't know, would you?" I said.

When I left him that day a part of me died. I knew I was losing the only person I had ever loved, the only consolation was that the hospital had said that they wouldn't do a biopsy unless they could offer treatment.

Was Wilf yet again to cheat the grim reaper or had his luck run out? As I lay in bed that night I can say without a doubt that if the devil had come wanting my soul I would have given him it on the understanding that my man was allowed to live. The following day, whilst Wilf was in theatre, I went to a church in Boston to light a candle for the bravest man I ever knew. Down on my knees I made a deal with God. It went something like this,

"If you can't save him, take him quickly. I don't want him to suffer." I think God granted that prayer.

I visited Wilf in Nottingham a few days before he came home. Paul and Becky went off to speak to the oncologist. Although Wilf was still very weepy, I was surprised at how well he looked, his speech was improving as his brain settled back down. We would get the results of the biopsy the following week. He had suffered blinding headaches for weeks before his biopsy. However, he was to make the transition from this world to the next without morphine or any mind-blowing drugs.

Wilf was to come home the following Monday. I knew that Paul and Becky had been told a lot more than they were saying after we left the hospital that day. I sat on a bench for a few minutes to collect my thoughts and clear my head. I looked at Becky.

"You may as well tell me, I need to know what is going to happen."

Becky sat with her arms around me. "Are you sure you want to know?" she asked.

I nodded, tears streaming from my eyes. I listened, the sobs shaking my body, as they told me that no matter what treatment was offered it would make no difference. Wilf had very little time left.

I was heartbroken but, more than that, I was so bloody angry. I'm a loose cannon when the red mist descends. I blamed everybody, right from the GP, the hospital, God for letting Wilf be taken from me. I even blamed Wilf – how dare he leave me alone?

Monday came around and my man came home. He was very upbeat. We sat until the 'witching hour' listening to the old sixties music that Wilf loved. He told me again about Colin, a disabled lad, who Wilf and his mates protected and looked after – taking this lad to the pubs, clubs and wherever they went. I had heard this tale many times but it still made me smile. Colin used to tell Wilf, "Don't sit by me Burrows. How can I pull a bird with you sitting there?" When Wilf used to sing, Colin would shout 'Candy Man' – he loved the song. Wilf would take him on stage and Colin would help to sing 'Candy Man'. Woe betide anyone who didn't applaud. Colin was well looked after by these lads. At last Wilf told me how he felt after his prostate operation. His confidence had taken a nose dive. He felt useless and unloved. I blamed myself for this. I thought that this must have been a failing in me, why hadn't I seen this coming?

Wilf also spoke about his regrets – all the years he spent on a bar stool, precious time that he wished he'd spent with us. He admitted to being the biggest flirt ever – how he loved the way ladies chased him. He told me, 'hand on heart 'that he'd never cheated on me, the chances had been there but he had turned them down.

I asked why he pressed the 'self-destruct' button so often.

Apparently this stemmed from his teenage years. Yes, he was a teddy boy, yes he was a rebel but he just needed someone to love him for himself, not the image he portrayed. People had expected him to act like a prat in his teenage years. When he celebrated being twenty-one, I was only sixteen, still a kid. He deeply regretted his first marriage. How he wished he'd stuck to his guns. Right up to the time he'd said, 'I do' he wanted to run. This marriage was doomed from day one. They had nothing in common. If Pauline had told him a day later than she did that she was pregnant he would have already had told her it was over. Wilf lived a 'Walter Mitty' life whilst he was in that marriage. We fell asleep in each others' arms just like a couple of teenagers that night.

We spoke a lot over that week. I didn't know it then but these precious days would be some of the last times I ever spoke to him.

CHAPTER 40: GOODBYE MY LOVE

I was fighting an inner battle with myself regarding Wilf's daughter, should I ask if he wanted to see her? I'm afraid I made that choice for him. For the time he had left I decided that no-one had better upset or distress him, I would tear their heads off.

He spoke about his boys and how proud he felt. He spoke of how he loved his grandchildren and how much Becky meant to hm. We laughed remembering the night out with the boys that resulted in him being brought home in the dustbin wagon. He was on crutches as well. He spoke of how he lost his chance to play football for Sheffield, apart from the fact that he hit the nightclubs instead of training, his father had stepped on his dream. He ended up with an apprenticeship. He'd been working for two weeks before his parents realised he'd left school. The last thing he wanted to be was a textile engineer but he stuck it out and qualified.

He admitted that he had seen the future through the bottom of a pint glass but there had always been some lady looking 'cow-eyed' at him, wanting to mess up his lovely black hair. He said that it was at that time he felt the loneliest ever. As we talked, I knew I was burying my head in the sand as he was already deteriorating.

The phone call from Paul brought more devastating news. It was the worst case scenario, the most aggressive type of tumour, already at grade four and growing rapidly. I so wanted to keep Wilf at home until the end but I knew this would not be possible. We lived outside Boston and getting help in the night was an impossibility. I told Wilf that he was the bravest man I'd ever met. He faced everything head on. It was so cruel that the thing he dreaded most was losing his mind. This was going to happen. There was nothing I could do or say to prevent it.

We were due to go to Lincoln the following week to plan his treatment. He had to have a mask made to protect his face during radiotherapy. He saw his consultant. She looked so young, a little girl with a short skirt. After Wilf went for his blood test I spoke to her privately. I needed to know what to watch for and how bad it was going to be. Would he lose his sight? She thought this was unlikely. I asked her not to tell Wilf that he was dying. He wouldn't have been able to cope with that. She promised not to, saying that unless he asked her the question she would say nothing. I wanted to know how long he'd got. She replied that it was impossible to say. Radiotherapy had been known to stop the growth of this type of tumour and some people had lived a number of years. She said that the main thing was to try and keep his strength up as the treatment was very hard to bear.

She gave me a glimpse of what to expect. "If I could choose how I wanted to die," she said, "I would choose a brain tumour. They get weaker, they sleep deeper and in the end they just drift away without fear, without knowledge of what's happening." I guess that's what you class as a good death.

By this time Wilf's mobility was almost gone. However,

the consultant did think it was possible to get some of it back. As far as his speech was concerned, the cancer had taken that for good. He could still make noises and we had to try and determine what he wanted. This used to make him so angry. He couldn't understand why we didn't give him the drink he wanted, why we tried to put him to bed when he wanted the loo. Scott used to sit with his dad and feed him his favourite sweets – jelly babies and Malteasers.

The next time we went to Lincoln was for Wilf to have a special CT scan so that the correct area could be targeted.

It was a painful and tiring journey for Wilf. Paul expressed his concern that the journey on a daily basis would be too much for his dad. The hospital did say he could be admitted for the duration of his treatment if we thought this would be better. This was the last time that Wilf attended Lincoln County Hospital. The next time he was to travel to Lincoln it would be to his final destination.

Things were becoming much harder to cope with. Wilf became very aggressive at times, usually with me. He was still able to talk a little, just after he'd taken his steroids, but his speech soon faded again. One day he got very upset and told Scott and I to get out of his house and let him die in peace. That night Scott was very upset. "Why are we looking after that old man in the bedroom?" he said.

I got angry, "That's your dad you're talking about. He's devoted his life to caring for you," I snapped at him.

"That's not Dad," Scott replied. "We lost Dad days ago."

Wilf had a disturbed night. I was having to put pads on

him then to keep the bed clean. He hated it. After working in the care industry himself he'd once told me, "If I get to the stage of having to wear nappies, give me an overdose."

If I had to leave the house to go to Boston to the bank or pay bills he became very distressed. Paul had to keep ringing me to see if I was on the bus home. He was a handful, I must admit that. I had carers coming in at night to help him to bed but that soon became a pointless exercise. If they were late he would already be in bed (having insisted that I put him to bed). This was no easy task. Nine times out of ten his legs would let him down. Scott and I struggled between us to get him settled. At times he was very nasty. I have arthritis in my hands and my thumb joints and wrists become swollen, it's a very painful condition. He would twist and squeeze my hands, he knew this caused me a lot of pain. Maybe this was payback for putting him in nappies. Paul and Scott both said, "It's not Dad, it's the tumour."

One night I was very upset and couldn't sleep. I'd made myself a cup of tea. I sat by the bed with my head on Wilf's chest, sobbing. He was fast asleep for once. Then I felt his hand stroking my head. "You will be fine, my love. You will manage to do it all without me." I was stunned.

He hadn't spoken properly for ages.

"I don't want to manage without you. I can't cope without you," I replied. He just kept stroking my head. When I looked at him he was sleeping again.

Next morning I asked the St Barnabas nurses to bath him. Wilf hated being sweaty or smelly, I knew this from previous times when he'd been ill. We'd had a bath seat delivered so the nurses put him in the bath and washed his hair. It was a big mistake on my part. I guess I was closing my mind to the fact that he was getting weaker day-by-day, even though he was still eating and drinking well. As they got him out of the bath, he collapsed. Between the three of us we got him into his chair. I was beside myself. "This is it," I thought, he's dying." None of us could find a pulse. When we did it was faint and irregular. The paramedics had been sent for. A first responder lived a few doors away. He was first to arrive with oxygen. When the paramedics arrived they did a heart trace. Wilf's blood pressure had always been low but after his heart attack in December 2011 the doctors put him on blood pressure medication to keep it low and he was still on it. He came to with the oxygen and was promptly put back to bed by the nurses. I rang his GP for permission to reduce his blood pressure tablets, after all, he was dying, what difference would it make? I had to wait for a GP to come out and see what he thought – laughable really if it wasn't so bloody sad.

My man was dying. He'd been my man for nearly forty-three years. I wondered how I could carry on without him.

I couldn't see a way forward. The strain was showing on us all. Paul and Becky were due to go on a cruise. They had been looking forward to this, it would be their twenty-fifth anniversary. They cancelled it. I felt so sorry but they wanted to be near Wilf. They knew, as I did, that his time was growing shorter. The only thing we could hope for then was a miracle.   I soon learnt that miracles were in short supply.

I used to sit and watch Wilf sleep. He looked so peaceful.

I would cast my mind back to the first time we went to Scarborough. I called it his 'dark glasses era'. We had been in a pub near the seafront. Wilf was all in black, the reason for the glasses being he'd drunk too much the night before. His eyes looked like 'piss-holes in the snow' (his words not mine). We both sat by the juke-box. I was drinking coke, he was on tomato juice (after I'd put him on a 'red card'). I was a Roy Orbison fan. After putting some of my favourites on I went to the loo. When I returned there were two young ladies sitting in my place. Wilf was being Mr Charming, as usual. They thought he was a singer, hence the glasses. I sat down on the nearest chair. "Take off the shades, Wilfie baby, they think you're someone famous." We had a good laugh about this – I have the photos to prove it.

After I had been to the cinema with Wilf for the first time I assumed he was my fella, how stupid was I? I found out how stupid I was that week.   I went out on the Wednesday night with a few girls from the office. We went to a pub we liked that had live music on Wednesdays. I could hear someone singing before we even got inside. I knew it was Wilf. I was last through the door. There he was, 'Mr Sex on Legs' doing his walkabout with the microphone. We sat down at a table in the corner. His face dropped when he spotted me. I made my hand into a gun and pretended to shoot him. Yeah, you guessed it, he was crooning to a couple of kids, if they were over eighteen I was a Chinaman. I thought, "Well Burrows, you just blew it with me." Maybe, at twenty-one, I was too old for him? These girls were certainly too young for a twenty-six year old man. I was livid but no way was I going to let him know it bothered me. Christine spotted him. "Isn't that your fella getting up close and personal with the teeny boppers?" she asked me.

"I've been out with him once but I don't like to rough it," I replied. It was well-known that I only dated office guys. I was in jeans and boots that night, was I looking for trouble? I saw a young lad who worked in Despatch standing at the bar. Kevin was also there. "Right," I thought. "Which one is going to have the pleasure of getting smoochy with me on the dance floor?" If I picked Kevin, who was now a married man, I didn't want his wife on my case. I stood talking to Kevin, he'd his arm round me and we were laughing together. Wilf's face was like thunder. Kevin kissed my cheek. I moved on to Dave from Despatch. He was only young but we all called him 'Dishy Dave'. He was very good-looking, a bit like Ricky Nelson.

"You fancy a dance, Dave?" I asked.

We had danced before at a Christmas works do. Now with Dave I could jive but with Wilf I never learnt. The next number was slow and we smooched around the dance floor. Wilf retaliated by asking 'sweet little sixteen' to dance. I didn't care. Yeah, right, who was I fooling, I was as jealous as hell. I put my head on Dave's shoulder. I wasn't even going to look Wilf's way. Later on he made a beeline for our table.

"Hello sweetheart. Fancy a dance?" he asked me.

"No thanks," I replied. "I prefer younger meat."

He glared at me and left. We totally ignored each other at work for the next couple of days. On the Friday I was sitting in Victoria Park eating my fish and chips. He sat down on my bench. "This is stupid," he said. "It was only a song. I always walk around when I sing."

I ignored him.

"I only asked her to dance because you were hung round Dave's neck. Cradle snatching now are you?"

"Not at all," I smiled sweetly as I added, "Dave's only three years younger than me."

"So you fancy him more than me, do you?" he sneered at me.

"I would fancy any man who could keep it in his pants."

"Oh, stuff you. I sang to her, I didn't sleep with her."

"In your dreams, Wilf, you will always be as you are now, a ladies' man. I don't want someone I have to watch all the time. It wouldn't work with us," I said.

Now I was sitting watching him sleep. He was sixty-nine and we'd been together a lot of years. I loved him just as much then as I ever did.

The following morning the nurses left him in bed. He wasn't best pleased about that but they were concerned that he was going to have a repeat performance and pass out on them.

At about three o' clock the following morning I awoke to find him choking. I ended up sitting by him for the rest of the night, keeping him upright. At around four o'clock he spoke again to me very clearly. I was standing by the bedroom window waiting for daybreak. The nights are long when you're awake whilst all the rest of the world sleeps. He called me by my nickname.

"Dor, my love, can you get me some help. I feel really poorly."

I had already rung the Marie Curie night nurses. I had looked at Wilf's throat earlier. It was ulcerated. I thought it might be thrush or that it could be something connected to his brain condition. I couldn't understand why he was choking. It could be that he was aspirating and his drinks and food were going into his lungs, not his stomach. We had moved another step nearer to the inevitable conclusion.

A male nurse and a health care assistant finally arrived from Marie Curie. The nurse asked where the 'as required' box was. I had no idea what he was talking about. He explained that when patients get to the palliative stage the GP should prepare a box of medication containing anti-sickness injections, morphine and other heavy-duty drugs. You kept this box in the house so it was there when needed. He listened to Wilf's chest, which sounded clear. He left me with antibiotics. As Wilf didn't have a chest infection, these were of little use. The anti-sickness injection Wilf needed couldn't be given. I left an emergency message asking a GP to call before morning surgery. It was nearly 11.00 am before he arrived. The St Barnabas nurses made Wilf comfortable and phoned Paul to say he was deteriorating. They warned me that 'this could be it', the end was close.

The GP wanted Wilf to be admitted to hospital. He said it

was clear I couldn't cope, not with Scott to care for as well. Wilf was very sleepy. I told the doctor that I wasn't having him messed around in A & E. He agreed and Wilf was admitted straight to the CDU at Pilgrim Hospital, Boston. Paul didn't want him to go there, he wanted him in the hospice at Lincoln. I put my foot down – how could myself and Scott have visited him in Lincoln? Paul stayed with his dad to make sure he was being cared for appropriately. We were still hoping for treatment which was due to start on 20th September but we were all beginning to think that Wilf would not be strong enough to cope with two weeks of radiotherapy. Anyway, we knew that only time would tell. Paul was going to ring Lincoln County Hospital to see if his dad's treatment could be moved forward. This was not possible as they only had two machines and one was awaiting repair.

It was now 2nd September. Paul was camped out in Ward 7B with his dad, working from there. I visited daily, sometimes with Scott. It was when I was leaving his bedside one afternoon as I bent to kiss him he drew back from me. It was obvious, from the look in his eyes, that he had lost all knowledge of me. It had happened. I had lost the love of my life forever. I was devastated. At home I was crying non-stop. I knew deep in my heart that Wilf would not come back to me, he had left, never to return to my arms. He remained on Ward 7B until 11th September. The standard of care for the dying was not good. I had refused permission for him to be catheterised. This was the promise I had given Wilf. Unfortunately, this meant that I often found him very wet and cold. His drinks were now being thickened. I made it quite clear to all staff that he must not be refused food or drink. As far as I was concerned they could keep the

Liverpool Care Pathway in Liverpool. Paul was not happy about the standard of care given to his dad.

When the Oncologist visited Wilf for the last time she confirmed that he was too weak for any treatment. The tumour was by then very large. He was beyond help.

When I arrived the next afternoon Wilf had been moved to a private room. As Scott and I walked into the room he was trying to climb over the cot sides. He wanted to wee. I gave him a bottle. It was pointless. He was soaked in urine and very cold to the touch. I rang the bell. It took fifteen minutes for anyone to answer. I lost my temper.

This had been brewing over the last few days. I told the staff that Wilf had been nearly over the cot sides. I asked when he had last been changed as he was soaking wet. They said he was checked every hour. I ranted back, "It's not enough. Is this how Pilgrim Hospital cares for the dying?" I told the Staff Nurse that I was taking Scott downstairs for a coffee and that when I got back I expected my husband to have been made comfortable. I also told her that he needed more blankets as he was very cold and requested that whoever kept leaving the radio on, didn't because the noise hurt his head. I told her that if I found it on again I would 'shove it where the sun don't shine'. I said that I wanted my husband to be monitored on a one-to-one basis until Paul arrived and that if this were not possible I would return with a member of the press plus a photographer. It seemed to do the trick. This was the last straw for Paul. He arranged for Wilf to be transferred to St Barnabas Hospice at Lincoln the following day, it was the right decision. I had amazed myself, I had got my point across without being arrested.

Paul made himself comfortable in the chair for his Dad's last night in Pilgrim Hospital. The strain was very evident. Paul was tired and he was very emotional, just managing to hold it together. Although Paul lived only minutes from the hospice he asked if he and Becky could have the flat upstairs. He didn't want his dad left alone for a minute. When the time came to move Wilf, Paul was fine until they put him onto the trolley. He had just realised that they were taking his dad to the place where he would die. Paul crumbled but by the time he'd followed the ambulance to St Barnabas Hospice he'd composed himself again. The care Wilf received in the hospice was amazing. They were waiting for him with a warm blanket. He was soon settled and comfortable. He was never left wet or cold. Every care was given. I can't praise the hospice staff enough.

Over the following three days Wilf went downhill very quickly, sleeping longer and sleeping deeper. It was just as his consultant had said, he was peaceful and never agitated. We sat by his bed for hours watching him slip away. Part of me was dying too. Over the years I had always thought I would be the first to go. I know it sounds morbid, but I had imagined my death scene many times – I would die in Wilf's arms. He would protect me in death as he had in life. I would have sold my soul to the devil to save my man. I believed I was never going to be able to cope with his loss. I had looked in the mirror that morning and there was something different about me. I realised then what it was. Over the years Wilf had always said that my eyes sparkled. He said he could see right into my soul. By then my eyes were dead. The sparkle had died slowly as each day passed and Wilf slipped further away from life. His life force had always been so strong. As I closed my eyes I could see him in his element singing his favourites, strutting his stuff on the dance floor. I couldn't bear it, my love was dying. It was now Friday, 13th September. I didn't know it, but both Paul and I were begging him not to die on Friday 13th. Stupid really, what difference would it make?

At about 9.30 pm that night Paul called on his mobile. I thought, "This is it."

"What's happened?" I gasped into the phone.

"Nothing Mum," he replied. "I'm sitting with Dad. Say goodnight to him. I'll hold the phone by his ear."

Remembering what I'd been told from my work in care, that hearing is the last sense to go, I said 'goodnight' to my precious man for the last time. I loved him so much that I couldn't bear for him to leave me. I begged God for more time. It was selfish of me I know. Wilf was ready to go.

That night I dreamt of Wilf. He was in his black suit and was his younger self. We walked hand-in-hand through a field. He kissed me and then he walked away, looking back many times, waving and smiling. The faster I walked the further away he got. Then he was gone. I was up and drinking tea by five thirty. At six twenty the phone rang. I knew before I answered that my love was dead. That was what the previous night's dream was about. He had come to say goodbye to the woman he loved. It was Becky on the phone. I could hear Paul crying in the background. She said,

"He's gone. He's left us. I can't believe it."

Paul and Becky then told me what had happened that night. At just past midnight Wilf had sat up and reached out his arms. His eyes were open and he was looking at something above their heads. His face broke into a beautiful smile and then he sank back on the pillows. Paul and Becky both said that they had felt something leave the room. From that time until 6.20 am his body slowly closed down. Then he took his last breath on this earth and fell asleep forever.

Scott and I made our way in a taxi to Lincoln. I was keeping it together for Scott's sake because of his health problems. Nobody knew just how his dad's death would impact on his health.

I found Wilf just the way he'd died. Paul had asked the nurses to leave last offices until we had seen him. He was laid on his side, one hand under his cheek, he used to sleep like that. His other hand was resting on top of the covers on his pillow. By his head the nurses had placed a small sprig of flowers. His eyes were slightly open but the light had gone forever from them. The smile was still on his lips. I wondered who had come to claim him back. The room was very cold. When I touched him and kissed his lips he was stone cold and stiff. My heart broke into a thousand pieces. I could not imagine my life without him. I gathered him into my arms and held him for a few moments. This was all I had now. I would have given a king's ransom to have had a few more moments to spend with him. I said my goodbye. It was the hardest thing I've ever had to do. I left the room, not looking back. I had to walk away. I knew that my love was now in a different place.

Scott sat by his dad's bed for a while, touching him, telling him how much he loved him and how he would miss him. I sat quietly sobbing. Paul and Becky had already said their farewell. Pip and Beth had said goodbye the previous day. I thought I would feel a sense of relief when he was gone and was suffering no more, his earthly life over, but I didn't. I was so angry at the world. I felt that everybody had let him down, including me. He would not see Pip graduate nor Beth take her wedding vows. He had been cheated of so much.

"Well, Wilfie baby, it's been an exciting and mostly enjoyable journey through life with you. We were always meant to be together. We lived life in the fast lane. We gave life a good bashing. In the end we were still together. I shall never love again."

The next few days were a blur in my memory, my eyes forever red from crying. But I'm a good carer. You get up next morning and it's business as usual. I left the funeral arrangements to Paul. The only thing I requested was that Wilf should not be embalmed. It was an invasive procedure. It was unnecessary. This also ensured that Wilf's coffin would remain closed as his body would deteriorate quickly. Wilf had told me that he wanted no-one to see him in a coffin. He wanted us to remember him as he was, a joker, sometimes a pain in the arse, but he loved us all so much. He was the bravest man I've ever known. He handled everything life threw at him and still managed to crack a joke. It is hard to say if he knew he was dying. He did ask Paul if he was. Paul had replied, "Well it's not looking too good at the moment." But he never gave up until the tumour took everything and he returned to a childlike state. I hope that when my time comes I can be that brave though I doubt I will. I just hope Wilf comes for me and I will go willingly, just to be with him again.

Over the following few days I cleared out everything of Wilf's. I just kept one fleece jacket that he had loved. I carefully selected his clothes for the funeral.

He had told Paul he didn't want his ashes scattering. I had to keep them until I died and then we would be scattered together on the hillside at Scarborough where he told me he loved me for the first time.

Wilf's funeral had been planned for 24th September. This gave me plenty of time to do my crying. I wasn't going to let him down this time.

On the Monday before the funeral Paul had asked me to write a few words to be read out at the service. At first I refused, but I started writing and ended up with two A4 pages full. Both Becky and Paul cried when they read the words. The problem was who was going to read them on the day. I knew I couldn't without breaking down. Caroline said she would but she was worse than me for tears. Liz had also said she would be honoured to read them. In the end we had a funeral celebrant called Richard Sayer who did a great job. I explained to Scott that if he wanted to say a last goodbye he must do so before the curtain closed around the coffin. Scott and I chose the music between us, there were three songs. The first was Patsy Cline's 'Just a closer walk with thee'. Wilf had always said he wanted this song at his funeral. He used to cry when he heard it played. Well Patsy sang out as we followed Wilf in. Before Richard said his piece I took Scott over to the coffin and placed his hand there. Scott cannot whisper quietly so everyone heard him say,

"Goodbye my dad. Heaven says hello."

I could hear Caroline sobbing at the back and also Liz. Scott returned to his seat. I placed my forehead on the coffin to compose myself. I said my last goodbye to the love of my life. He had left footprints on my heart. Beth placed a red rose on his coffin, a last gift from Grandad's Princess. As the curtains closed, Elvis sang 'Peace in the Valley', another of Wilf's choices. The last song, however, was chosen by me. It wasn't hard to pick. It was Roy Orbison's 'Candy Man' which Wilf had sung so many times with his mate, Colin. Wilf would have wanted everyone to leave with a smile.

We made a collection for the hospice to help them continue with the work they so lovingly perform for those in their care.

Over the next few weeks I descended into disarray. Scott always got his meals and medication but it was Caroline who was holding me up. She held me whilst I cried and she comforted me and Scott. She listened to me raving about the care Wilf had not received. She was always there. I can never repay her. I thank God for her being a part of our lives. Between her and my family I managed to carry on.

Then strange things started to happen. The bathroom light would switch itself on and off at night. I saw a shadow pass by me in the kitchen whilst I was making up Scott's medication. One morning very early I was making tea when someone blew in my ear. This was something Wilf would do when we first got together, creep up behind me and blow in my ear. I was convinced he was around. Paul thought I'd lost the plot. I don't know what

Becky thought. She was too polite to say. The crunch came one night when I woke up to find someone standing at the side of my bed. I can't say for sure that it was Wilf but it scared the life out of me.

The next day in Boston I wandered into a charity shop called The Love Shack. I was chatting to the lady behind the counter. She had lost her husband a year previously. There was a chap in the shop talking to the manageress. After he left she came to talk to us. I said, jokingly, "What I need is a good medium."

She replied, "Why didn't you speak up. The chap who just left is a medium."

I was dumbstruck. She gave me his business card. I wondered why I had been in that shop that day, until then I hadn't even known it existed. I kept that card in my wallet for days wondering if I had the courage to ring. Then one night about 9.30 pm I was in the loo. The light went on and off repeatedly. "Right, that's it Wilfie baby," I thought. I sat on my bed and rang Mr Arthur Wright, Medium in Boston. He has since become Reverend Arthur Wright and a dear friend. He came to see me one Tuesday whilst Scott was out. Liz had said that it was best not to involve Scott as he could get carried away with situations. Mr Wright had already asked me on the phone if my husband had lost his speech before he died as he'd had him chattering in his ear for days. By the time Mr Wright left he'd given me a whole new outlook on life. He'd told me things that only I knew. In fact, when he left I smiled for the first time in ages.

"Thank you Arthur for giving me hope for the future." I urge anyone who is suffering to contact him. He is an amazing fella.

Things still carried on happening but I was never frightened again, it just proved Wilf was around as he always said he would be. As I told you before, my hands were not much use to me but from then on I found I could manage bottle tops and cans where before I'd always had to ask Wilf to open them. Any decisions I had to make, I would sleep on them, the answer would be in my head by morning.

CHAPTER 41: GRIEF

What is grief? It's a feeling that takes hold of you, leaving you emotionally dead. On the day my husband died I felt him leave me, the hurt so deep in my soul. The sparkle in my eyes was dimmed forever. I opened my wardrobe door. Seeing his clothes hanging there was tearing me apart. I sat on the bedroom floor surrounded by his belongings. My task was to choose what he would wear on his last journey, a journey he would make without me. It wasn't difficult, ever the teddy boy, he would meet his maker wearing jeans, his favourite black shirt, a pink tie, his deep red jacket and trainers. To complete the outfit, a hankie would be tucked in his top pocket and his medallion which read "Wilf & Doreen Forever" (on the reverse side were the words "And how") would be in his jeans pocket.

To believe he had gone forever was something I couldn't contemplate. How could a man who I had spent the bigger part of my life with be ripped away from me in such a cruel fashion? Not happy with just taking him, the cancer deep in his brain took everything he was. He was reduced to a child- like state, his memory wiped, no feelings left. It was as if he had never known me, he looked at me with a stranger's eyes. I would never again hear him say how much he loved me. Instead I saw him draw back when I tried to kiss him, and shunned any attempt to cuddle or try to comfort him in his last few days.

I was overcome with an anger so fierce, I cursed everybody, the doctors, the hospital, God for not saving him. Finally I cursed him. How dare he leave me? I had always thought that he would be there forever. Who would hold me in their arms as I crossed the big divide between this world and the next if it wasn't going to be him? I painted on my face the look which said "I'm fine, I'm coping, life moves on," but that was all 'crap'. I was dying inside, loneliness gripped me with its cold talons dragging me ever forward toward the point of no return.

My son, Scott, was struggling to cope alone, his disabilities and complex medical issues making it even harder. His father was gone. The strength of the anger I felt frightened me. I had to pull myself together. I'm a carer. I'm not allowed to be ill or be indisposed by grief. I swore if anyone said to me the words, "Time is a great healer," I would tear their heads from their bodies – just like the prawns on my plate. Talking of which, I just moved my food around, even attempting to place it in my mouth I thought would choke me. My weight responded by dropping at a rate of knots. I knew this had to stop, but I was quite happy to stay in this comfort zone with my memories and music from the sixties. I had downloaded all the love songs Wilf had sung to me as he walked around with the mike entertaining the ladies. My world had been him and now he was no more.

When he came home it was in a scatter tube with the image of a beach at sunset. There he sat on my cupboard, a battery candle always lit (so he would never be in the dark), fresh flowers in a small vase and the picture of his little dog, Scamp, who he had loved so much. My older son commented, "It's not good to make a shrine to Dad." Why, what should I have done, put him out by the bins to be emptied with the rest of the rubbish? He still stands there now, the candle is only lit on special dates, but the picture of little Scamp is always on guard. Fresh flowers appear on birthdays, but he will stay forever sixty-nine, never changing as time moves on. In my mind he will always be the good-looking guy in the drape suit who had won my heart so many years ago. Whoever said "Time Heals?" Well, guess what? It doesn't. The tears spring readily to my eyes even now, the hurt is still there, the emptiness still leading me down the long winding road to nowhere.

Very soon your journey through my life will be over as I bring my book to an end. I will close with a copy of the words I wrote for Wilf's farewell.

* * * * *

We are here today to say goodbye to Wilfred Robert Burrows, my husband and Paul and Scott's dad.

Wilf was born in Keighley, West Yorkshire, on Monday 15th November 1943. He was a keen sportsman and swam for his county.

He started his working life as a textile fitter and later retrained to work with young adults with learning disabilities.

Wilf was the original teddy boy, he was the best dancer and singer in the youth club and always had a keen group of admirers. However, not a lot of people got to know the real Wilf Burrows. He was a quiet, sometimes insecure, man who loved his family and worked hard to support them.

He would not want me to waffle on about him so I shall tell you what he thought and spoke about in the last few weeks before his illness took away his speech and mobility.

He admired Jill and Colin for moving all the way here while Jill was dealing with her own health problems.

He had a special place in his heart for Becky and the way she cared for him in the last few days of his life showed she really deserved that special place.

His two lads were his pride and joy and he was so proud of them both.

Pip was his teacher on how to throw a Frisbee, he described Pip as a free spirit, someone who would travel far and wide but would always come back home.

Beth was his little princess and he hoped she would meet someone who would take good care of her, but he'll be keeping a watchful eye on her, just in case.

I can't forget Liz, who has become one of the family. Wilf described Liz as "good people" but would ask her if she was qualified and would be hoping she was dressed properly for the occasion today!

Margaret he said was a foxy lady, that was praise indeed coming from him.

And last, but not least is Caroline, our very own "Dipsy". She cries at sad cartoons, has a heart as big as the world and keeps me sane, she dries tears, gives lots of love, does all the ironing and keeps us all smiling.

Well that's what he thought of you all, what he thought of me is my secret.

He was the love of my life, with him life was never boring. I must carry on my journey now without him. Goodbye my love, you left footprints on my heart.

Wilf died on 14th September 2013 and words alone cannot express how much he was loved and how much he will be missed.

*   *   *   *   *

If you have travelled with me I hope you enjoyed the journey. I've tried to tell my story truthfully. Sometimes a bit of humour crept in. I wanted to get across to you the true picture of Wilf, the man I shared my life, my hopes and my dreams with.

There will never be anyone else for me. So as I say goodbye I hope I managed to show you the love and devotion we shared for each other, even in the times of hardship, a love so strong it survived and blossomed even across the threshold of life after death. Thank you for reading my story.

AFTERWORD

Sitting here, reflecting on all that has gone before is a very sobering experience. As a small child I was so ignored by my parents that I thought I was invisible. However, I was a determined little soul who was going to make it no matter what. My parents disinterest in me gave me another idea – I thought perhaps I had been adopted and was not really part of the family. Well, that didn't worry me a lot either. When I became a teenager it was far too late for me to be given boundaries. Oh, I always asked for permission before I did anything or went anywhere but if I got a negative reply I just did it anyway. This got me into a lot of trouble but my parents were so disinterested in me that they couldn't even be bothered to punish me. I guess I must have been a nightmare to them.

Looking at Wilf's childhood, his parents were never there for him either. As a teenager, when he started smoking and coming home reeking of booze, instead of getting him into line they just let him get on with it. So at fifteen he was already well-known by all the landlords of the local pubs. He was also hanging out with lads that were much older than him. He'd also learnt how to use his fists. He would treat females very well until he got what he wanted then he would drop them like a hot potato. This could be said about a lot of lads in the sixties. When he came chasing my tail I was only twenty but I'd had a failed marriage behind me and had a toddler. What struck me as strange was the fact that I could remember very little about my first husband. I can close my eyes and try to picture what he looked like but nothing appears. I don't know about his childhood. In fact, I know nothing.

When Wilf and I first met we were both hot-headed and determined to get what we wanted but then we fell in love – a new experience for us both. A small piece of my heart remained with Kevin for many years but I realised, quite quickly, that my life wasn't mapped out for me to marry Kevin. However, I still have a soft spot for him today and was upset to find I had no pictures of him to put in my book. I destroyed all memories and any pictures I had of Dudley, my first husband. Although, if I hadn't met him I wouldn't have had my eldest son, but none of this counts now.

I believe that a book opens with your name on it the day you are born. Each day a page turns, until there are no more pages left.

I can say, with hand on heart, that I have only ever loved one man, any before him were practice runs.

Any woman who marries a man believing she can change him is onto a loser. He'll only change if he really wants to. I consider myself very lucky. I spent a lot of my life with a very special guy. Thinking back to all Wilf's friends who married young, not one couple stayed together. Two of his friends committed suicide, they were a mixed up bunch really.

I remember going with Wilf to the Marquis of Granby pub which, at that time, was considered quite posh. I hadn't known him very long. We were meeting an old friend of his who he hadn't seen for a while. At first it was fine until this idiot started offering us drugs and started openly snorting coke.

I turned to Wilf. "I'm out of here. I don't do drugs. If you do, Wilf, don't bother contacting me again."

I left. When I looked round Wilf was trying to catch me up. "I'm sorry about that sweetheart. I thought he'd sorted himself out. I've never taken any drugs. Even I have some standards."

So you see the problems the kids have today were also around in the sixties. Drugs were around and being sold in the pubs and clubs in most large towns.

Unmarried mothers – another blemish on the sixties, if this happened to you it was frowned on. You were considered a slut, the sort of girl a guy wouldn't take home to meet his parents. Couples living together were another issue. You had to be very brave to live with a guy without a ring on your finger. Wilf and I lived together for a while before we got married but we just didn't 'give a shit' what people thought about us.

When Teddy Boys first started showing up they were considered to be evil. It was thought that they would bash old grannies over the head for a few coppers. Well, Wilf was a Teddy Boy, as were most of his friends, and I can't remember one old person who'd been assaulted by a fella in a drape suit and 'brothel creepers'.

So it would seem that most generations have similar problems although in the sixties families tended to live closer to parents and grandparents. Consequently, if any lads were seen misbehaving it wasn't long before the jungle drums were beating. Mum or Dad would be waiting to dish out the punishment, which included going to the person they'd upset and apologising.

Wilf was very respectful to his elders. One night we were in the King's Head. An oldish fella collared Wilf. His daughter had been chasing my man before he met me. She was peeved that he wasn't interested. Wilf tried everything to avoid trouble when he was with me. He knew I hated fighting.

"I don't fight old men. If I offended your daughter, I apologise," he said.

As Wilf walked away the guy swung a punch which caught him on his cheek. My heart stood still. I thought,

"Oh, God, he'll kill him."

"You can have that one free, as I said, I don't fight old fellas. Just teach your daughter that 'no' means 'no'. If you fancy your chances, let's take this outside or let me and my lady enjoy our drinks."

Wilf again started to walk away but stopped when he heard the words, "She's no lady."

What happened next was a blur, it happened so fast. Wilf turned on his heel and the old fella hit the deck. The landlord was standing watching this. Wilf apologised.

"Sorry, mate. I gave him every chance to walk away."

"He's been asking for that all night. If it hadn't been you, someone else would have put him down," the landlord replied.

As the fella staggered out, the landlord shouted, "You're barred."

All the trouble put a dampener on our evening. We nearly had the same thing again the following week. This time it was Pauline's new bloke. He was sitting with two mates giving us the evil eye. Wilf waited until he went to the toilet and then followed. I kept my eyes on his mates but they stayed put. I think they had been drinking all day – they looked pissed. Wilf returned to our table. I grabbed his hands to check his knuckles. He started laughing, "I wouldn't waste my energy on that prat, I offered him outside, he grovelled, end of."

I was to come across Pauline's fella again. I'd taken a part-time job doing the wages where he worked. I stood handing out wage packets. I noticed him in the queue looking very uncomfortable. The men on the shop floor could be a bit saucy with their comments. I just ignored them, moving onto the next man. Then he was in front of me. I handed him his wages, informing him he'd also got a tax rebate. He muttered, "Thanks." I just smiled. The problems had been between Pauline and Wilf, nothing to do with us. It was funny though, he was very much like Wilf but a bit taller. Wonder if he and Pauline managed forty-two years like we did?

All this just reinforced my decision to leave Keighley for good. Wilf's illness held things up but we managed it. I must admit he struggled at first in a new place but before long he was back to the charmer I fell in love with. I would tear a strip off him from time to time but would always stand his corner against all comers. Did I miss Keighley? The answer is a definite no. I still think that Wilf did sometimes.

Well now Wilf is no more. It will soon be two years since he left us. Like it or not, life moves on, it has to. Scott and I live in Lincoln now in a bungalow that Paul bought us. I am in touch with Julia after thirty years. I don't know if we'll ever meet up. Only time will tell. I have new friends now, some of them male. Will I ever marry again? The quick answer is no, I could never live with another man. I enjoy male companionship. It's no fun eating out alone. Will it ever be more? Who knows.

We also lost Scott's little dog, Izzie, which left a big ache in Scott's heart. He now has a new little girl called Annie. She will never replace Izzie. Pets are like people. You can never replace them, they are all individuals. We are all getting older. People in our lives are moving on. We were very sad to lose Liz. She helped Scott and I through the most difficult period in our lives but she has now moved on to pastures new. Scott has some new support workers now but Caroline is still with us, still my rock in troubled times. What the future holds? Well who knows? If you read my story, I hope you enjoyed the journey through my life.

Printed in Great Britain
by Amazon